Your Towns and Cities in the Great War

Sheffield
in the Great War

On the front cover is a vehicle used by the volunteer-organized Personal Comforts Depot to transport food and other items for patients in Sheffield military hospitals. The Depot is described in Chapter Seven.

Author's royalties from this book will be paid by the publisher direct to the Royal British Legion for use in the Sheffield area.

Your Towns and Cities in the Great War

Sheffield
in the Great War

Peter Warr

Pen & Sword
MILITARY

First published in Great Britain in 2015 by
PEN & SWORD MILITARY
an imprint of
Pen and Sword Books Ltd
47 Church Street
Barnsley
South Yorkshire S70 2AS

ISBN 978 1 78303 641 7

A CIP record for this book is available from the British Library

Printed and bound in England
by CPI Group (UK) Ltd, Croydon, CR0 4YY

Typeset in Times New Roman by Chic Graphics

Pen & Sword Books Ltd incorporates the imprints of
Pen & Sword Archaeology, Atlas, Aviation, Battleground, Discovery,
Family History, History, Maritime, Military, Naval, Politics, Railways,
Select, Social History, Transport, True Crime, and Claymore Press,
Frontline Books, Leo Cooper, Praetorian Press, Remember When,
Seaforth Publishing and Wharncliffe.

For a complete list of Pen and Sword titles please contact
Pen and Sword Books Limited
47 Church Street, Barnsley, South Yorkshire, S70 2AS, England
E-mail: enquiries@pen-and-sword.co.uk
Website: www.pen-and-sword.co.uk

Contents

Preface and Acknowledgements   8

1   **'The War That Will End War'**
This was the 'Great' war   12
The catastrophe unfolds   14
Counting the cost – people, animals and money   19
Death, injuries and sickness   19
Shell-shock   21
Animals at the Front   26
Billions of pounds   28

2   **What Sort of Place Was Britain?**
King and Empire   30
A country divided   36
Votes for women   36
Trade union unrest   39
Conflict in Ireland   40
Some welfare benefits   42
Everyday living   45
Ready for war?   48

3   **Sheffield Before the War**
Politics, the press and the churches   51
Roads and transport   54
Housing and local facilities   61
Medical and welfare services   66
Entertainment and social activities   71

4   Autumn 1914: British Recruits and Belgian Refugees

The war cloud bursts   80

New soldiers   82

Recruiting offices   89

The first few months of war   90

Homeless Belgians come to Sheffield   98

5   Born in Germany, living in Sheffield

Germans in pre-war Britain   107

The 'enemy in our midst'   111

Riots, repatriation and internment   116

What happened to internees?   122

Naturalized Germans in the city   127

6   1915 and 1916: Adapting to war

Restrictions, regulations and the Defence of the Realm Act 133

Sheffield in 1915 and 1916   137

News from the Front   139

Propaganda and morale at home   146

Propaganda from the government   147

Propaganda from the community   149

Conscription and military tribunals   152

Aeroplanes, Zeppelins and government insurance   156

Hospitals throughout the city   160

The Third Northern General Hospital   162

Wharncliffe War Hospital   171

Voluntary Aid Detachments (VADs)   173

The Silver War Badge   174

7   Giving and doing: the City's Voluntary Work

Contributing clothes, food and vehicles   176

Providing a service   183

Helping soldiers   184

Helping the city   187

Giving money   190

| | Money for the nation | 190 |
| | Money for people in need | 193 |

8   **Industry Responds to War**

	National factories	203
	Controlled establishments	203
	War service badges	204
	Dilution and women workers	206
	Working conditions and health	209
	The city's factories	209

9   **Sheffield in 1917 and 1918**

	Conscription, tribunals and conscientious objectors	217
	Shortages and rationing	221
	Prisoners-of-war and influenza	225
	The armistice and peace	225

Chapter Notes	231
Indexes	263
Person Index	263
Subject Index	265

Preface and
Acknowledgements

The enormous catastrophe of World War One has given rise to many debates. Was Britain right to enter the war? Should peace have been sought at an early stage? Should the generals have made different decisions? Was it worth it? These are of course major questions, but we also need to learn about individual people. Soldiers and other troops sometimes kept diaries, but very little has been written about their families back at home.

So this book focuses on the Home Front. It tells a story of activity, change and distress in Sheffield. Local events are set into a national framework, and over 100 photographs and drawings illustrate how the city acquired a new life. For more specialist readers, Notes at the end of the book provide additional information, and two Indexes make it easy to find people, topics and places.

Sheffield in this period faced many problems that were entirely new. The city's Great War is described in two companion books rather than a single, large volume. Both books cover the full period and each can be read independently of the other, but they have slightly different emphases. The first (this one) pays particular attention to the earlier wartime years, whereas Sheffield's Great War and Beyond, published in mid-2015, also looks in more detail at munition production, food shortages and other developments in the later years. Each book is self-contained and each one fully extends across the entire war. In addition, the second book also looks at the immediate post-war years, when poverty and yet more pain descended on the city.

Sheffield in the Great War opens with a brief summary of the fighting itself, looking at its enormous cost not only in terms of money but also in the huge number of men killed or impaired. Life before the war is next reviewed before moving on to Sheffield in the first few months of fighting – enthusiastic volunteering and the surprise arrival of hundreds of refugees from Belgium. The following chapter asks about the many Germans already in the city. How were they treated? Some had married Sheffielders, but they were widely regarded as spies waiting to join an enemy attack.

Later developments in the city are then covered, showing how families gained news about their absent menfolk and how anti-German propaganda was used. A Zeppelin attack is remembered, and new munition tribunals are introduced and illustrated. Particular attention is paid to the sudden creation in the city of around thirty entirely new military hospitals to cope with what became more than 70,000 sick and wounded men.

Sheffield women organized themselves to help these new hospitals and their patients, working to supply food, clothes and other items. Women also moved into the city's greatly-expanded munition factories, and the book describes Sheffield's crucial role in the production of armaments and equipment. Readers are introduced to the newly-formed Ministry of Munitions, the country's national factories and controlled organizations, and the ways in which women gradually took over many jobs that were previously restricted to men. The book's final chapter covers the stresses and problems of the later war years, looking at military conscription, conscientious objectors, prisoners of war in the city, food shortages and eventually rationing. The local impact of the worldwide influenza epidemic is explored, and events in Sheffield on Armistice Day are given particular attention.

Material for this book has been gathered from personal diaries, family collections, archival material, hard-to-find newspaper and other items. Hundreds of hours have been spent studying the city's newspapers, council minutes and other documents, and in this work I have received considerable help from the staff of Sheffield's Local Studies Library and Archives. I am extremely grateful to them.

In addition, I would particularly like to thank three people whose assistance has been enormous. Dean Hill has been a wonderfully generous provider of information and guidance across a wide range of the book's topics. His in-depth knowledge was always available (see also www.sheffieldsoldier.co.uk, with website management by Stuart

Reeves), and he resolved many of my uncertainties about the details of military life. Second, I have been greatly helped by Clara Morgan, Curator of Social History at Museums Sheffield, who kindly provided information, followed up my many queries, and made available items from the Museums' collection. Third, Dave Manvell offered to work on the digital restoration of unclear images, and his work on illustrations in almost every chapter has been greatly appreciated.

As well as those three invaluable sources of support, many other people kindly responded to requests for information on websites or at meetings, and I have been hugely impressed by their generosity and helpfulness. This book and its companion have gained considerably from their willingness to assist in the venture, and I thank them once again for their kindness: Don Alexander, Neil Anderson, David Baldwin, Christine Ball, Colin Barnsley, Peter Bayliss, Christine Bell, Pauline Bell, Keith Burnett, Eric Chambers, Nigel Clark, Paul Clarke, Michael Collins, Miles Connell, Chris Corker, Yvonne Cresswell, Dawn Crofts, Peter Davies, Michael Deal, Alison Duce, Malcolm Dungworth, Sylvia Dunkley, Mike Dyson, Dan Eaton, John Eaton, Jonathan England, David Flather, Richard Ford, Graham Frith, Thelma Griffiths, John Grove, Judith Hanson, Stephen Hardcastle, Angela Harpham, Ken Hawley, Doug Hindmarch, Chris Hobbs, Derek Holdsworth, Christopher Jonas, Roy Koerner, Erik Lonnedahl, Annette Manvell, Anthony Marshall, Peter Mason, Roy Millington, Barbara Moffatt, John Moore, Dorothy Moss, Gerald Newton, Pat Oldham, Panikos Panayi, Robert Proctor, Jane Salt, David Sandilands, Elaine and Peter Scott, Mark Sheridan, Anthea Stephenson, Christine Stirling, Mark Tiddy, Ian Trowell, Geoffrey Tweedale, Joan Unwin, Brian Ward, Stephen Woollen, and members of Sheffield History Forum (http://www.sheffieldhistory.co.uk/forums).

Sheffield Libraries and Archives kindly permitted reproduction of six images from Picture Sheffield: s09387, s10739 (thanks also to H D Sports), y00132, y00146, y00235 and y00251. Other organizations that have generously provided material and granted permissions include Kelham Island Museum, the National Trust, Manx National Museum, Museums Sheffield, Sheffield Hallam University, Sheffield Local Studies Library and Sheffield Newspapers. Thanks very much to all of them.

Preparation of this book has extended over several years, and I fear that a few helpers may have been omitted from that list. I hope not, but sincerely apologize for my error if that is the case.

Thanks of a more general kind are due to the charitable organizations that have worked to assist the military and civilian victims of the Great War and subsequent conflicts. With that in mind, my royalties from this book will be paid by the publishers direct to the Royal British Legion for use in the Sheffield area.

Peter Warr
May 2014

CHAPTER 1

'The War That Will End War'

The war between 1914 and 1918 created horrors and pain beyond anyone's expectation. European countries unleashed tragedy on an unimaginable scale, millions died and millions more suffered. Buildings were obliterated, people in many countries endured years of threat, danger and distress, and huge debts were built up for repayment across many later years.

This was the 'Great' war

From its very early days the conflict was labelled the Great European War or the Great War'[1]. *(Notes for more specialist readers are provided at the end of the book.)* It was 'great' because it was huge, not because it was a great experience. Recognizing that the fighting had extended to non-European countries and also took place at sea, politicians and the press soon described it as a world war'[2]. A second large conflict between 1939 and 1945 made it necessary then to look back to the *first* of two world wars[3].

During and immediately after the Great War, people could not imagine it happening again. Within a few weeks of its commencement on 4 August 1914, British author and social commentator H. G. Wells published a series of influential newspaper articles (in Sheffield as well as elsewhere) referring to 'the war that will end war', arguing that a clear victory and the resulting international arrangements would prevent later conflict[4]. He – and many other people – justified this war because of its expected positive impact on the future.

Display Box 1.1
TROOP NUMBERS IN FOUR YEARS OF WAR

Estimates differ widely between some publications, and all figures here and elsewhere are approximations.

The Allies
(Total about 38.6 million troops)
- Britain: about 5.6 million troops
- British Empire: about 2.7 million troops
- France and Empire: about 8.4 million troops
- Italy (from 1915): about 5.6 million troops
- Russia: about 12 million troops
- USA (from 1917): about 4.3 million troops

The Central Powers
(Total about 21.5 million troops)
- Germany: about 11 million troops
- Austria-Hungary: about 7.3 million troops
- Turkey: about 2.2 million troops
- Bulgaria (from 1915): about 1 million troops

Allied countries from the British Empire included Australia, Canada, India, New Zealand, Newfoundland (separate from Canada until 1949) and South Africa. In addition, several other nations were involved in the war, often for less than its full duration. Thus Germany was for some or all of the time opposed by Belgium, China, Greece, Japan, Liberia, Portugal, Romania, Serbia, Siam (modern Thailand) and several Central and South American states.

Several countries in Europe remained neutral: Albania, Denmark, Holland, Luxembourg, Norway, Spain, Sweden and Switzerland.

Wells' encouraging phrase was picked up and used by American President Woodrow Wilson when he sought in the spring of 1917 to persuade the US Congress to enter the war. Sometimes expressed more briefly as the war to end all war, the idealistic wording came in later decades to seem inappropriate as it became clear that wars were still part of international life. More common nowadays is the label Great War or

First World War, sometimes stated as World War One and perhaps abbreviated as WW1.

The Great War is often recalled mistakenly in Britain as between merely the home country and Germany. But it involved two large groups of nations – sometimes described as the Allies, including Britain, and the Central Powers, those in the centre of Europe. The principal countries and their approximate overall number of troops[5] are shown in Display Box 1.1.

The catastrophe unfolds

The origins and course of the Great War have been described in many dozens of publications through the century that has followed. We are not concerned with causes, military strategy or details of specific battles here, but a brief outline of developments can be helpful as a background to events at home.

Much of the fighting took place in northern France and Belgium along what became known as the Western Front. A front is the line of troops nearest to the enemy, and in western Europe that line soon became more-or-less fixed all the way from the Belgian coast to Switzerland. There was more movement in eastern Europe as battles took place in Austria, Russia, Serbia and neighbouring countries. Fighting also occurred in other parts of the world, such as Africa, China (briefly), Egypt, northern Italy and the Middle East[6]. War was also waged at sea, with naval blockades and surface and submarine attacks, and in the air through airships and aeroplanes.

The conflict started with disputes between single European countries, but others soon became drawn in through a multiple chain reaction of formal or informal agreements. When a disagreement between Austria-Hungary and neighbouring Serbia escalated into a declaration of war on 28 July 1914, the two opposing countries were soon joined by others. Austria-Hungary was immediately supported by her ally Germany, and Austria's opponent Serbia was backed by Russia. Germany was already prepared to attack westward to knock out Russia's ally France, while its own ally Austria simultaneously fought Russia in the east. The chosen attack route was through Belgium, a neutral country whose security had previously been guaranteed by both Germany and Britain[7].

Up to then Britain had traditionally remained detached from continental quarrels, mainly treating them as local disputes that did not directly affect this country. It was well-known here and abroad that Britain's concern was primarily to retain command of the sea in order to protect its empire and associated trade. More than half of British food was imported and open sea routes were essential. Britain had a large and powerful navy but only a small army[8], and Germany had some reason to expect that this island country would remain outside any disputes in mainland Europe.

However, when Germany threatened Belgium on 3 August 1914, the British government instantly objected, demanding that Belgian neutrality be observed. Not only had Britain previously offered to support that neutral country, but the defeat of Belgium would provide Germany with access to the English Channel and the ability to attack shipping and even this country itself. Germany had in recent years built up a strong navy and an extensive railway system, which had obvious military potential. Its militarism now challenged the previously-accepted balance of power in Europe and, when a British objection to the invasion of Belgium was ignored, Britain and its empire declared war on Germany at 11 pm (UK time) on 4 August 1914.

The people of this country widely believed that the conflict would be brief and that victory was certain: the British Empire was extremely powerful and the war would be over by Christmas. To meet the immediate need in August 1914, additional volunteers were sought and thousands of recruits came forward. By December more than a million men had joined 'Kitchener's Army'[9], and that number of volunteers had reached 2,500,000 by the end of 1915. Some young men were looking forward to a period of excitement and good comradeship, many were in a hurry not to miss what would be a brief adventure[10], and there was generally strong encouragement from the press, public and families.

As we now know optimism was misplaced. Although British troops served in several parts of the world[11], their greatest involvement was along the Western Front in Europe. Initially, an expeditionary force of 150,000 men, with about 1,000 lorries, cars and motor cycles and 40,000 horses, joined the much larger French Army to oppose the German advance. However, very soon neither side could make progress and each sought protection in an increasingly complex network of trenches. The new British recruits needed months of training and were not yet available, winter weather intervened, and the armies settled in defensive positions. No-Man's-Land between them was in some places as narrow as 30 metres but often extended to several hundred metres. Periods of trench life were made additionally unpleasant by dampness and mud from the high underground water-table and periods of intense rainfall. As later described by one observer, 'the mud wilderness [...] seemed to reach the utmost

Some results of war in Belgium: the Messines Ridge in 1917.

Mud, stagnant water, desolation and horses on the Western Front.

limits of ugliness and repulsion: greasy, blood-stained duckboards, smashed military equipment and debris, innumerable shell-holes filled with mire and stagnant water, the marks of wrath and death in all directions, and not one natural object of green beauty from horizon to horizon'[12].

In this setting successful attacks against the enemy were rare and progress was slow and painful. In the next four years huge numbers of British families lost their young men along the 90-mile British section of the Western Front. Among the battles still recalled for their massive killing and maiming were those of the Somme and Passchendaele. The Battle of the Somme opened on 1 July 1916 and dragged on for months, creating death and injury on a colossal scale. On the first day the British army attacking over open ground lost as many as 19,000 soldiers, and nearly 40,000 others became non-fatal casualties[13]. More than 500 Sheffield men were killed there on that first day[14]. In the next few months, repeated clashes on the Somme gave rise to more than 400,000 British casualties of all kinds. Also shocking was the extended Battle of Passchendaele in the autumn of 1917, which produced around 240,000 British casualties, including more than 70,000 deaths. These were terrible years – for other nations as well as for Britain[15].

Following a long build-up of deaths, mutilation and horror abroad and emergency regulations, food shortages and economic and social difficulties at home, the year 1917 was an uneasy one and the military outlook for Britain was bleak. At the end of January in that year, Germany initiated submarine attacks on merchant as well as military vessels, sinking around 1,000 ships and blocking essential supplies. The French and Italian armies (partners of Britain) were struggling, and a Communist revolution in Russia (Britain's ally in Eastern Europe) led to that country withdrawing from the war and Germany being free to move troop reinforcements from the East. German advances on the Western Front early in 1918 seemed likely to break the British line and a German victory was increasingly feared.

However, a few months later it was all over. By now the British Army was well equipped and armed[16], and the United States of America had joined the war in April 1917[17]. Conscription of American troops began almost immediately, but the creation and training of a new and complex army naturally required several months. It was only by the spring of 1918 that American strength on the Western Front became substantial, and the addition of nearly 2,000,000 US soldiers to the already-established

Australian, British, Canadian and French forces undoubtedly shifted the balance in favour of the Allies.

Furthermore, 1918 saw a change of Allied fortune in Eastern Europe. Peace was arranged with Austria, Bulgaria and Turkey, removing their support for Germany. That country's recent advances on the Western Front were reversed after successful Allied counter-attacks, and from July 1918 morale in much of the German army and navy declined. Some German soldiers turned to looting captured properties, and desertion became more common. Parts of the German army suffered in the expanding influenza epidemic from the middle of that year, and within Germany itself food shortages and economic hardship were becoming more widespread. By late 1918 Germany was ready to agree to a negotiated solution. The Emperor, Kaiser Wilhelm II, abdicated on 9 November, and an armistice[18] was signed on 11 November. The fighting at last came to an end.

During the war, Germany had developed advantages in submarine warfare but Britain became extremely effective in a key naval activity – the blockade of enemy ports. Any products that might strengthen enemy forces, industries or civilian populations became a target for blockade, and enemy countries were increasingly denied imports of foodstuffs and crucial industrial raw materials and machinery.

Air warfare had been entirely new in 1914[19], although balloons had previously been used for observation. The Royal Flying Corps (RFC) had been formed in May 1912 with separate military and naval wings, but the latter was separated in July 1914 as the Royal Naval Air Service (RNAS). Both services developed procedures for reconnaissance[20] and bombing of enemy sites, but the RFC (controlled by the War Office and working to meet tactical requirements on the ground) at first operated primarily in battle-zones, whereas the separate RNAS (based within the Admiralty) initially carried out sea patrols and attacks on strategic targets such as air-ship depots and submarine bases. The two were combined into the Royal Air Force in April 1918.

At the outset Britain had only a few dozen military planes, but by its end nearly 20,000 remained available for post-war redeployment. Considerable technical improvements were introduced during the war, including stronger air-frames and new alloy steels, wireless communication, and forward-firing machine-guns synchronized with a plane's propeller. Britain's success in the air contributed substantially to overall victory on the ground.

Many publications in the following decades have described events during the war, often emphasizing key battles between opposing armies. However, the Allies' victory also derived from success in financial terms. The enormous cost of the war led to continuing government worries that Britain might not be able to raise enough money in international markets to avoid bankruptcy. Some illustrations are presented below and in Chapter Seven. Without effective management of Britain's international finance, defeat would have been inevitable.

Counting the cost – people, animals and money
The Great War was like no other before it, and its impact was huge – primarily due to the millions of lives cut short or damaged. Although most of these can be counted and quoted, numbers are only estimates, partly because of the difficulty of collecting information in battlefield conditions. In addition, quoted casualty rates usually omit civilians as well as soldiers who became ill or died after the war had ended. For instance, more than 2,000,000 Russian civilians were killed during the Great War in addition to known military casualties.

Deaths, injuries and sickness
In respect of troops, it seems likely that across all the fighting nations the Great War directly caused substantially more than 10,000,000 deaths, and that maybe double that number were wounded. For Britain alone, approximately 750,000 soldiers, sailors and airmen died[21], and at least 6,000 of these had lived in Sheffield. Approximately 52,000 men left the city to fight (considerably more than half of the eligible male age group), and around 11½ percent of those died[22]. Nationally, the war's death rate for all the services together was almost 12 percent, made up of about 13 percent in the army, nearly 7 percent in the navy, and around 2 percent for the air force as a whole, but very much higher for men who flew the planes[23]. Women also died serving their country. The Imperial War Museum estimates that 700 were killed, mainly when providing medical assistance in the war-zone.

A small number of British deaths were very different. Some were purposely and legally shot by their own colleagues. The nation's Army Act permitted the execution of servicemen found guilty of serious offences, and during the Great War 300 British soldiers (most on the Western Front) suffered this fate[24]. Almost all had been convicted of desertion, but eighteen were executed for alleged cowardice and almost twenty for disobedience or quitting their post. Nearly 100 years later, in

2006, all of these men were posthumously pardoned, though their sentences and convictions remain in place. As pointed out by the Defence Secretary in 2006, 'injustices were clearly done in some cases – even if we cannot say which […] All these men were victims of war.' It appears that seven of them came from Sheffield[25].

The war also caused deaths a long way away from the battlefield. In July 1917, Sheffielder Cyril Hawley of Pitsmoor was training in the Midlands to be a pilot with the Royal Flying Corps. On his first solo flight his plane nose-dived and he was killed. In the city, 3-year-old Mary Butterill of Brightside Lane was killed by her soldier uncle's rifle. He was on leave from Salonica in mid-1917 and (as was usual) brought back his rifle. When the adults were briefly out of the house, young boys of the family discovered a cartridge in the soldier's coat pocket. As they played with the rifle and the cartridge, Mary was accidentally shot. In September of that year, an explosion in a Sheffield gasworks killed Private Ernest Mottershaw, one of the military guards there. And a Zeppelin raid on the city in September 1916 (see Chapter Six) led to twenty-eight more deaths. Nationally, several thousand British citizens were killed by air-raids.

What about deaths after the war had ended? Around twenty-five Sheffield servicemen are known to have died between 1919 and 1922 and other war-induced fatalities have yet to be added to official lists. For example, quarry worker Fred Sanderson of Stephen Hill, Crosspool, joined the Royal Field Artillery in January 1915. After serving on the Western Front he was invalided out with a military pension in 1917 due to endocarditis, an inflammatory infection of the heart. That was common in the trenches, where rats and fleas could carry the disease. Fred's death certificate in 1921 confirmed endocarditis as the cause. The war had killed him. Other known local unlisted post-war deaths are being brought together in the 'In from the Cold' section of www.sheffieldsoldierww1.co.uk.

In addition to around 750,000 British deaths, a further 1,750,000 men were injured. For those who became disabled, remedial operations and equipment or aids for daily living were primitive by modern standards, and hundreds of thousands of injured still-young men returned to shattered lives and family relationships that were often difficult and always less than they might have been[26]. Imagine your loved one having to go through life with (for instance) one or both legs amputated, being totally or partially blind or deaf, or crippled by rheumatism from conditions in the trenches.

Many military deaths and injuries arose from illnesses rather than from

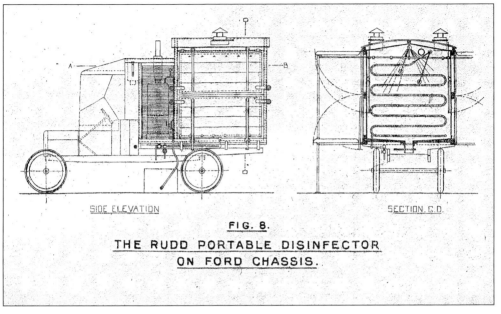

A mobile delousing van for disinfecting soldiers' blankets and clothes.

shells, bullets or bombs. For example, around 75,000 British troops were admitted to hospitals in France suffering from frostbite from very cold winters, or trench foot from waterlogged trenches. Several types of fever were transmitted by lice that became established in clothes and blankets. Delousing stations were provided, sometimes fitted in lorries or trains. In addition, dysentery was caused by impure drinking water, sometimes taken from pools in shell craters. And bites from the many trench rats could infect a soldier's kidneys or heart with potentially fatal results[27]. As in many other conflicts, war-induced sickness added greatly to the death and mutilation that resulted from physical injury in battle[28].

Shell-shock
Physical effects of war are often visible, but mental consequences can remain largely hidden within individuals and their families. The war's conditions and carnage also had a huge emotional cost. Imagine having to endure the front-line situation experienced by poet Robert Graves: '[the bodies] we could not get from the German wire continued to swell […]

Display Box 1.2
SHELL-SHOCK AND ITS TREATMENT

Dr Charles Myers introduced the term shell-shock in 1915 to cover a range of confused and often bewildering states. Patients could exhibit some partial combination of facial tics, nightmares, lost memories, inability to talk or walk, a jerky gait or shuffle, stomach cramps, sweating, unrelenting anxiety, uncontrollable shaking, diarrhoea, blindness, a fear of noises, repeated recollections of particularly awful events, paralysis, grotesque body movements or extended periods of silence. Different individuals exhibited different symptoms (never all of them), and these appeared to be linked to a person's battlefield activity. Excerpts from films from the period about the more extreme forms of symptom are available at http://www.wellcomecollection.org /explore/sickness—health/topics/ military-medicine/video.aspx?view= war- neuroses and also by searching for 'shell shock' at http://www. britishpathe.com.

Given that relevant brain or nerve damage could not be found, explanations in terms of physical harm were soon recognized to be incomplete, and attention turned to possible emotional causes and the need for novel treatments. Electric shocks and hypnosis were sometimes tried, but more common treatments were rest, improved diet and activity of a non-combat (e.g. farming) kind. Medical staff emphasized the need to rebuild a person's self-confidence and to seek to remove a possible sense of shame. Treatment was most often carried out near the front line with the aim of an early return to service, but more serious cases were returned to Britain where more than twenty asylums and clinics were requisitioned for shell-shock patients.

Similar problems have occurred in conflicts other than World War One, and nowadays the term post-traumatic stress disorder is more commonly used. Recent research has pointed to rates in the British army after active service, which are similar to those 100 years ago. Current treatments in terms of psychological counselling to maintain resilience can be seen as more sophisticated applications of the pioneering thinking introduced in the Great War.

---

the colours of the dead faces changed from white to yellow-grey, to red, to purple, to green, to black. These bodies or their dismembered parts had later, if and when it was safe, to be gathered and buried, and the stench of decay could be unbearable.'

Medical historian Leo van Bergen points to the prospect of 'mutilation from shrapnel or pieces of grenade […] asphyxiation from gas, or being burned or buried alive […] These were combined with the sight and burden of thousands and thousands of rats and other vermin like lice or flies; with constant deafening noise caused by the shells flying over from front to rear or vice versa; with hunger and thirst from lack of food and drinking water; with enormous fatigue caused by days without sleep and a knapsack weighing up to 40 or 50 kilos[29]. And these were combined with mud […] like a swamp into which the corpses disappeared and the wounded drowned. On top of that came the sheer endlessness of the war. A war that should have been a swift and glorious one became a war of years, years without any viable results.'

Coping with these conditions was far from easy, and for some the strain was too great. Emotional illnesses became officially recognized as the war proceeded, and from 1915 seriously disturbed behaviours and experiences were increasingly identified as 'shell-shock' and in need of medical attention. Symptoms were initially thought to be due to concussional effects on the brain, arising from extremely loud noises. But it became clear that many victims had no physical injury and that the condition could be due to mental disturbance at least as much as to physical shock[30]. Doctors working with these patients came to see that the label shell-shock was technically inappropriate, since the problem could occur without the nearby explosion of shells, and they preferred terms such as nervous shock or neurasthenia. However, the label shell-shock had the merit of avoiding a suggestion of mental weakness, and it became generally acceptable. It is still used widely today for being dazed and confused after great stress[31]. (See Display Box 1.2.)

It is unclear how many cases of shell-shock occurred in the British Army. A figure of 80,000 is usually quoted for the entire war, but that is almost certainly an underestimate and other commentators have argued for around 200,000[32]. Among Sheffield's shell-shock victims was Gunner George England, a hairdresser from Ellesmere Road. In the middle of 1916 he was the victim of a shell and gas attack and had to be dug out by colleagues from his front-line site. His serious injuries led to him being discharged from the army as an invalid, and he had to cope with lung problems and recurring shell-shock – at first every few hours and later every few days. His grandson describes him like this:

His body would be cowering and twitching as he was still experiencing the horror and pain of unwelcome unbearable memories. On returning to consciousness, he would be far, far away and take some time to return to this world. He would then drift off again; possibly the whole process could last several hours. His neighbours, his wife, his daughters and my dad all knew that his behaviour was wholly attributable to shell-shock, which was initially overwhelming and slowly improved in the years since the war. He literally heard the shells [...] contact could not be made with him.

Another sufferer was Dr John Stokes of Crookes, who was a lieutenant-colonel in the Royal Army Medical Corps. He was reported to have been greatly distressed, continually hearing the shrieking noise of a shell. While hospitalized with the problem in 1916, he committed suicide by cutting his own throat with a pocket-knife[33].

Given that commanders and medical staff (and some soldier colleagues) may have believed that affected men were fraudulently attempting to escape front-line duty, sympathy within a unit was sometimes limited. Many senior officers were known to believe that high rates of shell-shock were due to poor unit leadership, so junior officers may have been reluctant to accept its presence among their soldiers. Individuals themselves could feel shame about their apparent failure in comparison with their colleagues. In addition, the need for a large number of troops in post was always pressing, so retention in service would in all cases have been operationally preferable. It seems likely that cases of shell-shock were more widespread than official figures suggest. Prevalence was apparently about the same in officers and other ranks, but medical reports about officers often emphasized their heavy work-loads and responsibilities.

Following the war, emotional problems undoubtedly affected the mental health of many thousands of men, preventing a normal life. It seems certain that a large number of soldiers who escaped with their physical health more-or-less intact later suffered periods of depression, anxiety, panic attacks or horrible flashbacks. And, of course, that would also be the fate of many who, in addition, were physically disabled.

Display Box 1.3
HORSES IN THE GREAT WAR

Horses for the British army were obtained by the Remount Service, a part of the Army Service Corps. Purchasing officers toured the country seeking animals offered for sale or which they requisitioned and paid for on a standard scale. Animals were shipped from Remount Depots to the Western Front and other battle-zones for work in the cavalry or (mainly) to provide transport and haulage. In addition, hundreds of thousands were received and forwarded from the United States, Canada and other countries.

At the beginning of the war, cavalry units (regiments of Dragoons, Guards, Hussars and Lancers) were considered by many to be the fighting core of the army, with their traditional role in rapid attacks through the enemy's lines. Cavalry units continued to operate successfully in this way in some Middle Eastern campaigns, but trenches, mud and artillery bombardment soon showed that the traditional cavalry role could not be maintained on the Western Front. Instead cavalry units there gradually changed to serve as dismounted infantry troops.

Horses were mainly employed to transport materials, to pull vehicles, guns or ambulances, or to perform other supporting roles. For example, artillery bombardment became central to warfare in the static conditions of France and Belgium, and all armies had large guns that had to be hauled between sites. The Royal Field Artillery was responsible for larger guns and Howitzers near the front line, drawing those by teams of up to twelve horses, and smaller (also horse-drawn) guns were used by the Royal Horse Artillery. In addition, the Army Service Corps provided a continuous delivery of food, equipment, provisions and ammunition to the front line, often but not exclusively with horses.

Across all years of the war more fodder (in terms of weight) was delivered than were shells, with huge quantities of animal food needed every day. Maintaining animals' health was not always straightforward, and specialized medical care was provided by the Army Veterinary Service, sometimes operating in very difficult conditions. Field hospitals of the Army Veterinary Service treated around 750,000 animals during the conflict, and help was also provided through public donations to the Blue Cross Fund and the Royal Society for the

Prevention of Cruelty to Animals (RSPCA). These voluntary bodies supplied drugs and other veterinary requisites, and erected and operated animal hospitals in addition to those of the military authorities. Nevertheless, many affectionate relationships between horses and men were destroyed in these years.

Animals at the Front

As well as these human costs, animals also suffered in large numbers. Thousands of horses, pigeons and dogs were shipped to continental Europe to join in the battle – and most did not return. In 1914, civilian life in all European countries depended heavily on horses for commercial and personal transport, farm-work, and even to provide power in mines and elsewhere. Motor cars and vans had appeared around the turn of the century, but in 1914 the British army had few motorized vehicles and around 50,000 horses. As the force expanded after 1914, so too did the need for more animals – heavy draught horses, light horses and riding horses, as well as ponies and mules.

In total around 1,250,000 horses served in the British army during the war, and at least a third of those died. Overall estimates of deaths from all countries due to wounds and disease are usually around 5,000,000 horses, but no complete records are available. A letter to the *Sheffield Daily*

Horses serving as ammunition carriers in Flanders.

Mud adds to daily struggles on the Western Front.

Independent on 6 January 1915 pointed out that 'one of the greatest trials of the wounded lying on the battle-fields are *[sic]* the screams of dying horses'. Many horses that avoided shells or shrapnel died instead of exhaustion, disease or lengthy exposure to bad weather, perhaps finally having to be shot by their own officers or veterinary staff. Furthermore, it has been estimated that after the war 85,000 British horses were killed to provide meat for Belgian and French families, and around 500,000 were sold to local farmers. Only around 60,000 returned to Britain. (Further details are in Display Box 1.3[34].)

Information about animals other than horses in the Great War is sketchy and unreliable. Homing pigeons were used to fly messages (attached to their legs) from advanced positions to local command posts, and those birds had to be obtained, fed, trained and made available where required. Within British infantry battalions, the Royal Engineers (at that time responsible for signals and communication) provided pigeon-lofts as well

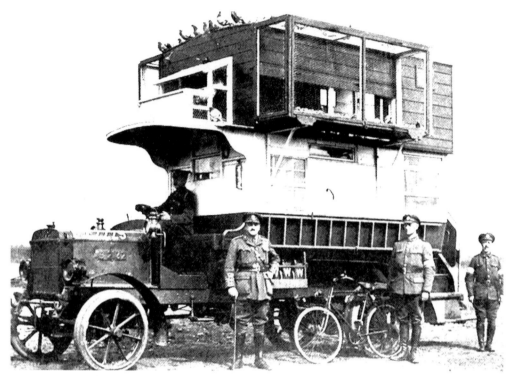

An early motor-bus modified to form a mobile pigeon coop.

as pigeons – estimated to total around 20,000 birds. Only a few documented cases of successful pigeon deliveries are available, and it is clear that many birds were killed or became lost in an unusual terrain.

Finally, the cost in terms of dogs' injury or death can only be guessed. These (also provided and trained by the Royal Engineers) were used in some places as sentries or guards and occasionally to carry messages. More often, dogs were attached to small carts for pulling those along. The army established a War Dog Training School in Britain and a central kennel in France. Unofficially, dogs sometimes served as pets to trench-based troops, with some breeds being rat-catchers as well as friends. It has been suggested that around 7,500 dogs were killed in action.

Billions of pounds

The Great War thus slaughtered a huge number of people and animals. What about its cost in terms of money? The government spent whatever it considered necessary and by late 1917 indicated that almost £8,000,000 was being spent each day – £66 a second. This was financed mainly by borrowing at home and abroad, although taxes on income, beer, tobacco, tea, coffee and other items were also increased. The government obtained large sums in this country through repayable loans from individuals, companies and banks as well as from sources in the United States and other countries. At the end of the war around £6,100 million was owed in this country and around £1,400 million abroad[35].

How much did the war cost at today's prices? A pound now is worth very much less than it was in 1918, but it is very difficult to calculate an up-to-date figure. Changes in the value of money over time depend on how those are computed, and several different procedures[36] might be used. In any case it is not clear which items should be included due to the war rather than being part of everyday expenditure. So estimates can only be rough. Recognizing that limitation, it is likely that the years of war cost Britain around a £1,000,000,000,000 at today's prices. Enormous debts had to be repaid in subsequent years – by increasing taxes on the population and by selling some assets. In addition, vital postwar reconstruction and other needed projects had to be postponed or cancelled. Irrespective of how it is assessed, the financial cost of the Great War was enormous both in its level and in its harmful consequences.

Over and above money, deaths and injury, other costs are less quantifiable but immensely important. A nation that had joined the war expecting success in a matter of weeks had suffered terribly and had become uneasy and considerably less sure of itself. The following years brought to Britain decline more than progress and disenchantment rather than a victor's pleasure.

CHAPTER 2

What Sort of Place Was Britain?

The Britain of 100 years ago was in many respects quite unlike today. People's hopes and fears were similar but (as now) life was shaped by what was known or usual or possible at the time. To help us understand life during the war let us first check out the previous years.

King and empire

> God save our gracious king,
> Long live our noble king,
> God save the king:
> Send him victorious,
> Happy and glorious,
> Long to reign over us:
> God save the king.

These words of the National Anthem were very much more part of everyday life in the early 1900s than they are today. They were sung routinely or spontaneously at social and public events of many kinds. The king and his family were widely felt to be essential elements of Britain, and royal activities were reported in detail in newspapers, magazines and the new picture theatres.

Between 1901 and 1910, the country was headed by King Edward VII (1842-1910). He was not crowned until the age of 59, and had spent his previous years (as Prince of Wales) largely in pleasure-seeking activities[37].

However, on taking over from his mother Queen Victoria (who reigned from 1837 to 1901), Edward worked hard to make himself visible and popular. He set out to meet a wide range of social groups and before long was being described as the people's king. Frequent public appearances included a visit to Sheffield in 1905 for the formal opening of the new university[38].

After Edward's death in 1910, public subscriptions in Sheffield made possible the erection of a memorial statue in Fitzalan Square (inscribed as a 'Peacemaker' who contributed to 'Peace, Unity, Truth and Philanthropy') and also the construction of the King Edward Hospital for Crippled Children in Rivelin Valley Road on a site presented by the Duke of Norfolk[39].

King Edward VII was succeeded in 1910 by George V (1865-1936). The city celebrated his coronation in a very loyal fashion, with band performances, fireworks, bonfires, decorated trams, and the planting of Coronation oak trees. Around 30,000 people watched a Britannia pageant by nearly

Only at the age of 59 did the Prince of Wales become King Edward VII in 1901.

After the death of King Edward in 1910, Sheffielders funded a statue that is still in Fitzalan Square.

Celebrating the coronation of King George V in Acorn Street, Shalesmoor, in 1910.

This 1910 coronation pageant of schoolchildren in Bramall Lane included a huge Union Jack.

15,000 children in Bramall Lane cricket and football ground, and the city's 80,000 school pupils were each given a specially-minted medal and souvenir programme.

George was a conservative survivor of the Victorian age, shaping his life around formality and strict obedience to rules. He had a strong sense of duty and, like his father, made frequent public visits to many parts of the country. His wife Mary had been a German princess before marriage and the king himself was related to many crowned heads of Europe. Descending from Queen Victoria and Prince Albert, George V's family name was the Germanic Saxe-Coburg and Gotha, and he was a first cousin of both Kaiser (Emperor) Wilhelm II of Germany and Tsar Nicholas II of Russia. The royal heads of Europe were closely interlinked in this period.

King George had very little involvement in parliamentary decision-making. Although he was in regular touch with key members of the government and, in theory, held the power of veto, his role in practice was mainly advisory and ceremonial. The aristocracy, represented by the House of Lords, had long been entitled to block legislative proposals from the (lower) House of Commons, but that power was (after a struggle) removed in 1911 by a new Parliament Act. Members of the House of Lords had been born into established families that together owned a large portion of the country. It has been estimated that in this period the richest 1 percent of the population held around 70 percent of the country's wealth. Often in possession of large estates, peers worked together through frequent social encounters and common styles of behaviour. They were the people who were most often appointed to top jobs.

The general public may have wondered about obvious disparities in wealth and privilege, but many were fascinated by aristocratic activities and upper-class social events. Newspaper articles regularly described top people's attendance at social functions, the clothes they wore, their success as owners in horse-racing, their grouse-shooting performance, or their involvement in charities. Social deference to individuals of title or high social standing was widespread. In a sense, they took the place of today's much-vaunted 'celebrities'.

George V encouraged the continuation of a society in which individuals knew their personal place and were expected to be comfortable with the status into which they had been born. He valued sharply distinct roles for husbands and wives, and considered strict social class distinctions to be essential for a stable and successful country. Advancement was commonly based on birth and background more than on experience or competence.

The upper- and lower-classes in Britain were widely separated by their attitudes, clothes, accents, values and lifestyles as well as by their wealth. However, the country's middle-class had expanded in recent years as new office and managerial jobs were created in the growing towns, and clerical workers, shop assistants and other non-manual employees were becoming more numerous. Particularly important in the lives of many middle-class people were social respectability and self-improvement, and activities were often directed at those. Book-reading and cultural activities were widely encouraged, and educational establishments for middle-class children still favoured classical and traditional themes.

Even the most prominent members of the middle-class were unlikely to cross the chasm into truly upper-class society, since that required inherited wealth and position. On the other hand, movement out of the working-class was possible for those showing effort and ability. That class was itself graded according to level of occupational skill, and a worker who had qualified as skilled, usually by serving a five- or seven-year apprenticeship, could sometimes earn double the wages of an unskilled labourer. Especially for unskilled men, periods of poor trade, unemployment or ill-health could push a family into poverty.

In the Britain of 1914, people were thus born into a social class in which they usually stayed. Dealings between the classes were based on strict hierarchical expectations and deferential behaviour, and everyone was very aware of differences in status and power. Unsurprisingly, in this layered society, members of the separate classes were sometimes suspicious or afraid of each other. For example, some middle-class individuals recognized the presence and problems of working-class poverty but they could see no solution, and the demands of many trade unionists sometimes caused middle and upper-class citizens to worry that they faced a potential upsurge of working-class rioting.

Nevertheless, all classes could see that they had in common something important – they were at the centre of the largest empire the world had known. Not only was George V the ruler of the United Kingdom of Great Britain and Ireland and of the British Dominions, he was also Emperor of India and the symbolic head of many other countries. At this time, the British Empire extended over nearly a quarter of the earth's surface and contained more than 400 million people. Its dominions (Australia, Canada, New Zealand and South Africa) were independent and self-governing, and more than forty other colonies were largely controlled from London, capital of the 'Mother Country'. The empire, 'on which the sun never sets',

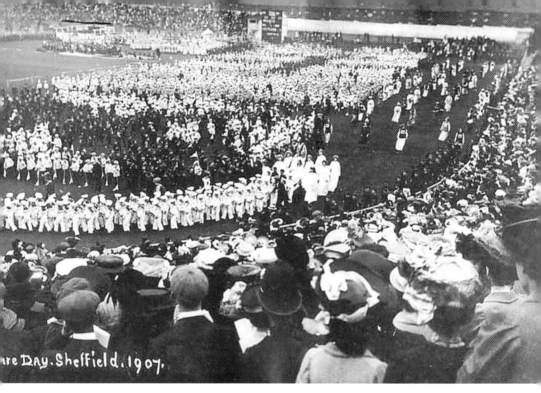

re Day. Sheffield. 1907.

Empire Day was celebrated in the city each year, here at Bramall Lane in 1907.

was a source of considerable national pride and the basis of Britain's financial and trade success around the world. It was generally viewed as part of the natural order of things, and celebrated particularly on each year's Empire Day (see Display Box 2.1)[40].

A country divided

However, more and more people were becoming uncertain about the state of the country, and change was increasingly debated. Doubts and disagreements were reported prominently in many newspapers and these contributed to a sometimes uneasy atmosphere in the pre-war years. Three of the period's difficult issues concerned votes for women, trade union unrest and conflicts in Ireland.

Votes for women

Britain in 1914 was a long way from being a full democracy. The country did not yet allow 'one man one vote', still less 'one woman one vote'. Less than 60 percent of British men[41] were permitted to vote for their member of parliament – only the ones who owned property valued at £10 or more or who paid an annual rent at that level. Additional unfairness came from

Display Box 2.1
EMPIRE DAY CELEBRATIONS

The school-day immediately before or on Queen Victoria's birthday (24 May) had in 1904 been designated as Empire Day. On that day school lessons and activities were dedicated to the magnificence of the British Empire, the greatness of the British people, and the positive influence of Britain across the world. Children were taught about their country's empire, aiming to build pride in its virtues and achievements and to encourage a sense of community with other Empire citizens. Parents and other adults joined in the annual preparations and large numbers attended the public celebrations.

Children were often dressed with colourful ribbons and patriotic finery or perhaps to represent a particular empire country. They had previously rehearsed for the day's pageants, and in many towns or cities (including Sheffield) bunting decorated public buildings. Parades, pageants, church services and concerts were held, eminent citizens made inspirational speeches, patriotic songs were sung, the national flag was saluted, and individuals came together for what was by now a major event in the nation's life. Newspapers added to the sense of occasion by publishing articles about the empire and its international greatness, and short films of events were shown in music-halls and cinemas.

The largest Empire Day pageant in Sheffield took place in Bramall Lane cricket and football ground, where around 10,000 school-children and up to 40,000 spectators were often present. As described by the *Sheffield Daily Telegraph* of 25 May 1906, that year's event 'culminated with the ceremonial saluting of the Union Jack by the assembled children, the public joining in, and Nelson's famous signal was displayed' and formally saluted' (i.e. 'England expects that every man will this day do his duty'). The *Daily Mail* described Sheffield's 1906 pageant as 'a spectacle on a scale of magnitude and ornamental detail never before attempted in England'.

Empire Day celebrations were very influential before the First World War. However, after the horrors of that conflict, flag-waving jingoism and implicit militarism was replaced by a more sombre outlook, and Empire Day gradually slipped out of public view. In 1958 its name was changed to Commonwealth Day, the second Monday in March, and it is still marked as that throughout the Commonwealth.

the facts that about 500,000 wealthy men could vote for more than one candidate, and women were completely excluded. In Sheffield, only about 75,000 men were eligible to vote in parliamentary elections out of a total male population of around 250,000 and no women at all could take part[42].

Although there had been campaigns for women's votes since before the turn of the century, it was not entirely clear what should be demanded. Votes for 'all women' would mean that, as a group, women became advantaged over men, since many men still lacked the vote. So some campaigners worked instead for equality – arguing for women being allowed to vote on the same restricted basis as men. But that would be unfair to the majority of women who were not householders or rent payers, as required by the current law. Others pressed for equality of a more radical kind, by redesigning the whole system to allow every adult to vote.

There was plenty of room for argument. In addition, a large number of people were opposed to change of any kind, either because of its massive legislative complexity or because they claimed that women were unsuited to political thinking and activity. Most of the groups campaigning for change came together from 1897 as the National Union of Women's Suffrage Societies (NUWSS), dedicated to pursue their goals in a peaceful fashion. However, the Women's Social and Political Union (WSPU), founded in 1903 by Emmeline Pankhurst with support from her daughters, came to have different ideas: they emphasized 'deeds not words'.

From 1905 the deeds of the Pankhurst 'Suffragettes' included disturbances at political meetings, smashed windows, setting fire to public buildings and assaulting prominent politicians. In 1913, a Suffragette died after throwing herself under the king's horse at Epsom, and separately Emmeline Pankhurst was sentenced to three years' imprisonment for a bomb explosion. Some Suffragettes in prison refused to eat and were instead force-fed by the authorities[43].

The force-feeding of Suffragette hunger-strikers was abandoned after public opposition.

Display Box 2.2
SUFFRAGETTES IN SHEFFIELD

Groups linked to the National Union of Women's Suffrage Societies (NUWSS) had been in Sheffield since the 1880s, and from 1906 the more militant Women's Social and Political Union (WSPU) joined them in the city. This set up an office and shop in Chapel Walk for distributing leaflets, selling fundraising items and organizing meetings and demonstrations.

Some WSPU protests set out to gain publicity from the annual Cutlers' Feast, an event that attracted considerable interest from the press and whose speakers always included at least one significant national figure. Demonstrators routinely gathered at the Midland Station to meet the early evening train from London and then congregate close to the (cordoned-off) Cutlers' Hall and in nearby streets. The police learned to expect protests and each year were out in force. On several occasions from 1908, Suffragette leaders attempted to gain entrance to the feast, sometimes trying through the back door by subterfuge or disguise. All attempts were detected and blocked by police but were reported in the next days' newspapers.

Between 1908 and 1911, the Yorkshire organizer for the Women's Social and Political Union was Adela Pankhurst, the youngest (third) daughter of the union's founder. Adela had previously held the same job in other parts of the country and her activities had led to several brief periods of imprisonment. Her campaigns in the city were sometimes noisy and boisterous but were free of serious public disorder. She lived at 45 Marlborough Road for at least part of this period, together with fellow-Suffragette Mrs Helen Archdale and her family. She also spent time campaigning in other Yorkshire towns.

Adela Pankhurst left Sheffield in 1911, gradually withdrawing from the WSPU, and in 1914 she emigrated to Australia. Her place in Sheffield was taken by 21-year-old Mollie Morris, who extended Suffragette activities (within a WSPU national policy) by planting fire-bombs in several of the city's letter-boxes; it appears that these usually turned out to be harmless. The group's meetings and demonstrations continued in the city up to the declaration of war.

These and other events were widely publicized, discussed and argued about, mainly by the middle-class rather than by working-class people. The number of women's suffrage-campaigning groups around the country reached almost 500 by 1914 (membership of the NUWSS more than tripled in the previous five years), and there were clear divisions and strong feelings throughout Britain. Several groups operated in Sheffield, and Display Box 2.2 illustrates how the WSPU became active in the city. For several years, Emmeline Pankhurst's third daughter Adela was the local organizer[44]. However, campaigning was brought to an abrupt end by the outbreak of war in August 1914, when proponents of electoral change (with a few exceptions) broke off their activities and turned to support the war effort. For example, Emmeline Pankhurst addressed meetings around the country, including in Sheffield's Victoria Hall in April 1915, urging that citizens' duty to the nation required their active support for the war (see Display Box 6.3 in Chapter Six). Wartime evidence about women's abilities and valuable contributions to society proved enough (in February 1918) to amend electoral law to benefit a proportion of women[45].

Adela Pankhurst was a Suffragette agent in Sheffield before the Great War.

Trade union unrest

For many working-class men, arguments about who should vote seemed personally irrelevant. For them, members of parliament were distant and unlikely to have much personal impact. Involvement with colleagues in a trade union seemed more likely to help in their everyday life. The number of trade unionists had been growing steadily since around 1900, and it surged from 1911 to about double the 1900 level at the outbreak of war.

The cost of living had been rising in excess of wages for several years, and real wages in relation to costs were lower in 1912 than they had been in 1900. Troubled by financial problems, several groups of working men decided in this period to use the most substantial weapon available to them by threatening to go on strike, and frequently doing so. In the years leading up to war, strikes became increasingly common and several caused national disruption on a major scale. In 1912, almost 41,000,000 working days were lost through strikes compared to around 3,000,000 in 1905, and between 1910 and 1913 the annual number of disputes was more than double the number in the previous few years.

In November 1910, following disruptions in different parts of the country by railwaymen, cotton workers and others, groups of miners across South Wales began an extended strike. Their local dispute gave rise to bitter scenes involving soldiers brought in from Salisbury Plain and policemen rushed from London. The next year saw a national railway stoppage and a widespread strike by dockers and seamen. Troops were called to a dispute in Liverpool and two men were killed. In 1912 there was a national coal strike in support of a wage demand, and other fierce disputes took place between employers and London dockers and carters. During 1913 and into 1914, trade unionists were laying plans for joint action by a triple alliance of miners, railwaymen and dock workers. A complete national shut-down was on the cards. In a sense the country was already at war – with itself.

This particular disaster was avoided by a worse one – conflict with Germany from August 1914. At that point patriotic opposition to the common enemy took over. Nevertheless, the general industrial atmosphere over the previous years had not been a comfortable one, as sections of the country repeatedly turned against each other.

Conflict in Ireland

Another kind of dispute was also very visible to the British public and it was clearly dangerous. Ireland seemed to be heading for a civil war. At the time the whole of that island was part of Britain, but relations between the mainly Protestant government in London and the Catholic majority in the south of Ireland had long been troubled. In recent decades Irish writers, politicians and a growing Sinn Fein movement had been arguing that Ireland should be separated from England – their country should have home rule. However, Ulster (in the north-east) took a different view, with its mainly Protestant population wishing to remain as members of the United Kingdom.

English politicians had been reluctant to accept the need for Irish home rule, but results from the 1910 general election caused severe practical problems for the government's day-to-day work. The Liberal party had been in power nationally since 1906 and had worked energetically to help the poorer members of society. The small Labour party (as its name suggests) also sought to assist working people and their families, with a particular emphasis on collective trade-union activity[46]. However, it had become numerically impossible for the Liberal government to carry out its legislative programme, including an Act to restrict the blocking power of the House of Lords, unless it received voting support from Irish Nationalist members of parliament. But they would not deliver their votes without a Home Rule Bill for Ireland. The Liberal party now proposed such a Bill, but the Conservatives expressed strong opposition. So too did many citizens around the country – including some in Ireland.

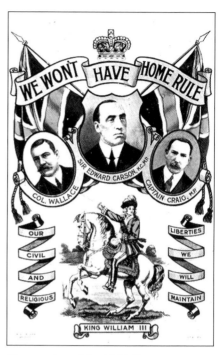

Signatories of the 1912 Protestant Covenant feared Catholic domination of Ireland if Home Rule were granted.

The centre of Irish opposition to home rule was in the north-east, where many Protestants saw home rule as a Catholic take-over of their lives. By 1912, a quasi-military Protestant force of Ulster Volunteers was active and threatening armed resistance. Around 250,000 men in the Belfast area pledged themselves in 'this our time of threatened calamity' by signing a Covenant to use 'all means which may be found necessary to defeat the present conspiracy to set up a Home Rule Parliament in Ireland'. By 1914, these Ulster Volunteers were known to be receiving rifles and ammunition from Germany and armed conflict within the country appeared imminent.

The Protestant Covenant also received support among some people on the English mainland, and a parallel English version was published in March 1914 urging any action to prevent the British army using force against fellow citizens who opposed home rule. By July, an opposing Catholic force of National Volunteers in the south of Ireland was itself armed and ready to fight the Protestants in the north. The British government alerted the nation's army and parts of the navy for action. Not surprisingly, the press and the public were gripped by this explosive situation – strongly-felt on all sides and apparently insoluble.

However, beyond Britain's shores conflict was looming on a larger scale and it soon became clear that the government had to focus on that. A quick end was needed to the Irish question, and on 30 July 1914 the Liberal government and the Conservative opposition agreed that a Home Rule Bill for Ireland was the only solution. That became law in September, but its implementation was deferred until after the war. The Irish crisis was over – but only for the moment.

Some welfare benefits
In parts of pre-war Britain there was considerable poverty, and families in difficulty had to rely for support on relatives, friends or charities. Older workers had to continue in a job long after the recent state retirement age to gain money to live, and state welfare benefits as we know them did not exist. Many politicians still thought that financial distress derived from a person's own lack of effort rather than problems and pressures from the environment. Notions of *laissez-faire* were entrenched in national thinking, such that personal responsibility was favoured rather than government intervention, and a welfare state was unheard of.

In that way, people in extreme financial need had to make a personal application for short-term assistance to the local Poor Law Guardians. These were elected by local citizens specifically to care for impoverished members of their community after setting and collecting rates from their community. The Guardians could use that money to provide some financial 'outdoor relief' to people in desperate conditions, perhaps requiring them in return to undertake work for the community, and indoor relief came from admission to a local workhouse[47].

The government required that workhouses should be unpleasant places, so that people would instead be encouraged to find jobs, and they were widely feared both for their poor conditions and because of the stigma attached to entering one. By 1914, many residents of workhouses were elderly individuals who had no money and who would never find employment – in effect living in what we would nowadays view as state-financed old people's homes. Other principal groups within workhouses were mothers and children unable to cope financially after the death or disappearance of their wage-earner, or men who were unable to find a job – sometimes disabled, and perhaps accompanied by their families, who would be placed in a separate section of the building. Sheffield had two workhouses, which will be described in the next chapter.

Members of the Liberal Party had long argued that the huge scale of working-class poverty was unacceptable. After coming to power in 1906, they set about making changes. In 1908 the government implemented an Old Age Pensions Act for poorer people over 70[48], and in the following year labour exchanges were introduced across the country to help cope with unemployment. Other Liberal innovations included a school medical service and free school meals for needy pupils. In 1911, procedures to pay some workers for medical treatment during illness were introduced, and men in a few trades became eligible for small payments if they became unemployed. Principal Acts are summarized in Display Box 2.3.

Welfare payments of these initial kinds were far from generous, but their introduction met with considerable opposition. Many workers as well as employers were unhappy about having to make weekly payments into the scheme, and the nation's taxes had to be raised to meet the additional expenditure[49]. Medical practitioners and chemists complained that payments made to them were inadequate, and Conservative members of the House of Lords repeatedly refused to accept the proposals. Deadlock about the 'people's budget' continued from 1909 to 1911 and forced two general elections – and eventually a curtailment of the power of the House of Lords[50]. More generally, many people in the country still disliked state intervention of any kind in their personal lives. Those were considered to be a matter for the individual not the government.

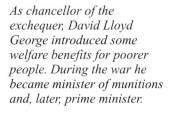

As chancellor of the exchequer, David Lloyd George introduced some welfare benefits for poorer people. During the war he became minister of munitions and, later, prime minister.

Display Box 2.3
OLD AGE, SICKNESS AND UNEMPLOYMENT BENEFITS

Pre-war Acts of Parliament introduced some welfare benefits, but only for certain sections of the population. In 1908 the **Old Age Pensions Act** created small pensions that were paid through a post office to people aged over 70. Recipients did not need to have made any previous contributions, but they had to meet requirements such as being of British nationality, having low wages, being a long-term British resident of good character, and never having been in jail or refusing work when able. Slightly larger amounts were paid to married couples, and a sliding scale ensured that better-off (but still poor) people received smaller sums. Initially around 500,000 older people were eligible, and David Lloyd George, Chancellor of the Exchequer at the time, claimed that the new pensions would 'lift the shadow of the workhouse from the homes of the poor'.

Three years later, the **National Insurance Act** introduced sickness and unemployment benefits for a proportion of workers. Both they and their employer were required to make weekly contributions, with employers confirming those by sticking a stamp on each person's insurance card. The Act's provisions were in two parts:

Health insurance covered medical treatment and the weekly provision of limited sickness benefits, but only if a person had previously made at least six months' contributions. Health cover was made compulsory for all manual workers, but self-employed and unemployed people were excluded. Sickness benefit was lower for women and in all cases extended for only twenty-six weeks. If needed thereafter, payments were halved under the heading of 'disablement' benefit. Crucially, coverage was provided only for an insured worker and not for family members. He, but not his family, became entitled to free medical treatment from a local doctor. Each insured person had to sign-up as a member of an approved society, which could be a trade union or one of the established friendly societies or insurance companies.

Unemployment insurance through the 1911 Act was also restricted to some people, in this case workers in certain trades – building, engineering, ship-building, iron-founding and a few others. Within those trades only workmen were covered, not clerks, foremen, managers or young people. Unemployment pay was restricted to people with a good record of previous contributions who were not out of work because of a trade dispute or misconduct, and benefit was limited to a maximum of fifteen weeks unemployment in any twelve months.

Everyday living

The Liberal government's innovations undoubtedly helped many poorer people. However, completely free medical treatment was many years away (the National Health Service was introduced in 1948), and doctors still expected to receive a fee from most patients. Major hospitals were charitable institutions that depended on money donated by the public (see Chapter Three), and medical examinations and treatment were basic by today's standards.

Most drugs were still derived from plants or animals and few synthetic chemical medicines had been developed. Ointments, tablets and potions were still mainly created in small quantities by local chemists, although mass-produced patent or proprietary medicines were increasingly sold by mail-order or through retailers. For instance, Sheffield newspaper-readers were told that a small dose of electricity 'repairs the broken-down human machinery by pouring a stream of new life into the enfeebled organs'. They also learned how Dr Williams' pink pills would: 'strengthen the nerves and banish all depression. They dispel pain and invigorate the system, and restore good health and a general feeling of good well-being'[51].

Men were on average about 4 inches (10 centimetres) shorter than nowadays (information is not available for women), and average life expectancy at birth was considerably below the current level – around 51 for men and 55 for women compared to present averages of about 78 and 82. Of course, many people lived beyond those average ages, which were strongly influenced by the very high rate of infant mortality. More than one in ten British babies died within their first year (now fewer than one in 2,000). People surviving into adulthood thus had a much longer life expectancy than the from-birth figure cited above. In addition, differences in health were sharp between the social classes, and infant and later mortality was (as now) greatest among poorer people.

In all social classes families were larger than nowadays. On average there were around four-and-a-half persons in each household, including nearly three children. Parents were expected to be married rather than living together without marriage, and it was difficult to obtain a divorce. A married woman's place was almost universally considered to be in the home. Women, especially middle-class, were expected to leave their jobs after marriage and devote themselves to their homes and families, while their husbands provided money from their jobs. Weekly hours of work were much more than we now expect, averaging for men around fifty-five, and periods of unemployment were common in difficult economic

Dental care was poor by current standards and several Sheffield companies dealt in second-hand teeth.

periods, especially among less-skilled workers. The official school-leaving age was not fixed at 14 until 1918, and many children before the war left school at 12 or 13 to move into jobs. Girls from working-class families often found positions as domestic servants or unskilled manual workers, and unmarried middle-class girls might assist their mothers at home or perhaps work as trainee schoolteachers, telephonists or assistants in high-class shops.

Housework was much more time-consuming and physically arduous than today. Electricity in houses was rare, especially in poorer districts. There was, of course, no central heating, and coal was used for heating and cooking. Domestic lighting came from gas. Plumbed-in baths and internal toilets were still uncommon, and bathing often took place in the kitchen (the warmest room in the house) in a metal bath, which at other times perhaps hung on a wall. Water had previously to be heated and transferred into the bath before being used by several members of the family one after the other. Most toilets of working-class houses (the majority) were in a nearby yard, and toilet paper could be torn-up newspaper.

Foxes were routinely killed to provide fur for fashionable ladies. This advertisement appeared frequently in 1914.

Wash-day for large families was particularly tiring. In the absence of running hot water separate heating was needed before washing could start, and the lack of detergents, washing machines, dryers or rubber gloves made the work difficult and unpleasant. A wooden 'dolly' was used to agitate items in the water, and additional dirt was removed by rubbing them against the ridges of a washboard. After rinsing, wet items were fed through the rollers of a mangle to squeeze out some of the water, and drying was on a rack in the kitchen or outside; rainy winter days presented major problems. Ironing was also hard work, with flat irons heated on the kitchen range and typically applied on the kitchen table covered by a blanket. All of this was considered women's work.

Making housework easier was a common theme in newspaper advertisements.

Food was very different from nowadays. Perishable items could not be transported far, and storage for long periods was not possible. Home coolers and food safes of various kinds were employed (perhaps using salt or ice), but it was usual to buy only small quantities of food to

Newspaper readers were regularly advised how to cope with pests in the home.

ensure it was eaten while still reasonably fresh. The lack of refrigeration caused frequent trips to shops or markets, with calls at many different retailers rather than at one-stop stores, thus consuming yet more time. Generally, the range of foods available was extremely limited by today's standards.

In terms of entertainment there was of course no television, and although radio had recently been invented there were no public broadcasts until after the BBC's first transmission in 1922. Middle-class families might have had a piano or a gramophone, and newspaper-reading was increasing, in part because new printing technology had led to reduced prices and better quality. However, plastic and similar materials had still to be perfected, and electronic equipment was decades away.

From the perspective of nowadays, life in 1914 was for many people restricted and hard. Four years of war made things worse.

Ready for war?

Britain had come to think of itself and its empire as largely self-sufficient. A pride in the country's 'splendid isolation' was widespread, and any military interventions were expected primarily to involve the British Navy rather than the army. In recent years the country's naval strength had been steadily increased, in part through construction of enormous battleships to ensure at least parity with Germany's fleet. It was widely assumed that Britain would continue to 'rule the waves', so a large army to fight on land was unnecessary[52]. Government policy was thus to maintain a strong navy backed up by a small army.

The country was unusual in Europe in that its army was made up of volunteers rather than conscripts forced to serve. In addition to a small force of regular soldiers (around 700,000 in 1914), the country's territorial force had been re-organized in 1908 for home defence. Territorial volunteers could not be required to serve overseas but could offer to do so, and part-time military activities had become very popular. In Sheffield there were several active territorial units, and many prominent citizens served as officers in them.

Like the rest of society, the regular army was based on a strict social-class hierarchy. Especially among older (and thus senior) officers, birth and family connections were particularly important. Senior staff's battlefield experience had mainly come from earlier cavalry engagements, and those men emphasized the primary importance of discipline, morale and firm leadership. They did not share the German interest in technological development and strategic innovation. As it turned out, both of those were soon to be in great demand.

JUNE 16, 1909.]　　　PUNCH, OR THE LONDON CHARIVARI.　　　423

THE GREAT WAR OF 19——.

Major. "IT'S PRETTY CERTAIN WE SHALL HAVE TO FIGHT 'EM IN THE COURSE OF THE NEXT FEW YEARS."
Subaltern. "WELL, LET'S HOPE IT'LL COME BETWEEN THE POLO AND THE HUNTIN'."

This 1909 Punch *cartoon saw conflict ahead and wondered about the army's readiness. An officer fears that war might interfere with hunting and polo.*

The British public, or at least its newspaper-readers, were well aware of disputes in several parts of Europe and had often been warned about Germany's apparent wish to impose itself on others. However, this country had traditionally avoided involvement in European conflicts and its intervention now seemed unlikely. Many British people preferred to ignore the gloomy predictions – Europe was somebody else's problem. So, although the British people might have vaguely expected to have to go to war, few were mentally prepared. The country had been largely preoccupied with other issues and the events of August 1914 came as a shock. As we now know, the repercussions of those events were extended and awful.

CHAPTER 3

Sheffield Before the War

A statue of Vulcan, the Roman god of fire and blacksmith to the gods, stands above the Town Hall. He is there to symbolize the city's great skills with metal. Describing the many 'reminders of the supremacy of Vulcan in his kingdom', Stewart Dalton tells us that during his childhood in Sheffield:

> The skyline was dominated by hundreds of smoking chimneys and the ring of metal meeting metal. Not only did the steelworks' smoke enter the lungs [...] but [...] steel could [also] enter the individual's psyche'[53].

That was some time after 1914, but Sheffield had long been a city of noise and smoke.

For at least seven centuries, tens of thousands of local cutlers, silversmiths and other metal-workers have passed their skills on to later generations. From the middle of the nineteenth century the city's manufacturing capacity expanded rapidly, giving rise to large factories in addition to the hundreds of small workshops. New steels were developed and produced in large quantities for railway lines, bridges and other features of the flourishing Victorian era, and widespread international trade (and hard work) brought profits from around the world. In addition, as was the case with Vulcan, weapons and armour were central. The British Association for the Advancement of Science declared in 1910 that

Sheffield 'is at the present moment the greatest armoury the world has ever seen', and in the years leading up to 1914 sales of Sheffield weaponry, shells and armour-plate were booming[54].

The town had been designated a city in 1893, and its town hall (with Vulcan on the top) was opened in 1897[55]. As in many industrial areas Sheffield's population had increased dramatically in the previous century, almost trebling between 1851 and 1901. Increases continued into the first years of the twentieth century, partly because the city's boundary was extended three times by 1914. In that year around 460,000 people lived in Sheffield, making it the sixth largest city in the United Kingdom[56]. The population was almost entirely white and from long-term British families, and marriage rather than living together was the usual form of family life. Women were generally expected to give up their jobs when they married, and births outside marriage were considered shameful.

Following the area's recent trade boom, the 1914 *Sheffield Yearbook* reported 'a considerable increase in the number of weddings among the Sheffield artisan class as a result of the prosperous state of local industry'. In addition, many middle-class families were now able to afford homes in outlying suburbs served by the city's new network of trams. However, in central and industrial areas, slums and poverty were widespread, and (as described in

Vulcan (here photographed by Pete Fisher) represents the city from his vantage point on top of the Town Hall. He was the Roman god of fire and blacksmith to the gods.

Chapter Two for the country as a whole) social and financial contrasts were very marked across the population.

Politics, the press and the churches
In 1914, the City Council's sixty-four members were evenly divided between Conservatives and Liberals. During much of the previous century the city's Liberal party had been in power and, although Conservatives governed Sheffield continuously from 1883, the Liberal party once again took over in 1901.The new council sought especially to help poorer people, for example by building working-class houses at High Wincobank and

subsidizing their rents from council funds[57]. In respect of education, Sheffield's school system had been greatly strengthened by the city's school board (operating from 1870 to 1903 within a national framework), and the Liberal party sought to continue that progress. For example, medical clinics were established in elementary schools, and free breakfasts were served to children whose parents were too poor to provide them.

Sheffield was also home to a developing Labour party, which had emerged nationally around the turn of the century[58]. The party's goal was explicitly to promote the interests of 'labour' in opposition to 'capital'. Those terms were widely used at the time, reflecting the sharp distinction between an employing class and a working-class. In addition, a minority of Sheffield Liberals viewed themselves as 'Liberal-Labour'. Although Liberal-Labour and Labour politicians shared an emphasis on the welfare of working people and their families, the Labour Party was distinctive in arguing that progress could only be made through the power of trade unions and workers' collective action and by aiming for common ownership of the means of production and distribution. A Labour councillor was first elected in Sheffield in 1905, and in each of the next few years the council had three or four Labour members and one or two Liberal-Labour councillors. At the outbreak of war, councillor numbers were as follows: Conservative twenty-four, Labour two, Liberal-Labour two, and Liberal twenty. In addition, the council included sixteen Aldermen[59]. In terms of national political representation, Sheffield had five members of parliament (MPs): three Conservatives, one Liberal and one Labour[60].

These MPs had not been elected by all the adults of the city. As described in Chapter Two, parliamentary voting was possible for only a part of the population – men who were not poor[61]. Both the Women's Social and Political Union (founded by Emmeline Pankhurst and others in 1903 to achieve votes for women) and the less militant Women's Suffrage Society had branches in Sheffield. In opposition to those the city also had a branch of the National League for Opposing Women's Suffrage[62].

The perspectives of the Conservative and Liberal parties were sometimes reflected in the city's two principal newspapers. The *Sheffield Daily Telegraph* more emphasized issues of interest to Conservative supporters, whereas the *Sheffield Daily Independent* had long been sympathetic to the Liberal party. In addition, the proprietors of the *Telegraph* also published other papers – the evening *Yorkshire Telegraph*

The parish church of St Peter and St Paul became Sheffield Cathedral on 1 May 1914.

and Star, a *Weekly Telegraph* and a Saturday evening *Sports Special*, widely known as the *Green 'Un*. A small weekly paper for trade union and Labour party members – the *Sheffield Guardian* – was published between 1906 and 1916[63]. In the absence of radio and television, newspapers were particularly important sources of information.

Up to a third of Sheffield's population attended one of the local churches, and social as well as religious activities often centred on church membership. The parish church of St Peter and St Paul became Sheffield Cathedral on 1 May 1914, and other city-centre churches included St Paul's, which stood in the present Peace Garden until 1938[64] and Catholic St Marie's Non-conformist denominations (Presbyterians, Methodists, Baptists and others) were at least as popular in the city as was the Church of England, and small numbers of Jews and Quakers were also active. Muslim and similar groups had not yet settled in the city.

St. Paul's Church & New Town Hall,
Sheffield.

St Paul's Church stood next to the Town Hall in the current Peace Garden until 1938.

Like other parts of Britain, Sheffield had experienced something of a religious boom after the middle of the previous century, but by 1914 there was clear evidence of decline[65]. Members of the working-class had on average always been less involved in religious groups, and now the middle-class was also turning away. Nevertheless, attendance was much greater than nowadays, and outlooks and social activities were still widely affected by the city's churches. Church officials routinely took significant roles in city events. Politically, members of the Liberal Party tended to be supporters of non-conformist groups and Conservative views were more likely to be consistent with those of the Church of England.

Roads and transport
The city included broad areas of open countryside, and farms operated

close to many homes. Parts of the centre had been redeveloped in previous decades and by 1914 the central layout was similar to that of today. But road surfaces and the traffic they supported were very different from now. Only around a fifth of the city's roads had a tarmacadam covering. Instead, nearly a third were surfaced with blocks (setts) made of granite, stone or even wood, and about half were compacted stone and rubble (referred to as dry macadam)[66]. Horse-drawn water-carts were used on the streets when necessary to keep down dust, spraying water from a horizontal bar at the rear of the cart. Outside the city centre, most roads were inadequately surfaced by today's standards, illustrated in Display Box 3.1.

Display Box 3.1
THE WORST ROAD IN ENGLAND?

In January 1915 the *Sheffield Daily Telegraph* published letters from several angry readers complaining about the state of the city's roads. Middlewood Road beyond Hillsborough received particular criticism, being described by some as 'the worst road in England'. An inspection by the *Telegraph* suggested that:

> For a large distance its condition is a disgrace to the responsible authority. Water runs down the hillsides on to the road, there is no channel to carry it away, it percolates into the road material and is churned up by the traffic, especially during wet periods such as we have been recently experiencing. It is quickly converted into a long course of mud and ruts, and sharp stones are loosened, which must cut the tyres of either the motor 'buses or any other vehicle going along the road.

Other problems in Middlewood Road were reported by a local doctor: 'I have twice broken the springs of my car on it.' No doubt many other local roads, especially minor ones in the suburbs, were at least as bad.

Tree-planting had recently become popular in some suburban roads, financed one-third by the council and two-thirds by residents making a request. Around 5,000 trees had been planted in recent years. For lighting, the city's streets in 1914 depended almost entirely on gas, with around 12,000 gas-lamps; less than 100 used electricity. Street gas-lights had to be lit every evening and extinguished in the morning by patrolling lamp-lighters. Since 1818, the city's gas had come from the privately-owned Sheffield United Gas-Light Company[67], but electricity was produced and sold by the council, which in 1898 had purchased the local supplier[68].

Trams in the city – originally pulled by horses – had been operated by a private company until that was taken over by the council in 1896. By 1899, a new network of routes was almost complete and electric trams were introduced. Running widely throughout the city and suburbs with eventually about 40 miles of track, these became immensely popular. Fares were low and Sheffield Corporation Tramways ran frequent services from around 4 am until after midnight, for example, passing Hunters Bar every two minutes for much of the day[69]. A few motor buses were introduced in 1913, initially avoiding the city centre and instead extending outwards some of the tram routes. For example, one initial service carried people from the tram terminus in Broomhill to fever hospitals at Crimicar Lane and Lodge Moor[70]. In 1914, the city had only ten motor buses, all with solid rubber tyres.

Sheffield centre was often busy in 1914, but walking or riding were not similar to nowadays. Horses were still very common, leaving dung and urine on the streets, and parking one's horse or carriage in the city centre could be difficult – perhaps in stables attached to one of the city's hotels.

By 1911, open-top trams were replaced in Sheffield by these fully-enclosed vehicles.

Display Box 3.2
PROBLEMS WITH NEW-FANGLED MOTOR VEHICLES

After years of working with horses, people had many problems with the new motorized vehicles. Local newspapers often reported disasters in the city, as in these two examples from the *Sheffield Daily Telegraph* of 1914:

FIRE IN A SHEFFIELD STABLE

Early yesterday morning an exciting fire occurred in a large stable at the rear of 457 Queens Road, and eight valuable horses had a narrow escape from being burned alive.

At the time of the outbreak there were twenty-one horses and sixteen vans in the place, eight of the animals being on the top floor near a hay loft. Just before five o'clock yesterday morning, a van […] was about to commence its journey, when it suddenly backfired, and in a moment the whole place was enveloped in flames. The fire was particularly violent in the hay loft, through which the horses on the top floor had to pass into safety, and […] the animals, terrified by the sight of the fire, refused to move.

When the fire brigade arrived, the hay loft was a blazing mass, and the plight of the horses […] was very serious. Two jets from the street main were at once thrown onto the building. The blaze was quickly subdued […] and the firemen after some difficulty managed to get the horses […] to safety […] The motor van […] was completely burnt out.

MOTOR LORRY RUNS AWAY

An alarming accident occurred in Broad Lane, and considerable damage was done as a result of a motor lorry getting out of control.

The lorry belonged to Mappin Brothers, brewers, Masbro', and was laden with beer. It was going up Brookhill when the steering gear went wrong, and the heavy vehicle began to run backwards. At the corner of Charlotte Street *[now Mappin Street]* and Broad Lane it collided with a gas lamp, which it knocked down. Then it crossed the road and crashed into the railings and wall surrounding the Applied Science Department of the University.

The railings, for a distance of about ten yards, were swept away, and several massive blocks of stone weighing altogether about a ton and a half were hurled into the yard below. There was no personal injury.

Petrol-engined cars had become available from around 1900, but they were expensive and unreliable, and they worked or failed to work in ways that people could not understand. Difficulties are illustrated in Display Box 3.2, and novice drivers' lack of knowledge was also shown after a collision with a tram in Abbeydale Road. The *Sheffield Daily Independent* reported that the car was removed to the side of the road and in order to examine the mechanism underneath, the chauffeur struck a match. This 'caused the whole car to be enveloped in a sheet of flame', requiring the attention of 'two motor fire engines'.

A small number of local companies now turned to car-making. For example, Burgon and Ball made La Plata vehicles from about 1903, Durham Churchill and Company produced their Hallamshire car before 1910, and Stringer and Company designed and made Winco cars in Wincobank. Meadowhall's Yorkshire Engine Company tried without much success between 1907 and 1910, and the Simplex Motor Company of Tinsley was prominent on the national as well as local scene; sponsored by Earl Fitzwilliam, that aimed at top-of-the-market purchasers[71].

In 1914 fewer than 1,000 vehicles were registered in Sheffield [72], and horses remained extremely important. They provided the power for many of the city's wagons and personal vehicles and were essential in some of the city's collieries and other companies[73]. A day-time census in 1910 of traffic on five main roads outside the centre revealed that horses and horse-drawn vehicles were on those roads almost five times as numerous as motor vehicles[74]. More than 150 accidents involving horse-drawn vehicles were recorded in the city during 1912, but around twice that number

This prototype motor-car by the city's Yorkshire Engine Company had its horn within easy reach of the driver.

The Sheffield Simplex Motor Company designed and sold top-of-the-range models.

involved motor vehicles – despite their relative rarity.

Horses towed almost all barges using the Sheffield Canal, with stabling for them provided both at Tinsley and in the city-centre canal basin. In addition, horses and carts delivered cargoes arriving by canal to sites all over the city and brought in materials for onward transportation by a horse-drawn barge. Drinking troughs were sited throughout the city. For street cleaning, the council used around fifty horses with wagons or carts, and many more worked on other council activities[75]. Much farming work would have been impossible without horses. The city held twice-yearly horse fairs, and regular (often weekly) sales took place at the Sheffield Horse Repository at 3-14 Broad Lane. For example, on one day in the autumn of 1914 this offered 'twenty-five horses, twenty carriages, 100 lots of harness, etc.'

JOHN HEATH & SONS,

CARRIAGE & MOTOR PROPRIETORS,

— AND —

FUNERAL DIRECTORS.

14. EARSHAM STREET; 653, ATTERCLIFFE ROAD,

— AND —

230, DUKE STREET,

✦ SHEFFIELD. ✦

MOTOR CABS.

Taxi companies also provided charabanc and funeral services. Heath's continue to operate from Earsham Street.

Horses still powered 'gins' by walking around a shaft to drive a corn mill or a colliery pump. This one at Killamarsh was not dismantled until 1943.

We do not know how many horses were in Sheffield at the time, but it seems likely that the number exceeded 10,000. All had to be housed, fed and cared for, and they gave rise to a wide range of jobs. Occupations listed in the 1911 *Directory of Sheffield* included horse dealers, horse keepers, horse breakers, horse slaughterers and horse hairdressers. The city then had more than fifty hay and straw dealers as well as horse-shoe makers and manufacturers of horse-nails, horse-singeing lamps and horse-clipping scissors. More than 350 men (and at least three women) were blacksmiths, about a dozen firms worked as wheelwrights or wheel-makers, and around forty of the city's men described their occupation as a 'groom'. Associated jobs in Sheffield in this period included harness-making, carriage-building, carriage spring-making, carriage-repairing and renting out horses or carriages for personal or commercial use. Individual police officers from time to time received formal congratulations for stopping runaway horses. The council paid individuals for the removal of horse manure and dead horses; and several insurance companies in the city offered policies that covered horses and cows.

Animals of other kinds were also central to many people's everyday lives, and pigs, hens or cows lived close to many homes. Sixteen cattle pounds were located across the city, for enclosing animals that had escaped. These were mainly attached to pubs, including in Haymarket, Attercliffe, Carbrook, Broomhill, Sandygate, Bents Green and Ecclesall[76]. Each year the council's veterinary inspectors examined around 500 cows based within the city boundary, and the authorities regularly took action in residential areas to 'abate a nuisance caused by the boiling of offensive matter for pig food'. Ploughing associations were flourishing in Dore, Fulwood and Norton, and each held public competitions every year[77]. The Sheffield Horse Show took place annually in Hillsborough Park, the city had its own branch of the Farmers' Union, and Ecclesall had a pig club. Local newspapers provided space for small advertisements by the public, with headings like 'Horses, Carriages, Dogs, etc', and specialized sales of cattle, calves, sheep and other animals took place in the city several times a week.

Members of the city's Cowkeepers' and Dairymen's Association operated about 200 farms in the area and each year that association set a standard local price for milk. (There was some concern about possible adulteration of milk. The city had around 600 milk retailers.) Other trade associations in Sheffield 100 years ago included the Coal Merchants' Association, the Coke Oven Managers' Society, the Confectioners' Association, the Medical Herbalists' Association, the Pawnbrokers' Association, the Pork Butchers' Association and the Sanitary Inspectors' Association. The city even had its own stock exchange, in Commercial Street, dealing in company shares and other securities and issuing its own daily list of prices.

Travel from Sheffield to other parts of the country depended largely on privately-operated railway companies. The city had two principal railway stations and around a dozen smaller ones. Trains of the Midland Railway Company called at what is now the city's main station in Sheaf Street, and the Great Central Railway Company ran trains through Victoria Station, which closed at the beginning of 1970. Those two stations were additionally used by up to six smaller companies, such as the Hull and Barnsley Railway and the North Eastern Railway. These also worked through goods stations around the city and had their own storage yards, from which they carried materials to and from customers throughout the city by horse-drawn carts or motor lorries.

Housing and local facilities

Large areas of the city were commonly shrouded in smoke, as thousands of factories worked for long hours and coal was burned in the city's almost 110,000 homes. In 1914, the council studied the city's atmospheric pollution by measuring the weight of ash deposited in different areas. The amount of soot landing on Attercliffe was 'considerably in excess of other towns' (more than 27 tons per square kilometre), but amounts measured in the parks were lower so it was argued that 'the average is not altogether unfavourable'. (By today's standards, that average was extremely unfavourable.) There was no way that Sheffielders could avoid smoke, especially in the poorer areas[78].

Between-area contrasts were also great in terms of the quality of housing. The Chamber of Commerce wrote that: 'Sheffield is essentially a city of workmen and works. Nine-tenths of the houses are working-class dwellings with low rateable values'. Nearly 20 percent of Sheffield's houses were of the back-to-back type, the building of which had been forbidden in the city for more than fifty years[79]. The central area contained many small courts, in which on average eight 'cottages' faced into a yard with a tap and external toilets. In 1911, the City Council estimated that almost 5,000 Sheffield houses were unfit for human habitation. On the other hand, many properties in middle-class suburbs such as Nether Edge and Ranmoor were comfortable, spacious and elegantly presented in their own grounds.

Families were larger than nowadays. The city's average household size was nearly four-and-a-half people, often with numerous children and perhaps other relatives or lodgers. Properties, especially the smaller ones, could be packed with people who lived in much closer contact with each other than we do today. Around 90 percent of houses were rented rather than owned, and many occupants moved frequently from one to another. Servants were still employed in many middle-class homes, often living away from their place of work and travelling there each day.

Electricity was uncommon in houses until the 1920s, in part because of the expense of installing wires and fittings throughout an existing building. Instead, gas lighting continued to be used in almost every home. That was dirty and smelly and the burning gas extracted oxygen from the air – a particular problem when windows were closed. Indoor temperatures were much lower than we are used to in our central-heated buildings, with coal fires lit only when absolutely necessary. Local dealers advertised coal deliveries by the ton, often from collieries within the city itself, with a range of types on offer such as the now-mysterious cobbles, nuts and brights.

Sheffield's water supply came from dams outside the city[80], and domestic provisions were primitive by modern standards. Toilets for around two-thirds of houses were located in an external yard and 10 percent were privy middens from an earlier generation. These required regular emptying by council workers officially described as 'night-soil getters-out'. Only about a third of the city's houses had internal water-closets in 1914, and many poorer families had to obtain all their water for drinking, cooking and washing from neighbourhood or in-yard standpipes. Supplies could also be interrupted by freezing[81]. A fixed bath was available in only around a quarter of Sheffield's houses, with most people instead bathing in a hand-filled tub – often in the kitchen or scullery where it was more likely to be warm. Even most of the new houses constructed by the council in Wincobank around this time had tip-up baths in the scullery; without pipes or taps these had to be filled with hot water from pots or buckets. In addition, slipperbaths, for personal cleansing, were attached to all of the city's swimming pools[82].

Telephones were available, but only infrequently inside a home. Instead most people had to visit a telegraph office within one of the city's post offices, both to receive calls and to make them[83]. Telegrams could be sent from telegraph offices, for which messages (charged by the word) were typed in by a member of staff. Other messages could be received by

'Coalmen' were familiar sights on the streets of Sheffield, in this case soon after 1900.

visiting the same offices or through deliveries made by telegram boys arriving on bicycles[84].

Telegrams were in effect the emails of the period, but they were expensive. Letters were cheaper and postcards were cheaper still. Picture postcards had become extremely popular in recent years for short messages[85], and frequent postal deliveries (up to six a day in Sheffield, with up to twelve daily collections) meant that mailed information could be received locally in a very short time. Postcard messages of the 'see you later today' kind were often sent within the city, and in addition mail could be dispatched later in the evening through post-boxes provided on certain tram-cars.

The Sheffield of 100 years ago provided many opportunities for shopping, with around 11,500 shops in the city. Most of these were small local corner shops, to which people (mainly women and children) could easily walk, but by now several department stores had opened in the city centre. There was no sign yet of supermarkets or out-of-town shopping centres. Many retailers were open later in the evening than is now usual, especially on Saturday which was payday, but Sunday opening was prohibited. The products on offer were, of course, packaged differently, and goods were placed behind counters on shelves or inside display cabinets for selection by shop assistants. Self-service arrived many years later. It was common for both department stores and local shops to deliver purchases if requested, and although credit was available to trusted customers, the technology behind credit cards had not yet been imagined. City-centre market halls were also important to many people. Twelve of those were administered by Sheffield Council, including the very popular Fitzalan Market, Norfolk Market, Sheaf Market and the wholesale markets for fish and other products.

In these and other respects, Sheffield and other cities were more self-sufficient than nowadays. Ownership of shops and department stores was similarly more local. We are now used to retail outlets belonging to large national or international concerns, but that was rarely the case in 1914. The hundreds of small shops were run by local people and several department stores in the centre had grown from small family businesses. Most of those have disappeared now, but a few of the original companies are still in operation. Atkinsons opened on the Moor in 1872, and other local firms of the period still active in Sheffield include jewellers H. L. Brown (now in Leopold Street, but then in Market Place) and confectioners Thorntons (now a national organization, but then in Howard

SHEFFIELD'S
ECONOMIC SHOPPING CENTRE

This advertisement for 'John Atkinson, 76-90 Sheffield Moor' appeared around 1905. Its text recommended the store's carpets, furnishings, furs, hats and children's clothes.

Street). Other shops have also remained in Sheffield, but have changed their name after joining larger companies. Cole Brothers (then at the corner of Fargate and Church Street) eventually became part of the John Lewis Partnership and is now in Barker's Pool with the John Lewis name[86]. A small number of local retailers even then were part of national organizations. For example, linked to the overall co-operative movement were the Brightside and Carbrook Co-operative Society and the Sheffield and Ecclesall Co-operative Society[87], both of which had large stores near the city centre and branches around the suburbs. Another beyond-Sheffield retailer in 1914 was Marks and Spencer, which traded locally in the Norfolk Market Hall and on the Moor.

Medical and welfare services

If you needed hospital treatment in 1914, you would probably have gone into a voluntary institution, such as the Royal Hospital in West Street (with an Annexe in Fulwood Road) or the Royal Infirmary in Infirmary Road[88]. These were called voluntary because they were charities that depended on voluntary donations from the public. Their medical staff were usually doctors who worked privately in the city and served in a hospital without payment. Voluntary hospitals remained the major providers of acute general medical care until the National Health Service was created in 1948. Some other kinds of hospital were instead funded by rate-payers and/or by tax-payers through the government; examples are described below[89].

Voluntary hospitals in the city and elsewhere were often short of money and had to work hard to raise funds in competition with each other. Each held its own fundraising campaigns and collections throughout the year, and groups and individuals organized their own activities to help. For instance, the village of Ecclesfield held an annual hospital parade with decorated floats and brass-band accompaniment, and the grounds of Holly Court, a large property in Millhouses, were opened each spring for visitors to enjoy a large display of daffodils with donations collected for the voluntary hospitals. In addition, churches sought funds on the annual

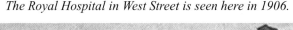

The Royal Hospital in West Street is seen here in 1906.

An annexe to the Royal Hospital was sited in Fulwood Road.

The city's other main voluntary hospital was the Royal Infirmary in Infirmary Road.

Hospital Sunday, the Hospital Saturday Fund campaigned in local companies through street collections and in social and musical events, and each year the Alexandra Rose Day called upon many hundred (mainly female) collectors.

Charities regularly published in local newspapers the names of donors and the amount of their contributions. Precise sums of money from legacies, regular subscriptions and single donations were cited for all to see, and large numbers of contributing individuals or employee groups were identified. Many factories arranged the optional deduction from wages of weekly subscriptions and it was generally accepted that individuals should give some of their own money to finance the hospitals available to them. In addition, donations of food, clothing and other items were frequently made by schoolchildren.

Particularly desirable for voluntary hospitals were continuing subscriptions taken out by individuals or organizations. These entitled the subscriber to nominate someone for admission and treatment in the hospital, with larger subscriptions paid by employers allowing them to nominate members of their workforce when required. More wealthy individuals without subscriptions were asked to pay some or all their costs, possibly being treated in a hospital's private wing.

In addition to these two general hospitals the city had two other voluntary hospitals caring for their own kind of patient. The Jessop Hospital for Women in Leavygreave, off Broad Lane, provided gynaecological and maternity services[90], and the Children's Hospital on Western Bank cared for the city's young people[91]. Both were unremittingly short of funds. Also dependent on donations and continuing subscriptions was the Edgar Allen Institute in Gell Street, which provided outpatient

The highly infectious tuberculosis was treated away from the city centre, for instance at Crimicar Lane Hospital.

medico-mechanical (mainly physiotherapy) treatment for musculo-skeletal problems[92]. The Institute offered free treatment for poor people in the mornings, and afternoons were reserved for paying patients. These medical charities were all competing for the same public money.

Three other types of hospital had greater security of funding. First, fever hospitals were financed by the City Council from local rates supplemented by government allocations. Of these, Winter Street Hospital was built in 1881[93], followed by Lodge Moor Hospital in 1887. The latter cared for patients with serious infectious diseases like smallpox, chickenpox, measles and scarlet fever. By 1914, Winter Street Hospital was used exclusively for tuberculosis. Patients convalescing from that illness were housed in sanatoria in Commonside and Crimicar Lane[94]. The fever hospitals communicated patients' condition through bulletins in local newspapers by giving each person an identification number known only to relatives and medical staff. An example is in Display Box 3.3.

Display Box 3.3
ONE DAY IN SHEFFIELD'S FEVER HOSPITALS

Regular listings in Sheffield newspapers included this one from 1914.

SHEFFIELD FEVER HOSPITALS
LAST NIGHT'S BULLETIN
The following bulletin of the conditions of patients in the Sheffield Hospitals for Infectious Diseases was issued last night.
1. Dangerously ill:- 739, 2674, 2784, 2624, 2670, 2762, 2787, 2697X, 2766X, 2795.
2. Very ill:- 2628, 2745, 2506, 2470, 2676, 2698, 2687A, 2801A. No change:- 2726, 2763. Slight improvement:- 2727.
3. Ill, but making satisfactory progress:- 2667, 2518, 2736, 2597, 2752 *(and 45 others)*.
4. Not so well:- 2610, 2542, 2509, 2492.
5. Progressing slowly:- 2244, 2426, 2764, 2760, 2519, 2749, 2717 *(and 90 others)*.
6. Satisfactory:- 2639, 2660, 2631, 2371, 2600, 2721 *(and 25 others)*.
7. Doing well:- All others not mentioned above.
8. Doctor wishes to speak on the telephone to:- 2287.

Second, mental hospitals (then called 'lunatic asylums') were funded by county councils. Locally, the South Yorkshire Asylum at Wadsley looked after around 1,700 'lunatics' in 1914, including around forty private patients who (or whose relatives) paid for the limited treatment that was available[95].

Third, hospitals in the city's workhouses, at Fir Vale, later part of the Northern General Hospital, and at Nether Edge, now converted to apartments, were financed mainly from Poor Law rates paid by householders. Providing care for extremely poor people, the Fir Vale workhouse, administered by the Sheffield Board of Guardians for the Sheffield Union in the centre and north of the city, had more than 1,000 inmates in 1914. About half of these were over 60 years of age. Also in its charge were around 300 orphans and other children, who were spread across homes in the city, and some 700 'lunatics'[96]. (County councils were required to subsidize provisions for pauper lunatics.) The workhouse at Nether Edge, operated by the Ecclesall Board of Guardians for the Ecclesall Union in the south of the city, had around 900 inmates and 500 lunatics, with around 200 children dispersed around the city including about eighty in Fulwood Cottage Homes near Blackbrook Road. By now the Nether Edge hospital included a maternity ward and an operating theatre[97].

Chapter Two has outlined how the 1911 National Insurance Act provided for working people's free medical treatment from a general practitioner on the local list or 'panel'. In 1914, Sheffield had around 170 panel doctors, and approximately 170,000 workers in the city were eligible for treatment. Since the Act applied only to people who were employed (almost all men), as many as two-thirds of the city's population (including wives, children and retired people) were ineligible. These either had to pay for their own treatment or choose to remain untreated.

The National Insurance Act had also initiated some financial assistance for workers during sickness and unemployment. However, unemployment benefit continued for only fifteen weeks and was restricted to a few trades. Payments were administered through the local insurance committee, and both the medical and unemployment schemes were organized through independent friendly societies (i.e., controlled by their members) that had been approved within the Act. Many of these were established long before 1911, collecting weekly subscriptions in order to provide financial support in periods of unemployment or to meet a family's funeral expenses. Some local societies (there were more than 300 in the city) were branches of larger organizations, such as the Hearts of Oak Benefit Society and the Equalized Independent Druids, but others operating only in the city included the Brightside and District Accident Club, the Sheffield Clerks' Association and the Sheffield Works Friendly Society.

Chapter Two also described how old-age pensions had been paid from 1909 to people over 70 with limited incomes. Sheffield City Council had established an Old Age Pensions Committee to handle claims and by 1914 several thousand older citizens were receiving small amounts each week. Generally, however, the welfare state had yet to become established, and people in difficulty depended almost entirely on their families and on charitable help.

Voluntary-funded organizations were thus central to the community's welfare. In Sheffield these included the Salvation Army's home for rescued girls, the Boys' Working Home in Broomspring Lane, 'to provide a home for boys in a state of destitution, and to afford them a measure of education', and in Paradise Square the House of Help for Girls and Young Women 'for the rescue of young girls placed in moral danger and from miserable surroundings'. A Catholic Boys' Hostel had opened in 1913 in Solly Street and this soon cared for around fifty boys under the administration of the Sisters of Charity of St Vincent de Paul.

The Sheffield Blind Institution had a school, residential home and workshops, the Boys' Charity (Bluecoat) School had moved in 1911 into new facilities in Psalter Lane, and the Girls' Charity School prepared its pupils mainly for domestic service. In addition, there were several orphanages in the city, the Guild of Help offered home visits to families in difficulty, and the local branch of the Cripples' Aid Society provided assistance to disabled people. The Refuge Home in Western Bank, 'for the restoration of fallen women', added to its donated income by operating a commercial laundry[98]. Welfare provisions 100 years ago depended crucially on a steady flow of donations and endowments from individuals and groups.

Entertainment and social activities
Life without radio (referred to as 'wireless' until the 1940s), television or music-on-the-move would be unbearable to many people today, but those were not available in 1914. Some middle-class families possessed a piano or a small domestic organ and sales of sheet music were booming. Also popular were gramophones – still sometimes referred to as a phonograph or a talking machine[99] – and several types of automatic player with names

like Pianola and Autopiano. For them a Music Roll Subscription Library rented out re-playable tunes from 76-80 Surrey Street. Newspaper content was more detailed than is usual today, and mothers and daughters were often kept busy sowing and making or repairing clothes. The city's Central Public Library loaned around 90,000 books a year and eight branch libraries, seven evening reading rooms and book delivery stations were also hard at work[100].

'Whit Sings' were still extremely popular, especially with Methodist families. On Whit Monday smartly dressed children walked in procession with bands, and often with their church's Sunday school banner, to one of the city's parks for communal hymn-singing. For example, in Meersbrook Park in 1912, around 12,000 people, including 7,000 children and teachers from twenty-two Sunday schools,

This Victor V phonograph, a 'talking machine' for listening in the home, was pictured in 1907.

were drawn from three different processions. Also popular were Empire Day pageants and associated festivities. These have been illustrated in Chapter Two's Display Box 2.1.

Public houses were very busy in 1914 and around 620 are listed in Sheffield street directories of the time. Public drunkenness had long been a matter of concern in large cities and as many as ten temperance societies were campaigning against alcohol in the city. The Sheffield Temperance Society held three open-air anti-drink meetings each week throughout the year in West Bar and a gathering every Sunday in the Temperance Hall in Townhead Street[101].

For some members of the city's middle-class, social activities could be based on private clubs. The Athenaeum in George Street had rooms for chess, billiards, newspaper reading and dining as well as a library and a separate room for ladies. Membership of the Sheffield Club in Norfolk Street was advertized to 'include the nobility and gentry of the neighbourhood and the leading citizens', and the Reform Club at the corner of Church Street and St James's Row had dining and reading rooms

Whit celebrations in Norfolk Park in 1912. A huge choir of schoolchildren was often conducted by Henry Coward.

on the first floor above shops and offices, and billiard and smoke rooms on the second floor. Masonic lodges and political clubs across the city were also important as male social settings, and members of the Literary and Philosophical Society met monthly in Church Street to hear lectures 'dedicated to the cultivation and advancement of literature and science'[102]. Away from the city centre, several social clubs were aimed specifically at working men or women, sometimes with support from religious organizations seeking to encourage temperance.

Sheffielders could also take advantage of one of the city's eight swimming pools. In addition to slipper-baths for personal cleansing, several pools advertized special facilities such as electrical, medicated, Russian or vapour baths. Separate bathing times for men and for women were usual, although mixed bathing was allowed in some baths at specified times only. Glossop Road baths had a separate pool for women and also a first-class men's pool, which was more expensive than the others. As shown in Display Box 3.4, water in the pools was not always fresh and there were occasional reports that it was 'darkish brown'.

Display Box 3.4
FRESH-WATER DAYS IN SHEFFIELD'S SWIMMING POOLS

Admission prices for swimming were generally doubled on days when the water was fresh. It was changed three times a week between June and September and otherwise twice a week. Schoolchildren were admitted for half-price outside school hours. Adult summer prices for 1916 were as follows:

	Fresh-water days (Monday, Wednesday, Friday)	Yesterday's-water (Tuesday, Thursday, Saturday)
Attercliffe	Two pence	One penny
Brightside	Four pence	Two pence
Corporation Street	Two pence	One penny
Glossop Road Women's	Four pence	Two pence
Second-class men's	Four pence	Two pence
First-class men's	Six pence	Six pence
Heeley	Four pence	Two pence
Park	Four pence	Two pence
Rivelin Valley (open air)	Free	Free
Upperthorpe	Four pence	Two pence

Grouse-shooting was still considered by some to provide good sport on the nearby moors, and hounds for fox-hunting were maintained by Earl Fitzwilliam. In addition, the Stannington Hunt had around twenty-five hounds for members to hunt foxes in the Rivelin area, and hare-hunting was undertaken by the Hallam and Ecclesall Pack and by Mr Butcher's Beagles.

Less wealthy individuals came together in sporting clubs of different kinds. No less than forty-eight bowling clubs were affiliated to the Sheffield Amateur Bowling Association, and bowling greens within the city's parks had more than 100,000 users in 1913[103]. Sheffield in 1914 had around fifty hockey clubs (separately for men and women), and most of the city's eleven privately-owned golf clubs were open to both sexes. Tennis players could belong to one of about twenty clubs, including the Hallamshire Lawn Tennis Club near Hunter's Bar. Association football was also extremely popular, with a large number of clubs competing in several local leagues. For spectators, both Sheffield United and Sheffield Wednesday were in the first division of the football league, playing at Bramall Lane and Hillsborough respectively, with cricket also taking place at United's ground, as it was until 1973.

Many Sheffielders joined local or company angling clubs, or perhaps were members of their firm's sports society. And the city's Homing Pigeon Association was thriving. Cycling had been extremely popular for several decades and around twenty cycling clubs in the city arranged communal rides and other social events. Other Sheffield clubs in 1914 included more than a dozen for chess-players and about as many for draughts, a model aeroplane club, several horticultural societies, a bee-keepers' society and the Sheffield Chrysanthemum Society. On Saturday afternoons convoys of cars from the Hallamshire Motor Club would leave the city centre for locations, usually with a tea-room, in Derbyshire[104]. For the less wealthy, charabanc outings were popular. Another widely undertaken activity was the cultivation of a rented allotment, and more than 1,600 plots were provided by the City Council in eight different areas of the city[105]. Allotment regulations forbade gardening on a Sunday.

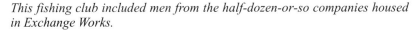

This fishing club included men from the half-dozen-or-so companies housed in Exchange Works.

This charabanc is setting out on a trip to Dovedale in June 1914, clearly not meeting today's safety standards.

In addition to activities of these kinds, amateur choral singing was extremely popular. Rehearsals and concerts were frequent, in church halls or larger settings such as the Albert Hall in Barker's Pool (on the site currently occupied by John Lewis department store)[106], the Temperance Hall in Townhead Street and the (Methodist) Victoria Hall in Norfolk Street. In the words of a subsequent account, 'the city teemed with capable amateurs […] *White's Directory* for 1910 listed no fewer than 240 private music teachers […] brass bands and military bands were numerous [… and] the enthusiasm for grand opera rivalled the cult of the choral festival'[107].

Audiences flocked to commercial theatres like the Empire Palace of Varieties at the junction of Charles Street and Union Street, holding 3,500 people, the Hippodrome in Cambridge Street, with 3,000 seats, the Lyceum, holding 2,500 in what is nowadays Tudor Square, and the Theatre Royal, close to the Lyceum[108]. Often featuring famous actors and entertainers like Scottish singer Harry Lauder or American escapologist

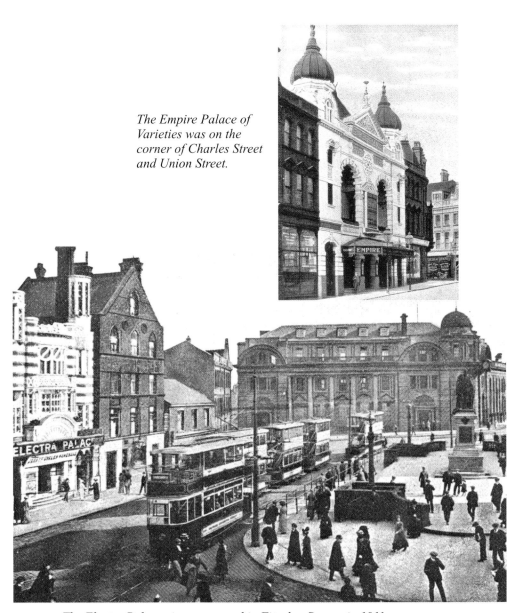

The Empire Palace of Varieties was on the corner of Charles Street and Union Street.

The Electra Palace cinema opened in Fitzalan Square in 1911.

Houdini, these presented a mixture of plays, short sketches, specialty acts and musical entertainment, but they were also starting to include brief film shows as customers were increasingly being drawn away to a new development – the cinema or 'picture theatre'.

The city's first purpose-built cinema, the Picture Palace in Union Street, opened in 1910 and was followed by the Electra Palace in Fitzalan

Square (1911) and the Cinema House in Barker's Pool (1913). By that year films were being shown in around thirty Sheffield cinemas, each capable of holding several hundred people[109]. They projected black-and-white and silent but subtitled stories or short episodes of activity by royal or other dignitaries, often with accompanying music from a pianist or small group of musicians. Several cinemas also offered other attractions, such as a tea lounge, a grill room or billiard facilities. The Electra Palace advertized 'five first-class tables' in its Lower Hall.

Travelling menageries and circuses were also popular. Between 1910 and 1913, Frank Bostock's visiting menagerie drew substantial crowds to a large building at the bottom of Hawley Street. Previously a roller-skating rink, the Royal Alexandra, this now became 'The Jungle', where visitors could view a large collection of animals and a range of bizarre shows and exhibitions. At its opening it was said to include 100 lions and 'the smallest and most perfect horse in the world', only 28 inches (70 centimetres) high. Later attractions included a boxing kangaroo, an educated elephant, a wrestling bear, a snake charmer, a rope climber and Anita the Living Doll[110].

Cinema House was in Barker's Pool, close to its junction with Leopold Street.

When in Sheffield, Frank Bostock's travelling menagerie was sited at the bottom of Hawley Street, here in December 1910.

Like other menageries, the Jungle was closed each winter and it did not re-open in Sheffield in 1914 after in 1913 advertising an intended world tour. In fact, it went to Ghent in Belgium. Its escapist displays were very popular, fitting well with many people's relatively simple tastes in a pre-radio and pre-television era. Even simpler, a Sheffield father was fined 40 shillings (£2.00) for exhibiting his 6-year-old son in a circus – the child weighed 12 stone.

CHAPTER 4

Autumn 1914: British Recruits and Belgian Refugees

Monday 3 August 1914 was a Bank Holiday in Britain. Local events included the Norton Agricultural Show and the Ranmoor Flower Show, and many Sheffielders were at the seaside or in the countryside. On the same day in Germany, decisions were being taken that would shatter the lives of millions. In support of Austria-Hungary, the German Kaiser confirmed his army's plan to attack France, with an initial assault through Belgium. As outlined in Chapter One, that provoked an immediate British response[111].

The war cloud bursts

Readers of the *Sheffield Daily Independent* on that Bank Holiday Monday were met with the headline 'War Cloud Bursts'. The *Independent* and other papers gave details of military activities in several parts of continental Europe and described how all British troop training had been brought to an immediate end in case the country became involved. On the next day, 4 August, British banks remained closed to prevent a panic withdrawal of savings, and the (evening) *Yorkshire Telegraph and Star* concluded that 'nothing can now prevent the outbreak of hostilities between this country and Germany'. In large letters it stated: 'WAR NOW INEVITABLE. GOD SAVE THE KING'.

At 11 pm (UK time) war was declared. King George issued a series of proclamations that placed the country on a war footing, and the next day the entrance to Sheffield's town hall was packed with people reading the statements displayed there. In a situation of great uncertainty, many were anxious about the future and about a major loss of trade and jobs. A large number took the precaution of buying stocks of food, and this surge in demand created shortages and pushed up prices. At the same time there was some relief that a decision had been taken. It was widely expected that the war would be successful and short, perhaps over by Christmas.

Military units were immediately ordered into action and in the next few days several Acts of Parliament gave the government considerable power over daily life and work. It took control of all the (privately owned) railway companies[112], and for the first time on 5 August issued £1 and 10 shilling notes. People were asked to exchange their gold sovereigns and half-sovereigns for these notes. Otherwise cash might run out as gold was hoarded[113]. The food-buying panic subsided after a few days and most previous opponents of Britain's involvement in the war, such as the Labour party and the women's Suffragette movement, came to accept the need to fight. Almost all national and local newspapers expressed patriotic enthusiasm for the government's decision and urged readers to support the national effort[114]. Taking up a phrase recommended by several London retailers, David Lloyd George, the chancellor of the exchequer, quickly urged upon the country that it would be business as usual.

That was not the case for Sheffield's pawnbrokers, who were soon overwhelmed by customers seeking to get hold of money. Many pawnbrokers closed down until the banks became able to provide more funds. Workers' holidays were cancelled in Sheffield's main armament works after the government ordered them to work night as well as day, and military band concerts in the city's parks were cancelled as musicians returned to active service. Police barriers were set up on twenty-six main roads into the city[115], and power stations, reservoirs and other public utilities were placed under guard. Police Sergeant Walter

The war expanded the job of Police Sergeant Manvell, who now also had to guard reservoirs in Derbyshire.

Manvell from Broomhill spent hours watching over the dams at Strines, taking a pet dog from the neighbourhood as company.

New soldiers

Although compulsory military service was widespread across continental Europe, it had long been viewed as unacceptable in Britain, and the British army was manned entirely by volunteers. Urgent steps were now taken to recruit more men. Early in the evening of 4 August, Sheffield's recruiting officer received an urgent instruction to start seeking men. Individuals with previous service in the territorial force, and therefore partly trained, were the first to be sought, but a wider range was soon in demand. The government appointed as Secretary of State for War the distinguished soldier Field Marshal Lord Kitchener (1850-1916), who immediately ordered a massive increase in troops whether or not they had previous military experience.

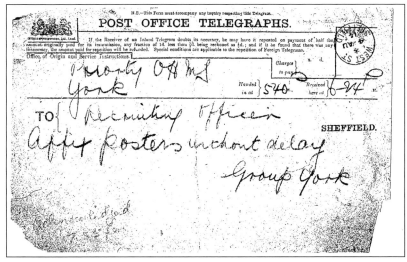

A few hours before war was declared, this 'priority' telegram was sent to Sheffield from the army's Northern Command in York.

MOBILIZATION.

All ex-Territorial Soldiers who are willing to rejoin the Colours should report themselves either personally or in writing to their former Corps without delay.

HORATIO MENDS,

Brigadier General.

SECRETARY,

West Riding of York County Association.

York, 4th August, 1914.

Sheffield newspapers published this recruiting request as soon as war was declared.

By 20 August 1914, recruiting advertisements in the city's newspapers were giving more details.

Your King and Country need you.

A Call to Arms.

An addition of 100,000 men to His Majesty's Regular Army is immediately necessary in the present grave emergency.

Lord Kitchener is confident that this appeal will be at once responded to by all those who have the safety of our Empire at heart.

Terms of Service.

General service for a period of 3 years or until the war is concluded.

Age of enlistment between 19 and 30.

How to Join.

Full information can be obtained at any post office in the kingdom; or

At any military depot.

God Save the King!

From 7 August, recruiting posters appeared in newspapers all over the country. For several days Sheffield's press included urgent requests from Lord Kitchener for men to join the army, and widely-displayed posters urged 'every patriotic young man' to 'answer the call'. Prominent in each case were the phrases 'Your King and Country Needs You' and 'God Save the King'.

Kitchener's initial recruiting target was for 100,000 additional men, but this was soon raised to almost a million and the upper age-limit for volunteers was lifted from 30 to 38. Early posters specified a wartime commitment of at least three years, reflecting Lord Kitchener's belief that a rapid conclusion was unlikely. However, many young men and their families expected a shorter conflict, and volunteers came forward in large

This striking image of Lord Kitchener was used in many different recruiting posters.

Among the advertisements in Sheffield's newspapers on 27 August 1914 was this one.

YOUR COUNTRY NEEDS YOU

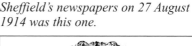

FOR KING & COUNTRY.

MEN URGENTLY NEEDED

FOR

HIS MAJESTY'S ARMY.

Men can join for duration of War, and will be discharged directly War is over.

Recruiting Offices:

10, St. George's Terrace, Brookhill.

429, Attercliffe Road.

534, Brightside Lane.

GOD SAVE THE KING.

numbers. Anti-German feeling was encouraged by newspaper and magazine repetition of German atrocities, barbarism, brutality, outrages and savagery in the 'murder of civilians' in Belgium. Recruiting speeches were given in local factories, creating enthusiasm that drew colleagues to put themselves forward as groups, and encouragement from friends and family was widespread. Prominent citizens and churchmen added their support and encouragement. Watchmaker and jeweller H. L. Brown[116] appealed to young Jewish men to enlist and rewarded each one with a high-quality watch. Several employers in the city offered money to employees who would enlist.

Local cinemas reinforced the mood by showing items about the war[117] in addition to their usual films. The Electra Palace in Fitzalan Square offered *War Specials in Pictures* and *German Atrocities in Belgium*. The Picture Palace in Union Street showed a 'thrilling story', *Your Country Needs You*, and Cinema House in Barker's Pool gave prominence to *England's Menace*. That was described as 'a great patriotic naval drama telling a pulse-stirring story of an attempted foreign invasion' and 'an astoundingly accurate forecast of the dangers of the present situation'. Concerts in the city also took on patriotic themes, emphasizing the nation's history and importance. On 15 October 1914, Madame Clara Butt, a distinguished singer of the time, was accompanied in the city's Albert Hall by the chorus of Sheffield Music Union in performances of *The Home Flag*, *Fall In*, *Harbour Lights*, *Drake's Drum*, *Land of Hope and Glory* and, of course, the National Anthem. Union Jacks were available at the hall to purchase for the war effort and were waved enthusiastically during parts of the evening.

With frequent reminders that 'Your King and Country Need You', volunteers were sought in the city for two kinds of military unit – those already established and in need of additional men and also for an entirely new infantry battalion. The established units mounted their own campaign in addition to the general effort. The Hallamshire Rifles asked potential recruits to present themselves at their Hyde Park headquarters and the Royal Field Artillery unit sought 'persons used to horses' including blacksmiths, saddlers and wheelwrights. Second, an entirely new unit was formed, which became the Twelfth York and Lancaster (Service) Battalion[118] – the Sheffield City Battalion known informally as Sheffield Pals.

Although the idea of a special Sheffield unit was discussed for some days in the local press, a principal initiative for action came from Sheffield

RECRUITS FOR R.F.A.

West Riding Divisional Ammunition Column (Foreign Service).

WANTED, at once, RECRUITS for the above. Special preference to Carters and persons used to Horses. Few Vacancies for SADDLERS, SHOEING SMITHS, and FARRIERS. Also SHOE MAKERS.—Apply Norfolk Barracks, Edmund Road, Sheffield.

(Signed) **H. E. AYKROYD,**

Lieut.-Col. R.F.A. (T.)

Commanding West Riding Divisional Ammunition Column.

Specialized recruits were sought for the Royal Field Artillery's work with horses.

Among its other wartime uses, the drill hall in Glossop Road provided facilities for enlistment in November 1914.

G. R.

3rd West Riding Brigade R.F.A. (T.)

(SHEFFIELD).

MEN WILL BE ENLISTED FOR THE ABOVE BRIGADE

AT THE

DRILL HALL, GLOSSOP ROAD, SHEFFIELD,

TO-DAY.

Vacancies for several Saddlers, Shoeing Smiths, and Wheelwrights;

Also 100 Gunners, and 100 Drivers,

To Complete Establishment of Divisional Ammunition Column.

Apply :—**MAJOR L. K. COLLEY,**

O.C. Depot.

University. The university's vice-chancellor, H. A. L. (Herbert) Fisher, was a strong supporter of Britain's involvement in the war, giving well-attended lectures on military and political themes in the city. Following an enquiry from the War Office and discussions within the university, Mr Fisher developed proposals to form a new Sheffield-based unit, and very quickly it was agreed that the City Council, local territorial units and the university would work together on such a scheme. The War Office by now was overburdened with other administrative demands and required that the city itself formed the unit and provided the necessary finance, clothes and training until it could be taken over[119].

The plan was announced in Sheffield on 1 September 1914, and volunteers were asked to report to the Town Hall on the next and succeeding days. Advertisements were hastily prepared for what was to be called the 'Sheffield University and City Special Battalion', and the university's initial poster sought men from 'the University and Public Schools', including from its own Officers' Training Corps. This narrow educational focus was soon adjusted to seek a wider range of backgrounds – teachers, clerks, shop assistants and others – but the emphasis remained

Initial recruiting efforts by the
new Sheffield City Battalion
were directed at university and
other educated men.

Later Pals posters noted 'the city expects
and the city knows that every man will
do his duty'.

on white-collar rather than manual workers[120]. A less restrictive title was
now chosen – the Sheffield City Battalion.

A few days later, men who had registered for the new unit were invited
by postcard to attend a medical examination and attestation (the formal
act of stating one's readiness to enlist). A temporary recruiting station was
established in the Corn Exchange in Sheaf Street[121], run by the local
Conservative and Liberal parties, each of which provided their own agents
and volunteer clerks. The battalion soon reached the required 1,000 men
and was officially formed on 10 September 1914.

No uniforms were available and initial training for most men was
carried out in civilian clothes. Members of the battalion continued to live
in their own homes. They were due to be accommodated in a hutted camp
to be built at Redmires on the western edge of the city, but that would not
be available until December[122]. Sheffield Pals stayed at Redmires until
May 1915, when they moved out of Sheffield for training in Staffordshire

Initial enlistment for the new City Battalion was in the Corn Exchange on 12 September 1914.

Uniforms and equipment were at first unavailable for the hastily-formed Pals, here on drill practice at Bramall Lane.

and beyond. Responsibility was taken over by the War Office in August of that year and the men, with eighty-nine horses and mules, sailed for Egypt in December 1915[123]. In the following spring the Sheffield Pals were sent to the Western Front, where they suffered dreadfully in the Battle of the Somme, which opened on 1 July 1916. On that first day more than 500 members of the battalion became casualties and this simultaneous death or mutilation of so many local men severely affected the city.

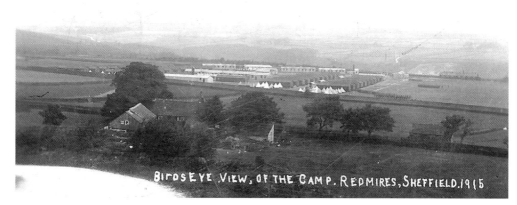

From December 1914, the City Battalion was housed at a new camp at Redmires on the western edge of the city.

Large crowds watched Sheffield Pals leave the city on 13 May 1915.

Recruiting offices

Although the Corn Exchange had been used for the new battalion, Sheffield's general recruiting office was at 10 St George's Terrace, near to St George's Church in Brookhill. Supplementary recruiting offices were established throughout the city, sometimes for short periods only[124]. A medical examination was compulsory to ensure that new soldiers met minimum standards of eyesight, height and other features, and a large number of would-be volunteers were rejected at that initial stage[125].

In the first few weeks of war, Sheffield's newspapers gave great prominence to the city's recruiting activities, with frequent suggestions that other north-of-England towns were doing better. The weekly numbers of new recruits were carefully monitored and reported in the press, and there were many complaints either about Sheffield men's unwillingness to come forward or about the inefficiency of the city's recruiting.

Display Box 4.1
RECRUITING IN SHEFFIELD: TWO DIFFERENT VIEWS

Recruiting facilities in Sheffield were initially overwhelmed by the large number of men wanting to enlist. At the same time, some people in the city were concerned that too many men were shirking. Here are the contrasting views:

1. In early September 1914 the *Sheffield Daily Independent* contained several reports and comments about what it described as 'Sheffield's Scandal'. For example, 'there are thousands of men in Sheffield anxious to join the forces. They are waiting, waiting in long queues outside little offices with staffs incompetent to do the work'. 'Men are going day after day to the recruiting stations full of patriotic enthusiasm and waiting for hours until their ardour is damped. Not a few have waited 10½ hours on the pavement and then been turned away.' 'One man [...] stood like a beggar at the gate [...] and was one of a crowd of 500 for whom arrangements could not be made. Yesterday morning he was there [again] at 10 o'clock and still at 3 in the afternoon he was still waiting. This is not only ridiculous, it is tragic.'

2. A subsequent letter to the *Sheffield Daily Telegraph* signed by 'A Britisher' complained about the city's 'Half-Hearted Recruiting'. 'Our recruiting is being done in a half-hearted fashion [...] I cannot understand how so many men, especially the younger end who (apparently) are eligible in every way to serve the country, and it needs all the men it can obtain, are not conscience-stricken or ashamed to be pursuing their ordinary avocations and pleasures as usual.' Other published letters made the same point.

Procedures eventually settled down and it is not surprising that the sudden demand on recruiting facilities had caused problems. For many years the army had sought only a small number of new entrants and was unprepared for the huge increase in 1914. Difficulties were compounded by the requirement to select and train a large number of administrative staff and to set up new procedures. Sheffield's initial recruiting contribution appears to have been up to the level of other large cities, but success brought its own problems. It soon became clear that the nation's mass recruiting had left behind too few skilled workers to produce material for the war.

Within two days of war being declared the local papers also published large advertisements headed ARMY HORSES WANTED. The army's chief purchasing officer announced: 'I am empowered by the War Office to impress all horses in Sheffield,' and he urged owners willing to sell animals to send them to the Sheffield Horse Depository at 8 to 14 Broad Lane 'where they will be examined and purchased if suitable at 4 o'clock pm daily'[126]. Pigeons were also needed to convey military messages and the Sheffield Homing Pigeon Federation asked its members to sell their birds to the government. The federation reckoned that they should be able to offer 1,000 birds capable of crossing the English Channel.

Other groups contributed in their own way. By 8 August 1914, Sheffield's Automobile Association and Motor Union was appealing to the owners of motor-cars and motorcycles to place those 'at the disposal of their country'. Motorcyclists were also sought, either with their own machine or to ride one provided by the army. Within a fortnight the city council had made available many of its horses, carts and motor lorries.

The first few months of war
From then on life in the city was dominated by war and by anxieties about the future. Some firms immediately reduced their working hours or laid-off part of their workforce. On 11 August 1914, the lord mayor formed a Sheffield Distress Committee to cope with the anticipated increase in unemployment and poverty. A Sheffield Relief Fund sought donations from companies and individuals, quickly raising a substantial amount of money for needy families[127]. At the same time the city's trade unions and co-operative groups set up their own relief fund for members, and the City Council developed plans for relief work in which unemployed men would be paid to assist with street-widening and other necessary tasks.

In practice, unemployment did not increase as expected. Some companies did initially suffer, for instance firms making silverware and luxury items, manufacturers depending on materials from Germany, and retailers specializing in German goods[128]. However, within a month many Sheffield companies were receiving orders to meet the needs of war – not only for armaments and steel but also for cutlery, razors and a wide range of supporting items. Elsewhere in the country, holiday resorts immediately lost thousands of visitors, and after only a week of war advertisements appeared in the local press seeking to convince Sheffielders that seaside attractions were still safe as well as pleasant.

BLACKPOOL.

OFFICIAL STATEMENT BY THE CORPORATION.

VISITORS to BLACKPOOL are hereby ASSURED

that all the conditions in BLACKPOOL are **JUST AS USUAL.**

Bread and Provisions as Cheap as in any Town in England. :: Abundant supply.

Charges at Hotels, Boarding Houses, Restaurants and Cafes as before the War.

ALL ENTERTAINMENTS IN FULL SWING
With Unrivalled Programmes.

STEAMBOAT EXCURSIONS DAILY

Tourist and Ordinary Bookings by all Railways.

BLACKPOOL BREEZES STILL BLOWING!

By 10 August, Blackpool needed to adjust its advertisements in the city's newspapers.

Shops in the city sought to turn a difficult situation to their advantage, promoting many articles in terms of their special value in wartime. John Atkinson's department store offered to mail its blankets to military recipients: 'if you want to help our soldiers, purchase a blanket'. On other days Atkinson's advertised material at 'practically' cost price to 'ladies who are interested in the making of soldiers' sleeping helmets, body belts, socks, etc'. Those items were being requested by the local newspapers and several women's groups for sending to the War Office. Pharmacists Boots, with branches in High Street and West Street, claimed that 'when its feet give out the army must give in'. They offered to send to the troops some of the company's Foot Comfort ointment on behalf of every purchaser. On other days Boots' Sheffield advertisements recommended vermin powder (against lice, described as 'the pest of the trenches'), anti-fly cream, iodine tubes and water sterilisers.

Tea specialists Arthur Davy and Sons, with shops in Fargate, Haymarket and elsewhere in the city, published drawings of foreign-looking soldiers on foot and on horseback with the text: 'India's magnificent loyalty in the Empire's hour of need has stirred the admiration of the world. Indian princes and Indian peasants, Indian troops and Indian treasure – all are being placed at Britain's service with touching devotion. You can do India a small service in return […] Show your gratitude to India in a practical way […] Buy our […] choice Indian blends [of tea]'.

Cole Brothers took advantage of the great increase in nursing requirements by promoting nurses' uniforms and hospital beds. Department store John Walsh advertised its stock of 'Regulation Army Blankets – suitable for use in army camps'. Jewellers H. L. Brown urged 'practical patriotism', asking for 'your kind assistance in this commercial crisis and so enable one of Sheffield's industries to emerge triumphantly in this industrial war'. T. B. and W. Cockayne's department store advertised regular 'patriotic concerts by the Belgian Quartette Jean', taking place every day in its restaurant for up to two hours. These were given by four sisters of the Jean family of Belgian refugees (see below), one singing

National **Appeal**
FOR
BLANKETS
TO-DAY!!!
JOHN ATKINSON
CAN SUPPLY
ANY QUANTITY
FROM . .
2/9
. . . EACH.
If you want to help our soldiers purchase a Blanket. We undertake to pack and forward to the War Office.

JOHN ATKINSON
Sheffield Moor.

City-centre stores found opportunities in the new situation.

and the others playing piano, violin and cello. On other days the store announced a 'Special Engagement of Miss Eva Rich to sing the National Anthems of the Allied peoples […] each afternoon from 3 to 5 o'clock'. 'At intervals during the Recital there will be a Fashion Parade' exhibiting clothes from the Allied nations.

Other Sheffield advertisements of this period are noted in Display Box 4.2. As Christmas 1914 approached, local newspapers gave prominence to suggestions about presents, especially warm clothes, to be sent to soldiers and sailors. One suggestion was a French-English pocket dictionary for use on the Western Front.

Cigarettes were extremely popular at the time, and retailers and other organizations were enthusiastic in promising to send packages to the troops. Tobacconist Wiley and Company in the Haymarket proclaimed that 'Your soldier friend would be pleased with a box of Wiley's cigarettes or a few cigars with your card or a message enclosed'. 'Give us your instructions and we will see it through' – at reduced prices[129]. In addition to retailers' promotion of cigarettes in this way, cash donations from the public were routinely used to buy cigarettes for troops. For example, the *Sheffield Daily Independent* asked for cash in order to buy gifts for 'the gallant men fighting our battle'. The paper reported in December 1914 that it had 'sent cigarettes by the hundreds of thousands to the hospitals and troops at the Front'. Further donations were now requested and each parcel would again contain 300 cigarettes, a quarter-pound of tobacco, a briar pipe and a box of matches, together with some eating chocolate, peppermints and packet of stationery.

By October 1914, businesses were finding new ways to boost sales from the war.

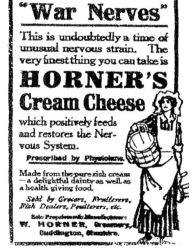

Helping soldiers was a common theme in many advertisements by Sheffield retailers in the autumn of 1914.

Display Box 4.2
PERSUADING PEOPLE TO SPEND

Retailers sought to attract customers by emphasizing the wartime value of their products, pointing to special benefits at this unusual time or spelling out their company's Britishness. Here are some excerpts from advertisements in Sheffield newspapers during the autumn of 1914. Many were accompanied by military or other eye-catching illustrations.

- **Our Soldiers at the Front Need Blankets Badly.** This is the time to show true patriotism […] Purchase from here. (Proctor and Son, drapers)
- **Support the British Corset Industry**. We appeal to the patriotism of every British woman […] Refuse to buy German corsets. (J. S. Blair and Sons)
- **Notice to All Volunteers, Territorials, Servicemen** […] We are offering all soldiers' clothing and comforts at practically cost price. (John Atkinson, department store)
- **War and the Complexion** […] The woman who values a good complexion needs to be on her guard against the war's damages and time's ravages […] War […] may very possibly hasten the relentless work of heavy-footed time. (Pomeroy Skin Food)
- **England's Glory Matches.** Every box you buy makes more work for English workers. Many other matches are made in Germany, Austria and other foreign countries. (England's Glory Matches)
- Throughout the war-swept area, Red-Cross conveyances of the allied forces are run on **Shell motor spirit** […] Insist on it. (Shell petrol)
- Of the tyres used by British dispatch riders […] **Dunlop tyres** are in a large majority. (Dunlop rubber company)
- **The Table Water of the Allies.** Perrier Water is not only being sent to the Front, but also to hospitals for wounded. (Perrier Table Water)
- **Buy Chappell's Pianos.** Every 'Chappell' piano sold provides employment for a number of skilled BRITISH workmen and food for their families […] Support our industries and help national employment. (Wilson Peck)
- **OXO is British.** It is made in Britain by a British company with British capital and British labour. (OXO beef cubes)

The Sheffield Daily Telegraph *collected money for 1914 Christmas presents for the troops, including through collection boxes on the city's trams.*

Newspapers' other requests for items to assist the troops were aimed specifically at 'our lady readers', asking for 'soldiers' comforts', such as socks, mittens, gloves, scarves, cardigans and other clothes. These were to be sent to a paper's Lady Editor. Before long cakes, jam, eggs, vegetables and other food items were sought for wounded soldiers in local hospitals. Each newspaper published the type and number of items donated by named individuals (nearly all women and a few children), and groups of women (often linked to a church) came together to make soldiers' extra clothes.

The Defence of the Realm Act (8 August 1914, with many later additions) restricted everyday activities and permitted the government to take over property or land as it wished. The purchase and distribution of much food and many materials became controlled by government officials, as did a wide range of prices. And industrial companies were increasingly required to work within procedures laid down centrally. Most of these changes were introduced hastily, and were sometimes incompletely thought through.

Newspapers in Sheffield and elsewhere gave great prominence to German soldiers 'brutal mistreatment or murder of Belgian citizens[130], many Germans in the city came under public suspicion, and companies started to complain of production difficulties caused by workers leaving them to join the army. Injured men began to arrive from the battle-zone, and schools and other buildings were turned over for use as military hospitals. Troops in the city were given free tram tickets and free entrance to specified sessions in public baths, and September saw the first Belgian refugees reach the city. The January 1915 edition of the *Sheffield Yearbook and Record* claimed that 'the city, like the country, settled down to a calm determination to see the war through'. At the end of August 1914, councillors agreed that no more local elections would be fought until after the end of hostilities.

Following a countrywide debate about the continuation or prohibition of football matches (considered by some to impair recruiting and essential efforts for the war), it was decided to continue professional and amateur games at a reduced level[131]. However, the annual Cutlers' Feast, the triennial Sheffield Music Festival and many other local events were abandoned for the duration. In November, the city's street lighting was reduced and the Intoxicating Liquor (Temporary Restrictions) Act banned alcohol sales in pubs and clubs after 9.30 pm on weekdays and after 9 pm on Sundays. The aim was to improve men's fitness for wartime work, and for a similar reason it became illegal for members of the public to offer free alcoholic drinks to soldiers.

In September 1914, Sheffield's chief constable established a volunteer Civilian Corps for men who were not eligible for active service. The Chief Constable's Civilian Corps (the 'Four Cs') provided instruction in rifle-use and military drill, with meetings held in the Jungle building at the bottom of Hawley Street, at Redmires and in other locations. More than 1,000 men joined in the first few weeks, providing in effect an earlier version of the Home Guard established in World War Two. (The Four Cs later became the Sheffield Volunteer Defence Corps.) Also popular were the city's rifle clubs, with more men than previously seeking to improve their marksmanship. Given that most members of these and similar groups also held jobs during the week, many activities became forced into a Sunday. Training sessions, rifle practices, route marches and so on all took place on what was previously advocated as a day of rest.

Although many of the city's workers were soon earning large sums (and working long hours) from the flow of orders received from the government, other families experienced great financial hardship. Soldiers' wives received a separation allowance, the size of which depended on their husband's rank. For lower-rank soldiers family income was barely adequate. This was also the case for pensions paid to the growing number of war widows. The number of poor children receiving free breakfasts or free dinners at school increased, and the local papers from time to time outlined aids to frugal living, including on one occasion no less a delicacy than tripe soup.

Newspapers every day reported events on the Western Front, at this stage retaining optimism about 'British dash and daring' and 'German demoralization', and claiming by October 1914 that 'German surrender [was] possible' in 'only a question of days'. However, newspaper articles about the fate of local men soon became common, with headlines like 'Local officer killed', 'Sheffield doctor's son wounded' or 'University man killed'. By November 1914, the *Sheffield Daily Telegraph* and the *Sheffield Daily Independent* regularly published long lists under the heading 'Casualties from the front line' or 'Roll of honour'. On some days these extended over eight complete columns. Within each group, men who had been killed in action, who were casualties or were still missing, were identified by name – not all from Sheffield although those were often picked out for special mention.

In December 1914, the killing and destruction reached Yorkshire. On the sixteenth of that month German ships attacked the east coast, shelling Scarborough and Whitby (towns well-known to many Sheffield holidaymakers) as well as Hartlepool to the north. Many buildings were destroyed and more than 100 adults and children were killed, and almost 600 injured. This surprise assault on British soil caused great outrage and anxiety. Not only were Britain's wars usually far away in distant countries, but the German mutilation of non-combatant civilians and children went beyond most people's view of acceptable warfare. It seemed to many that the brutal events in Belgium could soon happen here. The attacks, especially on Scarborough, were subsequently used to urge additional recruiting, with posters asking people to help 'avenge the slaughter of innocent men and women' or 'Remember Scarborough'.

Almost all of the country's churches supported military activity in the face of Germany's aggression, and special prayer sessions were held regularly throughout the city. At least forty Sheffield clergymen volunteered for service as military chaplains before the end of 1914, and many churches set up working parties to provide clothes and comforts for the troops or to raise funds to help families in distress. On the first Sunday of 1915 a Day of National Intercession was held in all churches, based on prayers for the nation and empire.

Some early recruiting posters emphasized Germany's aggression.

Homeless Belgians come to Sheffield

The pains of war were in these ways thrust upon the people of Sheffield. A rather different and completely unexpected development came in the sudden arrival of Belgian refugees. Starting in late August, tens of thousands of civilians and wounded soldiers left Belgium to escape the advancing German army. Some refugees moved into neighbouring (neutral) Holland, but Britain also offered assistance and within a few months more than 250,000 had arrived in the country – with around 3,000 coming to Sheffield[132].

A few Sheffielders had already started planning for their arrival. Linked to St Vincent's (Catholic) Church in Solly Street and the international St Vincent de Paul Society, a group that became the Sheffield Catholic Ladies' Association of Charity set out to help the refugees, most of whom were Catholics. By 7 September 1914, the group had obtained use of Shirle Hill House in Nether Edge rent-free from the trustees of the brewing family of S. H. Ward. This was to provide accommodation for up to 100 Belgian refugees, and by 12 September the Acting Belgian Consul[133] in the area, Arthur Balfour, managing director of Seebohm and Dieckstahl at the Dannemora Steel Works in the Wicker, had overseen the formation of a District War Refugees' Committee and a Belgian Refugee Fund. These now sought help of many kinds, starting with a money-raising concert and lecturette at St Vincent's Church Hall on 19 September, which was so popular that it was repeated two days later[134].

The District War Refugees' Committee, which also covered neighbouring areas and included a Sheffield sub-committee, immediately developed Shirle Hill as a receiving base. Other primary centres were provided by the Sheffield and the Ecclesall Boards of Guardians, and across the next few weeks individuals, groups and churches of all denominations made available (usually without charge) around 100 Sheffield properties to house Belgian families. For example, Ecclesall Church maintained or part-maintained nine refugee families, Upper Chapel accommodated others in two separate houses, Ranmoor Church rented and furnished a large property in Park Crescent, the Sheffield Jewish Refugees' Aid Society provided three houses in

From September 1914, many people in the city worked to help newly-arrived refugees from Belgium.

Ecclesall Road, the Stocksbridge Belgian Sub-Committee (part of the Stocksbridge Relief Committee) made available a house in Albany Road, and the university opened a hostel in Western Bank. In each case, groups were formed to provide clothes, furniture, utensils and coal for heating, to collect subscriptions from well-wishers, and to organize concerts and other fundraising activities. The City Council supplied free electricity to the Shirle Hill base for a period, and many tradesmen decorated or undertook necessary modifications to houses without charge.

The first group of around fifty Belgian refugees arrived in Sheffield by train on 21 September 1914[135]. They were met by volunteers and representatives of the Catholic church, who welcomed them to the city and organized bus transport to their initial accommodation at Shirle Hill. That process was repeated many times during October and November and less frequently in later months, with many reports appearing in local newspapers. For example, on 16 October 1914 the *Sheffield Daily Independent* described 'Striking Scenes at Sheffield Station':

> The grim reality of war was brought home to the people who were privileged to witness two scenes last night at Sheffield Midland Station – first the coming of 120 Belgian refugees to the city, and then a parade on the platform of nearly 400 wounded Belgians, a number of whom were for hospitals in Sheffield [...]
>
> Shortly after eleven o'clock the train pulled up in Sheffield Station, and as it came in sight revealing the war-worn warriors, the people on the platform cheered heartily and the Belgians responded with many signs of delight.

On the next day, the *Sheffield Daily Telegraph* reported the arrival of another 240 wounded Belgian soldiers, who were met by Arthur Balfour and other representatives of the Belgian Consulate, and also by Mrs Balfour 'wearing her smart uniform of her office as quartermaster of the Red Cross Hospital at Dore'. A large crowd of spectators was 'representative of every section of society in Sheffield'. Arrivals over the next few weeks were also greeted by officials and curious bystanders, and refugees continued to be of great interest as they settled into their accommodation. For at least an initial period Shirle Hill received a steady stream of well-wishers, who occasionally had to queue outside the gate before being allowed in for fifteen-minute periods.

Local newspapers also published many accounts of refugees'

Belgian refugees were initially housed in Shirle Hill in Nether Edge. Considerable help was provided by nuns and others from St Vincent's Catholic Church.

Many postcards in the city showed the new residents at Shirle Hill. One successful collector of money for them was this large dog.

experiences as they had escaped from the invaders, often by walking for days with very little food and sometimes carrying young children. In some cases, family members had become separated without knowledge of the whereabouts of each other before accidentally coming together again – occasionally only after arrival in Sheffield. One story is excerpted in Display Box 4.3.

Display Box 4.3
A TALE OF TWO BELGIANS

Excerpts from the *Sheffield Daily Independent* of 25 November 1914.

There is in Sheffield just now a wounded Belgian officer, who at the outbreak of war was a bridegroom of six weeks. The call of duty took him from his bride and his home, and without knowledge of how they were faring he fought the good fight until a German bullet put him out of action. With other wounded comrades he was brought to England and found a temporary home in the Third Northern General Hospital in Sheffield, subsequently becoming the guest of a well-known Sheffield citizen.

Meanwhile this officer's wife had to play her part in the terrible trial which had come for her country. Shortly after the departure of her husband, the town in which she lived was taken by the enemy and several German officers were billeted in her house [... They] eventually gave the lady permission to cross the Dutch frontier (which was adjacent) each day for the purpose of buying a Dutch paper, which the Germans themselves were glad to read.

One day the lady found in a Dutch paper a list of Belgian wounded, from which she discovered that her husband was injured and at the Base Hospital, Sheffield. From that moment all her thoughts were concentrated on escape. On each of her daily visits to Dutch territory for a few days she took some of her most valued and valuable possessions, and finally one day went to Holland for the usual paper, and did not return.

Ostend at that time was not in the hands of the Germans, and to that port the officer's bride directed her steps, then to Calais and across to Dover, where, she thought, her troubles would begin, as she knew nothing of England or the English language [...] Then an Englishman who spoke French solved the problem [...] He took the Belgian lady to

London, saw her in the Sheffield train, made all the arrangements for the journey from Sheffield station to the Base Hospital, and bowed himself out of the story.

The wounded Belgian hero was dining with his host when a telephone message informed him that his wife, of whose fate he knew nothing, was waiting for him at the Hospital in Ecclesall Road. One dinner at least remained uneaten. It was a happy reunion. The couple are still in Sheffield.

Wounded Belgian soldiers were treated in local hospitals or convalesced in houses made available by local people[136]. The civilians adapted to life in a strange country as well as they could. Some financial support was provided by the Belgian government, and this was supplemented by a city church or the War Refugees' Committee where needed. Collection boxes were placed in trams, and donations were widely sought of cash, food, clothing, bedding and furniture. Throughout the city, church groups, schools and others organized social events, concerts and similar activities to raise funds[137]. A clothing and clothing-repair department for refugees was set up in the Wicker, and families could also obtain clothes from a store run by volunteers in the Base Hospital. As aliens in the city, Belgians had to register with the local police and report any change of address. A few were fined for failure in those respects.

Belgian children attended schools in the city, sometimes receiving financial assistance[138], and a small number of Belgian teachers worked in Sheffield schools. Father A. de Broeck from Antwerp worked from St Marie's Catholic church throughout the war on behalf of the refugees, and in July 1916 the church (a cathedral from 1980) established its own school for Belgian children. A Belgian newspaper was created, the city's libraries obtained some books in French, and Sheffield University provided English lessons with the help of around fifty volunteer teachers. For a period, refugees could travel without charge on the city's trams and were given free admittance to Heeley slipper-baths once a week. The St Vincent de Paul Belgian Section made home-visits on a regular basis.

Belgian men of military age were required to return home and enlist for the duration of the war[139], and men who had previously worked for Belgian railways were sent to assist the French rail system. The War

Refugees' Committee was able to report in 1917 that 'employment has been found for every refugee who is capable of working'. Among the Belgian women were several accomplished seamstresses, and they obtained work, sometimes at home, for firms such as Redgates, which at the time sold ladies' clothes as well as sewing machines, prams and other items. In late 1918 a company was formed (Belbroid Lingerie) to market Belgian embroidery work from the city.

However, some refugee families suffered considerable financial hardship, especially those without a male wage-earner. In October 1915, local newspapers were still pleading for gifts of clothes and for material that could be made into clothes. The *Sheffield Daily Telegraph* of 16 October was by then alert to possible donor resistance:

> We wonder whether some of our readers, because they have found a 'black sheep' among the […] emigrants cast on our shores, have been disheartened and feel disinclined to give further assistance […] In the main our Belgian friends are worthy of, and in great need of, all the help we can give, and we can well afford to overlook the minority of those who have proved the reverse.

In the autumn of 1917, the City Council responded to Belgian requests by approving the opening of a slaughterhouse to provide horse-meat, and two horse-flesh shops opened in Westbar. That meat was popular with many Belgians and was much cheaper than the usual British preferences. The *Sheffield Daily Independent* of 29 September 1917 reported that 'apparently the ordinary Sheffielder has done nothing more than gaze on with curiosity and argue the merits of the food'. By November of that year the city had five horse-meat shops.

Belgium had become independent from the Netherlands in 1830, and each year the Sheffield Belgians continued to hold National Day celebrations. In 1915, after a morning service in St Marie's Church in Norfolk Row, afternoon events took place in Weston Park, where around 7,000 people were present for patriotic speeches, songs and dances from Belgian children, and an orchestral concert which ended with the national anthems of Belgium and Britain. The next year's National Day event instead involved a patriotic concert in the Albert Hall in Barker's Pool, and 1917 saw the fête again in Weston Park.

Over the years, the refugees to varying degrees became part of the community, and many made friends with local people, especially the children. In some cases romance blossomed, but problems did occasionally arise. One example is described in Display Box 4.4.

Display Box 4.4
A FRAUGHT RELATIONSHIP

From the *Sheffield Daily Independent* of 5 February 1917

There was a dramatic incident in the Sheffield Police Court, yesterday, when a Belgian refugee appeared in the dock, and in the witness-box stood a Sheffield soldier, who had been given special leave from the Front to see to the welfare of his children.

Facing the Belgian with flushed and angry face the soldier said:

'When I left England last August I left my wife and two children. She was a most devoted wife and took good care of the home. Through his getting her to drink he has got her into trouble and my children have been neglected for the last six months. It was while she was under the influence of drink to which she was not accustomed that he took advantage of her, and that was while I was out there fighting for his country. I had as nice a girl as any man could wish and he has led her off.'

The refugee, Jean Baptiste de Waele, aged 33, formerly of Brussels, was charged with contravening the orders as to registration of aliens by failing to notify his change of address and also by giving false information. It was stated by Detective-Inspector Fretwell that he had a wife and two children whom he had left behind in Belgium. He had been lodging in Hanover Street, and because of his conduct with the soldier's wife, who was also lodging there, was given notice to leave. The couple had since lived together as man and wife.

The magistrates, Messrs I. Milner and E. H. Banner, said it was a very serious case, and in order to act as a warning to others they sent the defendant to prison for three months, with hard labour.

In March 1918, Arthur Balfour[140] and other local helpers were formally thanked by the Belgian nation in a ceremony and musical fête in

Sheffield's Albert Hall. Colonel Arthur Connell, in charge of the city's hospital treating wounded Belgian soldiers, was separately made an Officer of the Order of Leopold I, and several Sheffield women, including Mrs Edith Watkins of Rosedale Road, also received medals from the country they had worked for. At the end of the war most refugees returned home despite the country's devastation. More than 1,400 left in two trains on 28 January 1919 and others returned later. Members of the Belgian War Refugees' Committee and hosts from the city were at the station to say goodbye, and the *Sheffield Daily Independent* of 29 January reported that 'at least twenty Belgians took with them Sheffield girls as wives, whilst conversely a number of Belgian girls remain behind having married Sheffield men'.

The *Yorkshire Telegraph and Star* in the evening of 28 January reported conversations with several of the departing men and women:

> An interesting personality amongst the throng was Mrs van Roosbroeck, of Antwerp, whose husband has been with the Belgian army all through the fighting. She and her bonny boy are returning after four years' absence. During the four years, Mrs van Roosbroeck has been 'doing her bit' for the cause by working on munitions at Cammell's. With all the vivaciousness of her race she said she wished to pay a tribute to the girls and women who had worked in the factories. 'They are a splendid lot,' she said, 'and I have had a very happy time amongst them. I shall always remember my happy time in Sheffield. In fact, I won't be allowed to forget it, because my boy speaks English perfectly. Good luck to the girls of Sheffield.

Little now remains of the city's contribution to 3,000 foreigners in distress. Among the stained glass windows of Upper Chapel in Norfolk Street is one with the wording 'I was a stranger'. This is identified as 'a memorial to the ladies of Upper Chapel who made and supplied 8,000 garments for the troops in the 1914-1918 war and arranged accommodation for Belgian and French refugees'[141]. A more prominent, but almost unknown, memorial is sited next to the disused Catholic chapel in City Road Cemetery. This was unveiled on 21 July 1921 and is inscribed: 'In memory of the soldiers of the Belgian army and of the refugees who died in Sheffield during the Great War 1914-1919[142]. May they rest in peace.' Forty-four names are listed, far from home but at least among friends.

This memorial to Belgians who died in the city was erected in City Road Cemetery in July 1921.

CHAPTER 5

Born in Germany, Living in Sheffield

Most people in 1914 Sheffield had been born in this country and were clearly British. But some came from other countries, including Germany – now the nation's enemy. How should they be treated? From the outset there was widespread public concern. Foreigners were at the time referred to as aliens, and anti-alien laws and regulations became more and more restrictive as the war developed. Large numbers of Germans became interned (held in special prisons) or repatriated (sent back to their home country), and others were treated with suspicion or active hostility.

Germans in pre-war Britain
When a national census was taken in 1911, around 51,000 German-born individuals were living in England and Wales[143]. Another 6,500 people of German birth had become naturalized as British after applying and paying for citizenship[144]. Around half of the country's German-born population lived in London, and Liverpool and Manchester each housed around 1,300. Within Yorkshire, most German-born individuals were in Hull (around 850), Bradford (around 550), Leeds (470) and Sheffield (390). Of these 390 German-born residents of Sheffield, thirty-six were British subjects whose birth happened to be in Germany and fifty-three were now British after naturalization. There were thus 301 non-naturalized German-born individuals recorded in Sheffield in the 1911 census[145].

A few prominent Germans in Britain were wealthy bankers or merchants, but most were in less exalted trades. German waiters were

Members of the Funk family came to Sheffield from Germany in the 1880s and later, and many were successful pork butchers.

common, especially in London, as were bakers and butchers. And in Bradford many Germans worked in textile firms. In 1914 Sheffield, a few were directors or managers of steel or cutlery firms, but most held manual or white-collar jobs. Several dozen ran their own retail shops as pork butchers, often employing members of their family or other German assistants. Many German men had arrived in Sheffield years earlier and were by 1914 settled in the city, perhaps with a British-born wife and with children who were British by virtue of their Sheffield birth. One such family is described in Display Box 5.1[146], and among others were the Funks. Some of those had come to Sheffield in the 1880s and by 1914 several were successful pork butchers in the city, often assisted by German relatives. A few names were changed, such as from Georg to George and Friedrich to Frederick'[147], at least one became naturalized, children were born and grew up as Sheffielders, and several sons served in the British army.

Display Box 5.1
FROM SINDELFINGEN TO SHEFFIELD:
THE KOERNER FAMILY

The German Empire was created in 1871, bringing together more than twenty independent states. One of those was Württemberg, in the south-west of the country, within which is the town of Sindelfingen. From there a pork butcher, Johannes Leonhardt, came to Sheffield around 1820. His business flourished, he changed his name to Charles Leonard, and he married a Sheffield woman. A stream of others arrived from Sindelfingen over the next few years, including Christian Heinrich (Henry) Hamm, who came to work in the town as a pork butcher and bacon factor around 1840. He became naturalized in 1860 and at the time of the 1861 census was able to employ in his shop five other ex-residents of Sindelfingen as well as his British wife.

One of Christian Hamm's employees was his niece, Christine Dorothee Hamm (1835-1889). In 1869, Dorothee married Gotthold Heinrich Koerner, also from Sindelfingen but then working in Sheffield. Gotthold (1840-1905) was one of five Koerners who had moved to the town at different times in the years following 1850. By the time of his marriage to Dorothee he too was a pork butcher, taking advantage of his wife's expertise acquired in her uncle's shop.

Dorothee and Gotthold Heinrich Koernerhad had four Sheffield-born [*and therefore British*] children. Two sons were employed as forgemen in the city all their lives, in Gotthold Edward's (1876-1921) case working for Jonas and Colver Ltd. Although Gotthold Edward's

German parentage had rarely caused him problems in earlier years, during the Great War he was often treated with suspicion. His age and munition job prevented service in the army, but his loyalty to Britain was sometimes disputed and he had to defend himself – in his customary Sheffield accent. After the sinking of the *Lusitania* in May 1915, when anti-German feeling was particularly strong, Gotthold felt it necessary to burn the long-valued family bible with its German associations. Nevertheless, one of his sons, Albert Frederick Koerner (1872-1944), served for two periods in the York and Lancaster Regiment (1893-1905 and 1914-1919) and later worked as a driver for Sheffield Corporation Fire Brigade. A German background was for him no longer an impediment.

Many Germans in the city were clearly industrious and helpful citizens, and were accepted and valued as such. But an undercurrent of anti-German feeling had been developing in the previous few decades[148]. One element of this was a general concern about Germans' impact on the labour market. It was often believed that they and other foreigners took jobs away from British workers, were willing to accept poorer conditions and drove down wage levels by accepting lower pay.

These economic doubts were accompanied by a national diplomatic and military concern. Germany's foreign policy in the early years of the twentieth century seemed increasingly to threaten international stability, and it was clear that her recently-strengthened navy now almost matched that of Britain; the two countries were shaping up as naval rivals. Many British newspapers and magazines were troubled by these developments and some politicians exploited them to encourage national opposition to Germany and Germans. It was frequently claimed that Germans abroad would support their country of origin ('once a German, always a German'), and that many in Britain were deceitfully waiting to join a German invasion that was imminent.

Linked themes were found in widely-read stories about German spies and possible attacks on this country. Spy novels became increasingly popular from the 1890s, with titles like *Spies of the Kaiser* and *Invasion of 1910*. The latter told about a German landing on the East Anglian coast leading to attacks on many parts of England[149], before a British counter-attack gained the upper hand. The assault was said to have been assisted by German spies resident in the country who, it was imagined, provided essential information and destroyed key railway lines.

Spies also figured in letters to the press, claiming that thousands of Germans – perhaps trained in warfare – were waiting undiscovered to act against the country in which they lived. Waiters and barbers were thought to be particularly dangerous, since they seemed in a position to hear about important political, military or manufacturing developments. Questions were asked in parliament about Germans allegedly storing ammunition or gathering information about key areas of the country.

In 1909, a government committee had examined possible German espionage. Although most of its evidence was weak, the committee concluded that spying was indeed common. As a result a new Secret Service Bureau was established in that year, and in 1910 another committee developed plans for dealing with aliens in a time of war. Among other suggested procedures to deal with possible threats, the committee drafted an Aliens Restriction Act for possible use in the future.

As war approached, the British public was in these ways alerted to possible threats from Germany. That country was increasingly active as a naval and military power, and it had more than 50,000 citizens in this country, widely thought to be gathering information and waiting to join an assault. Overt anti-German protests within communities were rare before the war, but the British were, in general, troubled. They were increasingly uncertain and ready to be tipped in a hostile direction.

The 'enemy in our midst'

The declaration of war on 4 August 1914 meant that many prompt actions were needed. The government had few detailed procedures worked out in advance, and the best way forward had to be found by trial and error in the light of developing experience[150]. So Britain's treatment of Germans in this country was repeatedly modified as time moved on. Sometimes, lengthy discussions in parliament were needed before changes could be made, but many parliamentary Acts were worded to permit rapid adjustment through subsequent Orders in Council. For example, that was possible with the previously-drafted Aliens Restriction Act, which quickly passed into law on 5 August. Initial and twenty-seven subsequent Orders within this Act contained restrictions of these kinds:

- aliens had to provide personal details to the nearest registration office, usually the local police station[151]
- aliens could not travel more than 5 miles from their home without a personal permit
- aliens could not enter or leave Britain without a permit

- 'prohibited areas' were established around military establishments and along much of the country's coastline. For example, whole counties such as Norfolk, Suffolk and Sussex were closed to aliens
- aliens could not possess, for instance, weapons or ammunition, cameras, signalling equipment, homing pigeons or military maps[152].

Although these restrictions were legally enforceable, continuous observation and complete control of every single alien was in practice not feasible. Furthermore, personal exemptions were often granted so that, for example, large numbers of German residents were individually allowed to continue living in their homes in prohibited areas. There was also some variability across the country, since many decisions were taken locally without a full knowledge of requirements and others' policies. In Sheffield the police immediately arrested all non-naturalized German men of military age. (See Display Box 5.2.) The men arrested were soon released, partly because there was not enough secure space in which to hold them, and instead they were required to report to the local police twice a week. German women and children, and men above military age were encouraged to leave the country and nationally several thousand did so in the next few months.

Newspapers were by now publishing detailed stories about events in Europe and about German soldiers' alleged cruel treatment of Belgian citizens. Not surprisingly, British people were concerned about these events, and were very alert to possible threats on their doorstep. Community pressures were building up to take action, and many members of the public were adamant – they wanted stronger restrictions placed on Germans.

For example, from someone identified as 'British to the Back Bone', the *Sheffield Daily Telegraph* published a letter in October 1914 that stated:

> I believe we have amongst us in Sheffield a number of Germans and Austrians, naturalized or otherwise, who are our deadly enemies […] Why do we allow them to remain? […] I would suggest […] that information be obtained and published as to the number of firms and business houses in Sheffield who regularly employ Germans or Austrians as their servants.

Spy fever was raging. Two waiters were arrested in Matlock Bath as possible spies and the London Metropolitan Police received more than

---

Display Box 5.2
ARRESTING THE ALIENS: SHEFFIELD'S
INITIAL RESPONSE

Excerpts from a *Sheffield Daily Independent* report on 8 August 1914

Since war broke out between England and Germany, many Sheffield people have been speculating on the presence in the city of German subjects […] But the police have not been asleep, and yesterday they had a busy and unparalleled time in dealing with the foreign population.

The bulk of the German male population, who are German subjects liable to the Kaiser's call, were formally arrested as prisoners-of-war and now lie at Hillsbro' barracks, where it is expected they will remain until peace is proclaimed […] Many of the women were sadly cut up when they found their husbands and sons were made prisoners-of-war, and several created little scenes in the vicinity of the Central Police Offices.

There was no antipathy shown towards the men, for the police carried out their duty in a perfectly friendly way and without ostentation. As a truth, many of the prisoners are quite excellent folk, and some have English wives […]

It is understood that there are about 400 German subjects liable to arrest, apart from Germans of British birth and women and children.

8,000 reports of suspected espionage in the first month of war. On 6 August, the *Daily Mail* thought it likely that 'Germans who are staying here may be serving their country more effectively *[i.e. as spies]* than by shouldering a rifle'. The paper later argued that 'the German spy network is so wide, so extraordinarily efficient, so immensely dangerous that it cannot be too severely repressed' (10 October 1914). That and other papers warned about possible German sabotage of water or electricity supplies, and many stories appeared about suspicious individuals taking photographs. The *Sheffield Daily Independent* of 14 August 1914 reported that a photographer 'who looked like a foreigner' had 'made good his escape on a bicycle and has not been seen since'. Other items concerned requests from abroad for picture postcards of the area. Allegedly, these might be intended for the enemy.

Writing in that October to the *Sheffield Daily Telegraph* about the 'enemy in our midst', cutlery manufacturer James Dixon at Stumperlow *[sic]* Hall had this to say:

> Are we going to wait until the enemy has landed on these shores, and then attempt to deal with the matter when it will be too late? […] Every precaution is being taken except the one that is a most vital one, and that is dealing with the enemy in our midst. There are thousands of Germans in England who are probably spies, and only waiting for the signal for the raid to be given to do their treacherous part of the work […] I firmly believe that a raid will be attempted by Germany, and I call on Sheffield to […] lead the way by holding a great public meeting to insist on the Government interning every German in Great Britain at once.

The *Telegraph* generally supported the Conservative party and sometimes argued for what we might now term more right-wing policies, frequently emphasizing its hostility to Germany[153]. Sheffield's other morning paper, the *Independent*, leaned more to the Liberal party and published several letters supporting Germans in the city. On 7 August, Edwin Unwin wrote to deny an 'unfounded rumour' that pork butcher Ferdinand Gebhardt had been assaulted because of something he had said about the war. More letters in praise of Mr Gebhardt were published in subsequent days, one pointing out that he 'has been a friend to many of our causes and also shown great kindness to poor folk in the neighbourhood of the Moor'[154].

Local concern was illustrated by a Public Notice in Sheffield newspapers on 12 October 1914. In capital letters throughout, this stated that 'THE EMPLOYERS AND EMPLOYEES ENGAGED IN THE CUTLERY AND ALLIED TRADES HAVE JOINTLY AGREED THAT NO REPAIRS TO GERMAN CUTLERY ETC. SHALL BE UNDERTAKEN OR EXECUTED AFTER THIS DATE'. In the next month, the Sheffield Chamber of Commerce urged traders to stop using the term 'German' in reference to German silver and instead refer to nickel silver. London hotels advertized in Sheffield newspapers 'No Germans or Austrians on the staff'.

Many Germans living in Britain were also uneasy. Throughout the country, there was a rush in 1914 to become naturalized, so much so that from August London stationers increased the price of the necessary forms by six pence. One naturalized German in Rotherham found it necessary to insert a Legal Notice in the *Yorkshire Telegraph and Star,* as shown in Display Box 5.3.

Display Box 5.3
SLANDEROUS STATEMENTS ABOUT A GERMAN

PUBLIC NOTICE.
THE WAR.
REWARD.

WHEREAS slanderous statements entirely without foundation have been circulated to the effect that FREDERICK CHARLES SCHONHUT of the Red Lion Hotel Rotherham has expressed hostility to England and sympathy with Germany and that he has destroyed a picture of King George and displayed with acclamation one of the Kaiser AND WHEREAS the said Frederick Charles Schonhut is a British subject and his sympathy is entirely with England and the untrue statements have caused and are likely to cause him serious loss and harm and he has never had in his house a picture of either the King or the Kaiser. WE on behalf of the said Frederick Charles Schonhut HEREBY OFFER a SUBSTANTIAL REWARD for reliable information of the names and addresses of any persons who have uttered or circulated or who shall hereafter make or repeat the statements complained of or any of them or any similar statements.

GICHARD and GUMMER,
35 College Street,
Rotherham.
August 7th 1914

Some Germans took steps to change their names in this period in order to suggest a more English background. For example, a co-defendant in Joseph Jonas's 1918 trial (see below) was Charles Alfred Vernon who, before August 1914, had been known by his full name, Charles Alfred Vernon Hahn. Other changes took place in the next few years. The local steel company of Seebohm and Dieckstahl (founded by Germans in

Sheffield in 1865) decided in December 1915 to adopt the name of its principal shareholder and managing director to become Arthur Balfour and Company Ltd. Edward Colver Glauert, son of the late Carl Glauert, a German industrial chemist and merchant trading in Sheffield, was also uncomfortable about his name. Drawing upon a link to the Wyckersley family of Broom Hall, he now became Edward de Wyckersley Swyft Colver – definitely not German. He served through the war honourably in a technical branch of the Admiralty.

A British-born coach and charabanc proprietor in Grimesthorpe Road took the same step. William Smith Dack came from a longstanding British family, but his surname suggested to some that he and his firm were German. So he now became merely William Smith. The royal family moved in the same direction – but not until July 1917, when anti-German feelings were particularly strong. King George V was a cousin of the German Emperor, and his family name – Saxe-Coburg-Gotha – pointed to his German ancestry[155]. Seeking further to demonstrate loyalty to Britain and to discourage potential opposition to the monarchy, the king declared that his family would henceforth be known as the House of Windsor, as it still is.

Riots, repatriation and internment

During the autumn of 1914, the government was faced with a range of other unfamiliar problems. It was becoming clear that the original expectation of a rapid victory was mistaken, and that long-term mechanisms for waging war must now be developed. In respect of Germans living in Britain, official thinking at first favoured tight restrictions on their everyday life with some limited repatriation. However, influential newspapers and much of the public kept up pressure to lock them all away.

A move in that direction became hard to avoid in the next few weeks. Anti-German riots erupted in some parts of London and some chief constables declared themselves worried about their ability to maintain public order. On 20 October 1914, the government announced that all unnaturalized men from Germany and Austria between the ages of 17 and 45 would be imprisoned. This process started on the next day.

In Sheffield, 108 men were arrested on 22 October[156]. They were held in the city's Central Police Station before travelling by train two days later to York. A local report of their departure is in Display Box 5.4. The *Sheffield Daily Independent* noted that the men were 'of widely different stations in life, ranging from heads and managers of firms to waiters and mechanics'. As throughout the country, Germans who had been naturalized (and thus were British) were excluded from these and later arrests. So too were wives and children and (on this occasion) men above military age.

Display Box 5.4
BY TRAIN TO INTERNMENT

Excerpts from a *Sheffield Daily Telegraph* report of 26 October 1914

ALIEN ENEMIES.
SHEFFIELD RESIDENTS SENT TO YORK.
The 108 Germans and Austrians of military age resident of Sheffield who surrendered to the police under the new Government Order were removed to York on Saturday afternoon for internment in the Exhibition Buildings of that city […]

The aliens have been accommodated at the Central Police Station since Thursday […] On Saturday afternoon they and their impediments were marshalled and taken in police vans and a Corporation motor 'bus to the Great Central railway station, where the men were embarked on a special corridor train. The majority of the aliens took their misfortune with philosophic good humour, though there were others who seemed inconsolable. The authorities certainly did everything to make the men feel at their ease.

Before the train left, the Deputy Chief Constable (Mr Barker) and Detective Superintendent Hollis passed down the aisle of the train exchanging cheery words with the foreigners. Everybody seemed well provided with tobacco, and a paper boy on the platform did a rare trade in copies of the *Yorkshire Telegraph and Star* and periodicals.

Though one or two men sat in gloomy isolation, most of them were busy chatting or reading, or engrossed in a game of cards. A posse of fifteen policemen, in [the] charge of Inspectors Andrew and Cottrell, travelled with the party to hand them over to the military authorities at York.

It was pleasing to notice that the people outside and inside the station precincts observed the best British traditions in their attitude towards the aliens. There was not the slightest suggestion of ill-feeling, but rather a spirit of sympathy and respect. As the train steamed out of the station the aliens smiled and waved farewells to the bystanders, who returned these courtesies with interest.

The arrested Sheffield men were subsequently passed on to other internment locations, but information about particular individuals is scarce. Many records about internment in this period have been lost or destroyed, and it is only possible to trace individual details from their own or a family's subsequent account. However, we know that, nationally, several thousand of those imprisoned in October 1914 were released after a few weeks. At this stage, facilities for accommodating, guarding and feeding large numbers of people were inadequate, and in any case many of the men were clearly valued citizens who supported this country[157]. For example, the Viener brothers (Adolf, Emile and Willie) were permitted to return to Sheffield, and subsequently their company (W and E Viener, later Viners[158]) made thousands of steel helmets for the army.

Parts of the press and several prominent politicians continued to demand more extensive internment. Spy rumours were still very common and British prisoners-of-war were allegedly being gravely mistreated by Germany – 'savagely misused, half-starved, deprived of medical attention and clothing, and treated with calculated ferocity', according to the (consistently anti-German) *Daily Mail*. Zeppelin air-raids on the east coast from December 1914 shocked the country, and these were alleged to have been assisted by signals sent by Germans on the ground. In this period, papers in Sheffield and elsewhere also reported torpedo attacks by German submarines without warning on British shipping, and in April 1915 local suspicions were further raised by an Austrian being fined £100 at Sheffield magistrates' court for possessing photographs of Liverpool docks and other places.

The enemy army used poisonous gas for the first time in April[159], and its horrific effects on British troops on the Western Front were described in the Sheffield press[160]. On 7 May 1915, the Cunard liner *Lusitania* was sunk by a German submarine off the west coast of Ireland, and more than 1,000 civilian passengers were drowned, many of them children, with bodies washed up on nearby beaches[161]. Photographs of the 'appalling barbarity' were published in the press, and Sheffield newspapers described the experiences of passengers and crew members and the anxieties of families awaiting news. A coroner's inquest charged 'the officers of the submarine and the Emperor and Government of Germany [...] with committing wholesale and criminal murder', and overt hostility to Germany and Germans swelled throughout the country.

Almost immediately, serious riots took place in the East End of London, accompanied by looting and the destruction of German property[162]. More than 800 arrests were made in the capital. Riots also erupted in Liverpool, Birkenhead and Manchester, and by 10 May 1915 they had spread to South Yorkshire. Crowds attacked shops thought to be German in Mexborough, Conisbrough and other towns, often targeting pork butchers and sometimes stealing their meat. Similar scenes followed in Rotherham, for example attacking the Red Lion Hotel and a shop kept by Ferdinand Schonhut (see Display Box 5.3 above). Anti-German violence and looting occurred for several hours in Sheffield on 13 and 14 May, mainly in the Attercliffe area and initially directed at pork butchers with German connections but gradually extending also to other retailers[163]. Crowds threw stones and flowerpots, and smashed windows and doors. Around a dozen shops were ransacked, and displayed union jacks were torn down rather than providing protection. A number of English-owned shops received attention because of an owner's German wife or employee, but others had no German links at all.

As described by the *Sheffield Daily Independent* on 15 May, 'women and men walked away with hams and flitches of bacon in their possession, women and girls wore links of polony and sausage as necklaces, while children munched pork pies and other delicacies [...] The crowd showed themselves ready to attack any shop if the owner was suspected of relationship with Germany. English pork butchers displayed Union Jacks, but even this did not always satisfy the crowd.' On the same day the *Sheffield Daily Telegraph* detailed riots from the early hours into the evening, including an attack on two shops in Attercliffe Common:

> Immediately the plate-glass windows had been shattered, it was only a matter of seconds before a combined rush was made on the premises. Window stays were forced down and doors were burst open, and the mob shrieking, jeering, screaming and yelling, pushed and scrambled and jammed each other as they crowded into the shops through the doorways and through the windows to clear [each] of its contents[164].

The local press again published critical letters from the public. In the *Telegraph* of 15 May 1915, 'Britain for the British' argued that: 'the fact that a man has lived in this country for twenty or even forty years is no guarantee. I would not trust a German. I know them [...] What are the local naturalized Germans doing? Defending the country of their choice, or busy making all the money possible?' In fact, many of the German-born Sheffielders who had become naturalized British subjects were beyond military age, and several (now or subsequently) had sons fighting in the British army[165].

On the same day, the *Telegraph* carried a letter from Ferdinand Gebhardt, written 'after tonight's demonstration opposite my shop' on the Moor:

> The public may not be aware of my history, but I am a native of the late kingdom of Württemberg, which the Prussians conquered in 1866. It was in consequence of such conquest that I decided at 14 years of age to get away from such militarism and make my home in England, where I have now spent 40 years of my life – 35 years thereof have been spent in Sheffield, and I have contributed to its rates for the past 28 years. I married an English woman (a Sheffielder), my children have been all born in Sheffield, and I am the grandfather of a Sheffield-born child, whose father is a Sheffield-born man [...] The English public can rest assured that I am not its enemy, having adopted its land as my home.

The riots were firmly ended by police intervention and subsequent fines by magistrates, but much damage had been done. Faced with disorder across the country, the government once again felt it had to take calming

The Weekly Despatch *of 25 October 1914 caricatured the internment of possible spies in this way.*

In this cartoon drawn by a patient in Carterknowle military hospital, a lady mixes up her words and wonders 'why ain't he interred'.

action. A new internment policy was quickly announced, on 13 May 1915. 'For their own safety and that of the community', all non-naturalized aliens would be 'segregated and interned, or, if over military age, repatriated'. German-born women in the country were also to be repatriated, but women of English birth now married to a German were allowed to remain. As previously, some exemptions from internment or repatriation were possible, for example for long-resident Germans with British-born wives and children or for Germans employed on essential munitions work, and internment tribunals were set up to consider applications and decide on action in each case. People who had been born in Germany but were now naturalized as British citizens were allowed to remain in Britain, apart from a few who were considered by the relevant committee to pose a particular threat.

Imprisonment on such a scale required the rapid expansion of secure facilities. During the summer of 1915 around 1,000 extra people were interned each week, raising the overall number of internees to more than 32,000 in November[166]. Repatriation out of Britain was somewhat slower, but by June 1916 around 10,000 foreign residents had left the country, either reluctantly or willingly.

Internment procedures and the administration of prisons were complicated by the fact that several different government departments were involved[167] and arrangements changed frequently. Further policy reviews took place in the summer of 1916 (after Lord Kitchener's ship had been sunk) and in June 1918 (after a particularly virulent campaign by sections of the press), but overall numbers of internees did not change greatly. Indeed, some reductions occurred in the later war years through individual releases and internees' deaths, and a small number of men were returned to Germany in exchange for British civilians. At the end of the war, almost 24,000 civilians were still interned on British soil.

What happened to internees?
When the government announced large-scale internment in October 1914, it was faced with a new and urgent problem. Where could the internees go? Many records of that period have been lost, but it is known that one initial action was to take over existing buildings[168]. For example, the halls of the Olympia exhibition centre in London and the horse-boxes of Newbury race-course were occupied by internees for some months. Established prisons in several parts of the country were used, and nine ocean liners were briefly rented – with wealthy prisoners paying for first-class cabins or high-quality restaurant service. Several other camps (illustrated below) also adopted hierarchical distinctions, permitting men with money to live more comfortably.

In some areas disused factories were turned into prisons, hastily surrounded with barbed wire and guarded with soldiers[169]. Near Wakefield, the grounds and buildings of a country house were developed into three separate camps. Each of these held internees from a particular group, for instance, all from German colonies or all previously businessmen in

More than 2,000 Germans were imprisoned in an internment camp in Douglas, Isle of Man.

England, but in each case internees at Wakefield paid 10 shillings (50p) a week for being in that particular setting.

In London, one internment prison was in Alexandra Palace, an exhibition centre whose halls and other buildings accommodated up to 3,000 internees, many for short periods on the way to other camps. However, the largest establishments were on the Isle of Man. Two separate camps, modified and developed in the course of the war, were administered in conjunction with the island's government. These – at Douglas and Knockaloe – catered for nearly 30,000 men in total, but they were very different in size and style[170].

Douglas Camp, on the east coast, had been a tented holiday complex. It was now used to intern around 2,500 men, mainly Germans but also some Austrians and a small number of Turks. Residential and other huts were constructed, and some tents were retained. The camp became divided into three sections – a privilege camp, a Jewish camp, and the so-called ordinary camp.

Occupants of the privilege camp (about 20 percent of the total) paid either 10 shillings (50p) or a pound each week for their shared or personal accommodation. They received better food in a restaurant with uniformed (also interned) waiters using high-quality cutlery. Alcohol could be purchased. Jewish internees, in their separate sub-camp, were provided with Kosher food and permitted to celebrate Jewish festivals. Most Douglas inmates were in the ordinary camp, and in all cases internment for a long period with an unpredictable end point could be very dispiriting. Some aspects of camp life are illustrated in Display Box 5.5.

Display Box 5.5
INTERNMENT IN THE ISLE OF MAN

A substantial number of men from Sheffield spent time behind barbed wire on the Isle of Man. Living conditions in its two camps were tolerable, but enforced idleness, lack of purpose and separation from family and friends were likely to wear a man down as month followed month. Personal motivation could become replaced by aimlessness, depression and mental lassitude.

How could time be filled? The pattern naturally differed from person to person and probably from time to time, but some activities were offered by the authorities and others emerged from the prisoners themselves. First, the administration of these huge camps required a substantial workforce. For example, the preparation of thousands of meals three times a day depended on a large number of organizers, cooks and assistants of different kinds. The camps also needed carpenters, plumbers, gardeners, clerks, hospital attendants, barbers, tailors, postmen, shoe-makers and refuse collectors. Inmates of the privilege camps employed personal valets, known by the military term of batman. These and other workers received some payment for their work, which remained optional.

It is likely that across the period around half of the internees had a job of some kind, often part-time or temporary. A small number worked elsewhere on the island, in road-building or on neighbouring farms. Other roles were in organizing the camp itself. Huts elected their own captain, and sections were partly administered through a committee overseeing recreational and some other activities.

A few internees worked to produce potentially marketable items, sometimes supported by volunteers from the Religious Society of Friends (the Quakers). The Society had set up its Friends Emergency

---

Committee, which contributed equipment and materials for making items such as brushes, baskets and furniture, and assisted with sales. However, since it was forbidden to sell internees' products through commercial channels, demand was limited.

A second form of activity in the camps was more clearly recreational. Some men passed time painting portraits or landscapes, and others took part in theatrical productions and orchestral concerts or in games of football, cricket, tennis or bowls, for which facilities were provided. Technical or academic classes of many kinds and levels were available, with fellow-interned teachers often highly qualified in their fields. And printing works were busy with the design and production of magazines, cards and documents.

The second camp was built at Knockaloe near the west coast. When fully developed, this housed as many as 22,000 internees in four different sections. It covered a very large area with a total circumference of approximately 3 miles. Living conditions were generally similar in each of its sections, although a small privilege camp was introduced in one of them towards the end of the war.

Almost no official documentation about individuals in Knockaloe Camp has survived and records of Douglas Camp are very limited. It is

Knockaloe Camp in the Isle of Man eventually held around 22,000 internees.

known that some Sheffield men were interned at one of the camps, including at least three members of the Funk family described earlier, but almost all details have been lost. Most internees remained in their camp until the end of the war, but some were released on license from late-1915 onwards to work on war-needed trades in several parts of the country. Transfers were presumably based on previous occupations as well as willingness, and at least four men were moved from Douglas Camp to work somewhere in Sheffield – presumably in munition or similar jobs. However, their activities in the city remain unknown[171].

For the families of interned men, having lost their breadwinner and an important source of support, life in Sheffield or elsewhere was often hard. Given the general anti-German atmosphere of the period, British-born wives of interned men may have been treated with suspicion and their children insulted by other young people. Dorothy Toyne, previously of Caxton Road, Sheffield, had married Robert Fritz in 1909. After his internment, she moved their three daughters to live in Matlock, and after the war her husband was sent back to Germany. She herself died in the influenza epidemic of 1918.

Sheffielder Michael Funk is pictured in Knockaloe Camp in 1915.

Financial assistance was available for needy families from the German or Austrian governments, initially administered through the (neutral) American embassy and its local consuls. By the end of 1914, Britain's Local Government Board was providing special grants for British-born wives of interned men. Other funds were sometimes obtainable through local or national charities, but little information is now available.

What happened to internees at the end of the war? Most were sent home. Men repatriated from Sheffield included Julius Freund, Professor of German at the university since 1908. He had been imprisoned in Douglas Camp from July 1915 and was dismissed from his university position at the end of 1916. In the opinion of the university council, at that point 'it appeared to be improbable that the state of political feeling would permit of a German subject filling a professorial post to the advantage of the university at the end of the war'[172].

However, in practice not all interned aliens had to leave after the war. Those wishing to stay in Britain were able to apply to an Appeals Tribunal for exemption from repatriation, and almost 4,000 applications to remain were successful for the country as a whole. Exemption was granted on the grounds of strong family ties, long residence and previous contribution to the community. Some men from Sheffield were able to remain but most details have been lost. The city's population of German-born individuals declined from 390 in the 1911 census to 176 in 1921[173], and their relations with British people were presumably difficult for some years to come.

Naturalized Germans in the city

Among the German-born people living in 1911 Sheffield, about fifty had been naturalized as British, and naturalization of non-enemy aliens continued into earlier years of the war[174]. The procedures for internment and repatriation described in previous sections applied only to men who had not been naturalized. However, many letters in the press or articles in newspapers or magazines failed to distinguish between the two groups, sometimes arguing that 'the call of the blood' would take priority over a mere piece of paper (the naturalization certificate). A number of politicians and campaigners continued to demand punishment without exception for all Germans in the country. Horatio Bottomley the stridently anti-German editor of *John Bull* magazine, addressed a Great Protest Meeting in Sheffield's Albert Hall in July 1916 'to demand immediate internment of all enemy aliens whether naturalized or not'.

Companies with possible German links were investigated and sometimes closed down – nationally around 350 had been shut by the end of 1916. The Poldi Steel Works, operating in Sheffield's Napier Street but also in several European countries, was wound up by the Board of Trade in that year, and musical instrument retailer Wilson Peck, trading in Leopold Street, was investigated and discussed in parliament for its close links to the Bechstein company in Berlin. After changes to ownership and management, Wilson Peck was allowed to continue[175]. Other Sheffield firms also received criticism in parliament, usually from one or a small number of MPs. Bohler Brothers of Renton Street was a branch of an Austrian firm, which was said to be kept going merely 'for the benefit of the enemy proprietors after the war', and it was argued that the Abrasive

Wheel Company of Tinsley should be closed because it is 'controlled by Germans and managed by an unnaturalized German'. This last manager was soon interned and no doubt the companies were monitored, but otherwise no official action appears to have been taken.

In 1917, the (non-naturalized) Viener brothers wrote to the Sheffield Committee on Munitions of War that 'we have not been receiving what we believe are our fair share of orders for helmets'. In fact, the committee had blocked any such orders because that company, W. and E. Viener, was being examined by the Board of Trade within the Trading with the Enemy Act of 1914. Approval was subsequently granted and helmet work was continued[176].

Even naturalized Germans faced hostile beliefs and actions, despite the fact that they were British citizens[177]. Confectioners and restaurant owners J. Lyons announced in the Sheffield press in October 1914 that all their naturalized German and Austrian employees were to be dismissed. Men with German backgrounds in senior civil service positions were regularly implied to be part of a 'hidden hand', which was somehow working secretly to assist their country's conquest of Britain.

Two of the city's naturalized Germans were particularly prominent – Paul Kuehnrich (1871-1932) and Joseph Jonas (1845-1921). Paul Kuehnrich moved from Germany to Sheffield when he was 17, initially becoming an employee of steel and cutlery manufacturers Marsh Brothers. Travelling widely in Europe, he was a very successful salesman. He was naturalized as a British subject in 1894 and by 1906 had created his own company. That soon expanded, linked to others in his ownership, and he quickly acquired a fortune and high public visibility[178]. He introduced many manufacturing innovations and his company was noted for several novel technical procedures.

Paul Kuehnrich was a striking bearded figure, known in earlier years for driving to his works in one of the city's finest carriages. Around 1912 he was wealthy enough to buy a substantial house, Holly Court in Ecclesall, and during the next few years he became the subject of rumours, criticism and even questions in parliament[179]. In one period of strong anti-German feelings, he reacted with a letter to the

Naturalized Paul Kuehnrich was a successful steel manufacturer in the city who was often viewed with suspicion.

Sheffield Daily Independent, complaining on 30 April 1915 that 'considerable mischief has been caused by certain Sheffield travellers spreading […] false tales over the country':

> [Allegedly] I had known already six months before the war broke out the exact date when the war would commence. I had always been a personal friend of the Kaiser, for whom I was a sort of chief spy. I had been rewarded by the Kaiser for some particularly good piece of spy work by being presented with Holly Court. I had a wireless installation. Holly Court was full of ammunition and guns were hidden there. There was enough dynamite at Holly Court to blow up the whole of Sheffield. Soldiers were being drilled by me at Holly Court on every Saturday and Sunday. The bed of the lake at Holly Court was concreted specially to carry the heavy guns. My business was financed by Krupp, and the steel which I sold was made in Germany.

The letter's failure to directly contradict the charges or to criticize Germany did not endear Paul Kuehnrich to the public, and he and his German-born wife were viewed suspiciously by many people throughout the war. However, he invited the police to inspect his property and to examine its lake. On two later occasions he was fined for breaking the law, first, in March 1916, for having inadequate lighting black-out in the bedroom windows of his house[180] and, in February 1918, for holding a stock of food (69lb of bacon) contrary to national prohibitions at a time of scarcity.

Paul Kuehnrich was a talented metallurgist[181]. He also brought together a substantial art collection and had a wide range of cultural interests. It appears from a poem seemingly written by him during the war (and kindly provided for this book by a Swedish friend of Kuehnrich descendants) that he saw himself as a neutral citizen with mixed sympathies – for both Britain and Germany. Four of the poem's six verses are in Display Box 5.6[182].

A German birth also contributed to the downfall of a second naturalized Sheffielder – Joseph Jonas, one of Sheffield's most successful industrialists and politicians of the time[183]. In the late 1860s he moved to London from a region that shortly became part of Germany and in 1873 he settled in Sheffield. Working initially as a travelling continental salesman for Seebohm and Dieckstahl, he soon set up his own steel company. He was joined by Robert Colver and the firm of Jonas and Colver greatly prospered with substantial European and American sales. It employed around 1,500 people in 1914.

Display Box 5.6
A GERMAN WITH MIXED VIEWS

Four verses from a poem believed to be written by Paul Kuehnrich in Holly Court after wartime criticisms:

> O! Have you heard of Holly Court?
> 'Tis a very fair demesne,
> With a very genial whiskered host
> And a bonny chatelaine.
>
> But, Alas! He is of German birth,
> Enough to raise suspicion
> In the minds of many plodding sleuths
> Who clamour for admission.
>
> They've searched each corner of the house
> For a wicked German spy:
> They've peeped into the billiard balls,
> And drained the lake quite dry.
>
> Remember, we are neutrals,
> My 'savage' spouse and I.
> So surely we may come and go,
> And they not reason why.

Joseph Jonas became a naturalized Briton in 1875, married a Sheffield-born woman in 1876, and was elected a Liberal councillor for Attercliffe in 1890. He became a magistrate and lord mayor of the city in 1904, and was knighted in 1905. He was active in public affairs, was a town trustee, and made major contributions of money, time and expertise to the university, especially its Applied Science Department. He was a member of the university council from 1905 to 1916. Before the war he served as the city's consul for Germany, being replaced in that role by the United

States consul once war had started. (USA was neutral for much of the war.) As the war progressed, Jonas and Colver Ltd. became increasingly active in producing special steels for armaments and aeroplanes ordered by the Ministry of Munitions.

Despite his public prominence and social position, Sir Joseph was uncomfortable about how he was being viewed during the war. Writing to the *Sheffield Daily Telegraph* and the *Sheffield Daily Independent* immediately after anti-German riots in the city (May 1915), he emphasized: 'I have spent the greater part of my life in serving Sheffield, the city of my adoption, in many capacities; in fact, I have held nearly every public position during the last twenty-five or thirty years, so that I need not assure the Sheffield public of my loyalty and devotion to the country of my adoption.'[184] In a follow-up letter a few days later, Sir Joseph wrote: 'I am doing everything that lies within my power to bring about the triumph of British arms, and so doing away with that system of militarism in Germany which I have persistently opposed since

Joseph Jonas came to Britain in the 1860s, was naturalized in 1875, and became prominent in the city.

my youth.' During the war his son Edward served as an officer in the Royal Engineers – a British subject born of a British mother and a (naturalized) British father.

Detailed information is lacking about Joseph Jonas during most of the war, but much has been written about events in 1918. In the summer of that year, a widespread anti-German campaign was reaching its height in the press and parliament[185]. Sir Joseph was charged in June with transmitting military secrets to a German company – but not recently. In 1913, when Anglo-German munitions contracts were often interconnected and contacts were frequent, he had received information about a new type of rifle to be built in Vickers' Kent factory. Following a personal request, he had passed this to a business contact who was a German competitor of Vickers[186]. At that earlier time Britain and Germany were not at war, but it was argued in 1918 that the Official Secrets Act covered potential as well as actual

Joseph Jonas's son Edward served in the Royal Engineers despite his father's German origin.

enemies. At the Central Criminal Court (the Old Bailey) in July 1918 Sir Joseph and a fellow defendant were cleared of conspiracy to injure the state but convicted of a misdemeanour – sufficient to fine him the large sum of £2,000. As a result, he was almost immediately deprived of his knighthood and was later removed from the local magistrates' list[187].

Many Sheffielders strongly supported Joseph Jonas, pointing to his long service to the city and his firm's important wartime output. On the other hand, it may be that some local people felt it appropriate that a man of German origin who had become extremely wealthy in this country should be brought down from his elevated position. Germans, naturalized or not, were widely viewed in terms of their country of birth, and being German in a British city during this period made someone noticeable and open to suspicion or worse[188].

On a less-exalted scale, the *Sheffield Daily Independent* of 30 January 1918 reported that 'a pitiful story was told in Sheffield Court yesterday, when Frances Knapp, wife of an enemy alien, of 4 Watkin Street, was sentenced to two months imprisonment for neglecting her nine children, whose ages range from 2 to 14 years. [... The] defendant had been persecuted continually by neighbours because she was the wife of an enemy alien [...] Free meals were given to the children at school, but, owing to the repeated taunts of the neighbours respecting her supposed nationality, she refused to let the children go and have them'. No doubt many other cases of hostility or overt aggression occurred, which did not reach the courts or the newspapers. Germany was the nation's enemy and, for many people, German links were no longer acceptable whatever their basis.

CHAPTER 6

1915 and 1916: Adapting to War

As 1914 turned into a new year, the nation's enthusiasm for war with Germany remained high. Recruiting levels were maintained and young men were keen to fight. However, as we now know, painful problems lay ahead. Deaths and injuries soon became commonplace, and distress at home became widespread.

Restrictions, regulations and the Defence of the Realm Act
The demands of war soon led Britain into what became a broad and lasting shift in national thinking. For many years attitudes had been based on the ideals of *laissez-faire* – leaving society to operate without the involvement of public officials. It had been taken for granted that communities would best flourish in a climate of private personal initiative and voluntary endeavour. Individuals' free choice was better than being organized by a government.

This national consensus was already breaking down in the early years of the twentieth century. The newly formed Labour Party was arguing for collective action and socialist control, and the Liberal government had accepted central organization by introducing state-sponsored insurance protection, pensions and some unemployment pay. The trend towards greater government control became unstoppable as the Great War asked more and more from the nation[189].

In many areas of policy the government first tried to make wartime changes through persuasion and encouragement, but lack of success often led to the enforcement of central regulations. This gradual slide occurred, for instance, in the production of munitions, which came under expanding government control from mid-1915, and the enlistment of servicemen, for whom compulsory call-up eventually replaced voluntary recruitment. Initial persuasion was eventually felt to have reached its limit, and coercion and decision-making by the state took over.

However, in some areas the shift to government control occurred with dramatic suddenness. Almost immediately after war was declared, the nation's railways were taken over, and exports of benzole and other explosive components were instantly prohibited. A wide-ranging act of parliament was quickly passed, on 8 August 1914, with the soothing title Defence of the Realm Act. Abbreviated as DORA, this Act and its amendments and follow-up regulations came to cover a huge variety of activities. The initial emphasis was on 'securing the public safety and the defence of the realm', but its restrictions gained force in many areas of life. By the end of the war there were more than 400 pages of Consolidated Regulations. Some of these are illustrated in Display Box 6.1.

In May 1915, the Liberal government was forced to accept a coalition with the Conservative and Labour parties, and over the following months a succession of new ministries, departments and committees felt it essential to introduce legally backed rules. It became usual to seek improved efficiency through state organization and associated restrictions on individual freedom, for example in censorship, price regulation, rent control, military conscription, industrial development, and a range of smaller constraints. A Liquor Control Board drew upon the Defence of the Realm Act to determine pubs' hours of opening, the strength of beer and the operation of breweries. A National Registration Act required all households to provide information about every adult member. Personal registration cards were issued and had to be carried at all times, and any change of address had to be reported to the new Local Registration Authority, in Sheffield's case located in the Town Hall. Some foreigners in the country were imprisoned, conscientious objectors were subject to legal processes and a huge range of components and raw materials could be bought and sold only by the government. Control boards of many kinds were created at local as well as national levels, and later in the war a national food controller introduced several types of rationing.

From 1915, public houses were forbidden to serve liquor except at lunchtime and between 6.30 pm and 9.30 pm[190], and credit payments in

Display Box 6.1
THE MANY FACES OF DORA – THE DEFENCE OF THE REALM ACT

This Act of Parliament of August 1914 and its later additions gave the government powers over many aspects of daily life. DORA regulations were backed by the threat of a trial in a court of law or, in some cases, in a military court. The Act or one of its subsequent Regulations made it illegal, for instance, to:

- talk about military matters in public
- spread false or damaging reports
- loiter near railway lines or bridges
- collect or publish information that might be of use to an enemy
- purchase binoculars
- provide liquor to a soldier on duty
- spread rumours that might cause alarm
- enter an enemy country without authorization.

Government officials, military authorities and police forces were empowered to:

- take possession of land or buildings and of power and water supplies
- erect and destroy buildings as needed
- enter and search any premises considered to be suspicious
- seize any material
- control the content of newspapers
- determine the opening hours of public houses
- arrest suspected individuals without a warrant
- take any other action considered necessary for the Act's purposes.

In addition to these general controls, other Acts made detailed interventions in specific areas of personal and commercial life.

pubs were prohibited. Also forbidden was treating another person to an alcoholic drink except with a meal. Households and business premises became required to black-out their lights in the hours of darkness, and street lighting was extinguished or shaded. Especially in the first two years of war, thousands of Sheffielders were fined for failing to mask their property adequately and local newspapers frequently published lists of prosecuted individuals and companies. A new Petrol Control Committee rationed supplies and petrol tax had to be paid in advance. Guy Fawkes night celebrations on 5 November were forbidden.

Many of Sheffield's companies became designated as controlled by the government. These had to submit their financial accounts to national officials and in almost all cases pay an excess profits tax. Munition production was subject to wide-ranging regulation and the Ministry of Munitions commandeered properties as it desired. Workers had to accept restrictions on their wage level, strikes and lock-outs were forbidden, and companies were forced to buy many materials at government-determined prices and sell their products for amounts fixed by

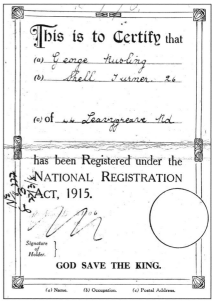

The nation's 1915 registration cards included details of a person's occupation and address, here in Sheffield's Leavygreave Road.

officials. Long lists of controlled items and prices were published and repeatedly updated. For two years from mid-1915, no workers in munition-related industries could move to a different employer without authorization through a leaving certificate from their last job. Workers disobeying management's instructions in a job could be, and often were, sent for trial and probable punishment at a newly-established munition tribunal.

Laissez-faire was thus washed away by the war, and big government and its officials took over. By the end of the war public expenditure is estimated to have been 52 percent of the nation's total compared to only 12 percent in 1915, and more than 80 percent of Britain's imports were channelled through state purchasing agencies. The country had changed, and much of the new thinking stayed with us.

Sheffield in 1915 and 1916
The city's initial anxiety about widespread joblessness and poverty soon declined. Government contracts gave rise to intense factory activity, and

huge expansion of munition works became necessary. To meet the need, around 10,000 additional workers came into the city.

Accompanying those changes, many day-to-day activities and experiences had to change. For 1916 the following year's *Sheffield Yearbook* reported:

> No street lamps are being lit, windows have to be darkened, shop doors display transparencies marked 'Shop Open', business ceases by 7 o'clock (compulsory closing of shops at 8), entertainments start earlier, and the tram service is suspended at 10.30 pm. Public clocks no longer strike, nor do church bells ring. Some churches have given up evening services. Others start at 6 pm instead of 6.30. To assist pedestrians on very dark nights white rings are painted round lamp-posts, tram standards and trees; curb stones are whitened, and the entrances to passages and the like. Many people were heavily fined before they were convinced of the need for darkening their windows.
>
> Wounded soldiers are among the daily sights of the city. Hospitals, schools and so on are used for them; and convalescent men are in the streets daily. Seats have been specially provided for them in all public places.
>
> Among the anti-Zeppelin defences, aeroplanes were conspicuous; and throughout the summer *[of 1916]* their manoeuvres, and looping the loop, were a never-failing source of interest. The nightly operation of searchlights conveyed suggestions of war.
>
> Women's work has developed in many directions. There are large new national munition factories staffed almost entirely by women, who, in shifts, carry on day and night. As the war develops, and more men are needed, the call for women workers grows.

The cost of living rose steadily, with food on average costing almost two-thirds more by the end of 1916. The government imposed controls on many food prices, but those had to be raised frequently to keep up with market changes. House rents also kept climbing in response to the arrival in the city of more munition workers, the loss of housing to factory extensions and the almost complete absence of domestic building. Successive national budgets raised taxes. In September 1915, income tax rates were lifted on average by around 40 percent, and duties went up on sugar, tea, tobacco, petrol and other items. Halfpenny letter postage was abolished and the price of telegrams was increased by 50 percent. The increased cost of living had its greatest impact on poorer people with fixed incomes. However, wage rates increased steadily and more hours at work became possible – unemployment was rare. World War One was for many a time of financial prosperity.

The English Cup Final took place in April 1915, when Sheffield United beat Chelsea 3 - 0, but many football clubs stopped playing for the rest of the war. (United and Wednesday continued playing, usually against local teams[191].) Bank holidays were cancelled in 1916 to allow factory work to continue, and in the summer of that year daylight working time was for the first time extended by moving all clocks forward one hour. The number of passengers on the city's trams surged, especially to and from the east-end factories. The demand for electricity and gas became so great that the city's supplies were sometimes restricted or interrupted. Companies lost key workers to the army or navy and often had to turn away new business. Hundreds of men left their city council jobs[192], and staff shortages developed in the medical services. As the army took priority some doctors were lost from civilian hospitals, and the panel of general practitioners offering free treatment to insured workers was frequently below strength[193].

Department stores and smaller shops coped with the loss of male staff with more female assistants. Many retailers continued to look for ways in which the war might help their business. During 1915, Mappin and Webb, of the Royal Show Rooms in Norfolk Street, advertized 'a Present for your Soldier Son' – 'Mappin's Famed Campaign Watch'. H. L. Brown of 65 Market Place could provide the badge of any regiment: 'If you have a friend or relative at the war, you should wear the badge of the regiment in which he serves. It is a mark of respect.' In June 1916, just after the start of general military conscription, John Walsh's department store in High Street advertized 'large airy depositories' to 'Married Men Called to the Colours' who might wish to store furniture in their absence.

Responding to a government campaign, the City Council released more land for allotments where families could grow food, but applicant numbers far exceeded the plots available. Enthusiasm for self-help was encouraged by local newspapers, for instance in a *Complete Guide to Vegetable Growing* aimed at women as well as men. Rifle clubs were also very busy. In 1915, Sheffield had twenty-two clubs with more than 2,000 members. Each had its own firing range such that, for instance, Pitsmoor Rifle Club practised in Roe Wood and the Brincliffe and Ecclesall club held meetings in Broad Elms Lane. Fences were constructed around Neepsend Power Station and other vulnerable sites, and military guards were installed. Unlit streets caused problems and more than twenty fatal accidents occurred during the winter of 1916-1917 – fifteen involving tramcars despite the requirement for continuous sounding of a gong at night. After being struck by a tram, Thomas Morrison, a tailor of Carterknowle Road, was awarded £660 for losing the sight in one eye.

The city's stock exchange continued business with thirty-six active members and daily quotation of prices. Plays and entertainment were still well-received at the Empire and Lyceum theatres, and cinemas were very busy with showings two or three times a day and in some cases continuously. Amid much disruption and despair, life had to continue.

News from the Front
As the people of Sheffield came to adjust in these ways, loved ones far away experienced dangers and horrors of a different kind. For families at home who wanted to learn what was happening overseas, news was very limited. In the absence of radio and television, newspapers were almost the only source of information and their content was often somewhat distorted – both by the government and by newspaper editors themselves. The government's Press Bureau acted as the principal channel of information from all official departments to the public. The bureau introduced a process of censorship to prevent the publication of information considered to be 'injurious to the naval and military operations of the British Empire' or 'likely to cause needless alarm and distress among the civil population'. Bureau instructions were in principle backed by DORA sanctions, but legal action was, in practice, rarely taken[194]. However, censorship meant that newspapers in Sheffield and elsewhere were able to report only certain aspects of the war. Even widely-published reports described as being from an 'Eye-witness' had been provided by a government war correspondent and were first reviewed by the Press Bureau – sometimes by Lord Kitchener himself[195].

Editors complained frequently, especially in the war's early stages, about the limited information supplied to them. However, they also exercised their own discretion, seeking to avoid the greatest excesses of the battlefield. Newspapers' wishes to maintain public morale and build optimism were reflected in the style of their headlines, for example the following (separately) in the Sheffield press during 1915 and 1916:

ENEMY'S HEAVY LOSSES
GERMANS KILLED IN THOUSANDS
SMASHING THROUGH THE GERMAN TRENCHES
GERMANY PREPARES FOR BAD NEWS.

The tone of reports was usually optimistic as far as the facts would allow. For example, the extended and death-producing Somme battles of 1916 were described as 'the Great Push' or 'the Great Advance', and murderous encounters were sometimes viewed as 'thrilling' or 'lively'.

In addition to material from the government's Press Bureau, the local papers also reported military life and death by publishing letters received by families or friends. (These were always censored before being accepted for posting.) Soldiers' letters were often cheerful, but they could be very explicit about the horrors of their situation. For example, Sheffield readers were told in separate letters:

We lost ten out of twenty-one in a troop. It was awful. I saw Mickie hit in the back with high-explosive shrapnel [...] There I was amongst ten of them, all wounded, screaming for help. God! I will never forget it. (November 1914)

It was death every inch of the way – a terrible sight. As we raced forward towards the guns our men simply fell as they were hit, and lay there in long lines as straight as if on parade. The Germans had six machine-guns on that hill alone. (May 1915)

You can just imagine standing beside a few of your pals, and every now and then one would topple over, either wounded or killed [...] Before the war came on I felt as if I should like a bit of a scrap, but I have had quite enough now [...] I have lost some good chums, chaps I had grown to like very much. The last I saw of one of them was hanging dead on the German barbed wire. I have seen them go to the attack as if they were going to a picnic, laughing and joking: the next minute they were bowled over like flies. (July 1915)

We were catching it badly in the supports. Parapets were flying about, and the dead and wounded were horrible to see. Stretcher-bearers were working like fury, still many of the poor wounded chaps were left lying in the filth and water all day [... Events which followed] held for us horrors indescribable. (October 1915)

Letter-writers' names and addresses were published, so readers were sometimes able to identify with soldiers they knew. More generally, casualties were listed several times a week in published Rolls of Honour. With separate sections for men Killed, Wounded or Missing, these often extended across several columns of a newspaper page. Published sets of photographs could show deceased individuals all from one Sheffield church or one school group, and in some cases brief life-histories of deceased men from the city were presented[196]. Following the tremendous number of casualties after mid-1916 (in the Somme and other battles[197]), these published lists were reduced in size and prominence. Local men continued to be recorded, but casualties from around the country were now included less often. In August 1916, Sheffield's lord mayor asked families worried about their missing soldier son to contact him so that enquiries could be made through the British Red Cross.

People in Sheffield thus received news of the war that was partial, often delayed and, in some cases, distressing. A message that a son was Missing could be followed by several weeks of non-information and anxiety. Families had to hope that their son or husband was alive and well, and letters and postcards were mailed in large numbers. Those from the Front had been censored and in some cases were limited to standard messages on a Field Service Postcard. But the worst could happen, and a family could receive the news they had been dreading.

The war had killed more than 2,000 Sheffield men by the end of 1916. Official communications about deaths included standard War Office forms completed for men identified either as Dead or Missing, and telegrams were sent in respect of officers. Weeks could elapse before a family received official confirmation of a death, but the Red Cross worked to obtain and send earlier information after particularly fierce battles. Private Arthur Greensmith, a trainee mining engineer of Kenwood Park Road, was killed in the City Battalion's Somme fighting on 1 July 1916 aged 22. He died before receiving an anxious note sent to him by his sister, and that was returned to her unread. It was almost a month before Arthur's father received a note from his son's company commander with news of his death, and a further month before he received official notification[198].

Occasionally painful mistakes were made. In December 1916, Private George Jenkins was reported to have died of wounds, and his Sheffield wife had to adjust and suffer as a widow in mourning. As long as eight months later, in August 1917, she learned that George was in fact still alive. In many other cases, families' anxious uncertainty was instead ended by the worst kind of news. A man declared to be Missing was later confirmed as Dead.

NOTHING is to be written on this side except the date and signature of the sender. Sentences not required may be erased. If anything else is added the post card will be destroyed.

I am quite well.

I have been admitted into hospital
  { *sick* } *and am going on well.*
  { *wounded* } *and hope to be discharged soon.*

I am being sent down to the base.

I have received your { *letter dated* _____
                          telegram „ _____
                          parcel „ _____

Letter follows at first opportunity.

I have received no letter from you
  { *lately.*
  { *for a long time.*

Signature }
  only. }

Date _____

[Postage must be prepaid on any letter or post card addressed to the sender of this card.]

(25343) Wt.W3497-293 1,760m. 4/15 M.R.Co.,Ltd.

The army's field service postcard allowed only basic and standard messages.

Some next-of-kin received both an official notification of death and a letter from a friend, junior officer or chaplain. Coalminer James Haynes had lived in Unwin Street, Darnall, with his wife Bertha and their four children. A lance-corporal with the Northumberland Fusiliers, he was killed in July 1916. His wife received this letter from his platoon commander, who tried rather formally to be sympathetic in a difficult situation:

I regret to have to inform you that your husband, Lance Corporal J. Haynes 16322, was seriously wounded on July 6th, and died before reaching the dressing station. I saw him very soon after he was hit, and he was unconscious and in my opinion died painlessly.

   He was a good soldier and man, and my sympathy goes out to you in the great loss you have sustained.

Warehouse assistant Leslie Cave of Cardiff Street was killed in action a year later, in May 1917. He was 29 and left a wife and three children. Another son was born soon after his death. A colleague (who was himself killed the following year) returned to his mother an undelivered letter she had written, together with his own note to her[199]:

Dear Madame, just a few lines to you hoping they will find you quite well as it leaves me at present. Well Madame I am very sorry to tell you that your son Leslie as got killed. He suffered know pain I was with him when the shell burst. I was very lucky to get out of it the same shell killed one more and wounded four. Madame I hope you do not take it to hard. I miss him a lot as he was my pal out here and we used to sleep together when we was out of the trenches. All the boys liked him he was brave and he died like a hero.

Distress for families at home could be all the greater because the absence of information led to a long period of uncertainty. The bodies of around 100,000 British men have never been identified, including more than 2,000 from Sheffield. Furthermore, after a death families were not able to mourn their loss at a funeral or visit a loved one's grave. All they had were the dead man's letters and possessions, which were eventually returned[200]. In addition to those mementoes, some families marked a death on subsequent anniversaries through an insertion in local newspapers. Two examples are in Display Box 6.2.

   In several dozen cases, deaths in battle were also detailed in the city's newspapers soon after they had happened. A colleague of Private Frank Pennington of Haworth Street, Walkley, serving with the Royal Welsh Fusiliers, wrote:

We were ordered back to fetch some more [ammunition …] The first man got killed as soon as he left the trench, and the same thing happened to the next man. Then Frank went, and he got about half way across the ploughed field when he fell. I saw him hold his hands up to his shoulder, and I ran to help him but they had me down through the leg when I was about five feet from him. I managed to crawl up to him and drag him behind a haystack, but I am sorry to say he died as soon as I got him there. I asked if I could take any word home for him, but all he could say was 'I'm going'.

Display Box 6.2
'IN LOVING MEMORY'

Among items in the *Sheffield Daily Independent* of 1 October 1917 were these anniversary memorials:

NELL. In loving memory of Pte. Henry Nell, killed in action
Sept. 30 1915.
Under the shade of the dear old flag
Out in a strange, lone land
Lies one of the best and bravest lads,
Slain by the enemy's hand.
From his ever loving Mother, Father, and Family.

STONES. In proud and loving memory of Harry, the dearly loved son
of George Henry and Louisa Stones of Station Road, Killamarsh,
who was killed in action Oct. 1 1916, aged 20 years.
Days of sadness still come o'er us,
Tears of silence often flow,
Memory keeps our loved one near us,
Though he died a year ago [...]
From his sorrowing Father and Mother, Sisters and Brother.

The *Sheffield Daily Independent* published a letter from a friend of Sheffield City Battalion Private Cecil Stanley Mason, of Briar Road, Walkley: 'None of us will ever face death more bravely [...] Stan, along with his comrades, was climbing out of the trench into No-Man's-Land, when a shell burst among them, killing three and wounding several others. He died instantly with his face to the enemy, setting a magnificent example of heroism [...] He was the most cheerful chap of the party during the time we were waiting for the word to go forward.'

Lieutenant P. K. Perkin had previously worked for William Hutton and Company in West Street. A soldier in the Sheffield City Battalion described in the *Independent* his officer's death on 1 July 1916: '[He] was well in front of his men and was encouraging them, and at the same time trying to work his way through the German barbed wire, when a hand bomb burst close to him, and he half fell, reeled and pluckily pulled himself together for another effort when another bomb burst which brought him down.' A chaplain wrote that 'Lieutenant Perkin was last seen sitting on the German wire calling on his men [...] He was not more than two or three yards from the German trenches.'

Also on 1 July 1916, Lieutenant Arnold Beal of Ivy Park Road was killed when he moved to a deeper crater shell. A wounded soldier wrote to Arnold's father: 'I tried to give him a drink, but only once did his lips move. He was past human aid, and died immediately [...] Then the Germans spotted us and we were in that crater fourteen hours, and at 11 o'clock on Saturday night we crept to our own line, leaving Lieutenant Beal and Lance-Corporal Emmerson and [another] dead man.'

Many similar battlefield experiences were described in the local papers. Such events were familiar to serving troops, but it is important to recognize that they were also known to many Sheffielders – albeit from a distance and with less intensity. Rationalizations for the slaughter were also well-

Sergeant-Major Joseph Siddall was granted leave from the Western Front to visit his sick wife in Walkley but, like her, he died in the city.

SAD HOME-COMING OF A HALLAMSHIRE SERGEANT.

Sergt. Siddall, of the Hallamshires, was summoned home owing to the illness of his wife. He returned half an hour too late, was taken to hospital, where he died of pneumonia. Photo is (1) that of the late Sergeant and (2) that of the funeral procession.

known. As reported in the *Sheffield Daily Independent*, one commanding officer wrote: 'May I remind you of the glorious death he died? Ever steady and true to his duty, at his post, like a good soldier, he laid down his life for the sake of his country. No nobler fate could be his.'

Military deaths also occurred on British soil. Towards the end of June 1915, 48-year-old Sergeant-Major Joseph Siddall was granted emergency leave from the Western Front to visit his sick wife in Walkley. Before the war he had been a file forger with Thomas Turner and Sons in Mowbray Street and had long been a territorial member of the Hallamshire Rifles. Sadly, Eleanor died shortly before her husband reached Sheffield. Her death and the subsequent funeral greatly distressed him and he spent long periods of day and night mourning at her grave in Walkley Cemetery.

For several days Joseph Siddall had been unwell with a chest infection and this gradually turned into pneumonia, as commonly occurred in Western Front soldiers. On 23 July he died in the city's Third Northern General Hospital and was himself accorded a full military funeral. Several thousand people lined the funeral procession's route from his house in Freedom Road. At its head were a party of rifle-bearers, a regimental band and soldiers from local regiments. Four hundred men of the York and Lancaster Regiment formed a guard of honour at Walkley Cemetery, and his coffin, draped with a Union Jack, was borne by six sergeants and accompanied by his two soldier sons. After the ceremony, rifle volleys were fired over the grave, now shared by the sergeant-major and his wife, and finally the *Last Post* was sounded.

These events were described in detail in the local press. In a city of apparently random deaths of sons and fathers far away, and an inability to share grief at a distant funeral or graveside, the war and its human significance had been vividly brought home.

Propaganda and morale at home
As in most wars, continuing support from the public was important for success. In the early stages patriotic enthusiasm was considerable, but during 1916 people were becoming weary of only limited progress and the increasing restrictions on daily life. Therefore, although the government's initial propaganda in Britain set out to increase recruiting and control information through censorship, later persuasion was aimed instead to maintain public morale and strengthen motivation to keep fighting.

Propaganda does not require that outright lies be told[201]. It advances a cause by emphasizing one set of facts and opinions and by distorting, denying or ignoring an opposing position. In those ways the government, mass media and information sources of all kinds repeatedly emphasized the nation's moral purpose and military valour while denigrating Germany, its achievements and values.

However, propaganda comes not only from government. People in Sheffield and elsewhere were each day exposed to a stream of messages and opinions, which of course also shaped their feelings about the war. Almost all newspapers and magazines showed support throughout, most churches stressed the war's moral purpose and the need for national persistence, and people were surrounded by volunteer and fundraising activities in unquestioning favour of the war effort. Society as well as government presented the conflict as essential and the enemy as evil, immoral and open to defeat[202].

Some recruiting posters built on encouragement from family and community.

Propaganda from the government The War Office initially worked to boost recruiting through posters based on patriotism, national honour and even the shame attached to not volunteering[203], and the Defence of the Realm Act prohibited publication of any clearly negative material. In addition to propaganda for the home population, the government was particularly concerned to influence attitudes abroad, working hard to persuade politicians, business people and the public in neutral countries, especially in the USA, to look sympathetically on the empire's struggle. Immediately in August 1914, the Foreign Office created a War Propaganda Bureau to strengthen the country's image in the world.

This bureau systematically supplied material to foreign newspapers, politicians and key individuals, and it increased the propaganda flow by arranging for distinguished authors to prepare pamphlets and other documents about Britain's honourable mission

Other recruiting posters played on the guilt likely to be felt by men who remained at home.

Fitzalan Square was the setting for many displays of weapons and war savings campaigns. This German gun was exhibited in 1915.

and the international need to conquer Germany. Most of these were published commercially with no indication of a link to government, and they were widely distributed abroad (after translation where necessary), and in this country by book retailers such as W. H. Smith, voluntary groups and private companies. The War Propaganda Bureau also disguised the official underpinning of many motivational war lectures, presumably including some in Sheffield, in which eminent speakers reviewed current issues in a way that bolstered support for the nation's effort.

Among other attempts to maintain public enthusiasm, the government sponsored war-related exhibitions around the country. For several weeks in April and November 1915, captured German guns were stationed in Sheffield's Fitzalan Square, attracting enormous interest. Later stages of the war saw the government turn to propaganda themes that had been of limited concern during the earlier patriotic fervour. With the nation increasingly weary of war and groups such as the No Conscription Fellowship and the Union of Democratic Control in active opposition, government posters and pamphlets shifted from recruiting to endurance-building. Thousands of talks and meetings were organized around the country for church and other groups or on employers' premises, often revolving around the brutality and dishonesty of Germany and the dangers of giving in to premature negotiations for peace.

In 1917 the government formalized many of its propaganda activities by creating a Department of Information with wide responsibilities. Headed by author, journalist and civil servant John Buchan, this worked to go beyond the previous focus on pamphlets and lectures by also sponsoring films to be shown in cinemas in this country and abroad[204]. Earlier government-provided films had mainly been brief, factual reports such as *Troops protecting Greek patriarchs*, shown in Sheffield in 1915, or pictures of *Dusty Indian warriors fighting for the cause of the Mother Country*[205]. Subsequently, films more often told exciting stories about German spies or brave British soldiers, or presented amusing episodes such as Charlie Chaplin's *Shoulder Arms*, which appeared in October 1918. Later years of the war also saw greater use of official war artists such as Muirhead Bone, Paul Nash and Wyndham Lewis to provide drawings or paintings of the Western Front, often for display around Britain[206].

Propaganda from the community Those official attempts to influence opinion naturally occurred in parallel with continuing everyday exposure to views about the war. Most people provided to each other a steady barrage of persuasion, usually that the war was necessary and (in some messages) morally essential[207]. Newspapers were full of patriotic and optimistic themes, in effect adding to the government's own messages. Especially later in the war, they frequently told readers how to economize in food, clothes, coal, firewood, soap, matches and other household items. Germany's brutality was emphasized, for example when Red Cross nurse Edith Cavell was executed by Germany in October 1915 for helping Allied soldiers escape from Belgium. Other 1915 headlines in the *Sheffield Daily Telegraph* included MERCILESS KILLINGS, WARFARE MADE BUTCHERY and NON-COMBATANTS AS SHIELDS.

The German execution in October 1915 of British nurse Edith Cavell caused outrage in British towns and cities.

In May 1915, a national committee chaired by Lord Bryce, with members including H. A. L. Fisher, the vice-chancellor of Sheffield University, examined previous stories of German troops' atrocities in Belgium. The committee concluded (without any checks on actual events) that the atrocities (described to include rapes, baby-bayoneting and cutting off children's hands) had indeed occurred. The Bryce Report (citing 'murder, lust and pillage') was widely publicized in Britain and other countries (copies were made available for one penny), and its conclusions were discussed at length in Sheffield newspapers.

Religious groups also looked positively on Britain's role in the war. Union Jacks were placed in churches, and sermons, lectures and literature urged support. For instance, the Dore and Totley Parochial Magazine of September 1914 drew upon material in *The Times* newspaper to argue against 'the most deadly peril that Britain has ever known'. Father Oswald Dolan of St Marie's Catholic Church in Norfolk Row repeatedly urged men to volunteer to fight, and in 1915 he enlisted as an army chaplain (as did other clergymen). The Feed the Guns (fundraising) Campaign in Barker's Pool in October 1918 opened with a religious service conducted by the Bishop of Sheffield. The city's schools also played their part. Pupils were taught patriotic songs and learned about the country's fight against Germany and about the empire's world-wide importance. They were (for instance) taken in April 1918 to the Albert Hall in Barker's Pool to see *With the Empire's Fighters*, and later that year a large number were taken to the Mappin Art Gallery to view war pictures provided by the Ministry of Information.

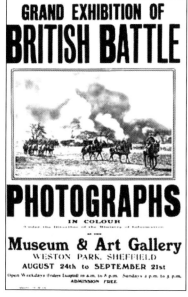

Schoolchildren gave pocket money for ambulances or to buy war savings certificates. School thrift campaigns accompanied lessons in household economy, and pupils provided food and other comforts for soldiers in hospital or for the city's Prisoners of War Help Committee. Teachers' encouragement was often based on requests from the government. For instance, in the spring of 1917 a National Welfare and Economy Campaign (with a local exhibition in the Cutlers' Hall) included essay-writing competitions about how to economize during the war. The log book of Ranmoor Council School reports that on 30 April 1915[208] 'work was stopped at 11 am today as all the

This was one of several special war exhibitions at the city's Mappin Art Gallery. It was extremely popular.

children were employed in helping to make respirators for the army. 320 were made.' Outside school, magazines for boys featured weapons, war heroes and famous victories, and some girls' papers provided materials and instructions for embroidering patriotic pictures.

Display Box 6.3
SUFFRAGETTE EMMELINE PANKHURST INSPIRES
THE CITY
Excerpts from *Sheffield Daily Telegraph* 21 April 1915

RECRUITING SPEECH BY MRS PANKHURST
APPEAL TO SHEFFIELD

Mrs Pankhurst, the leader of the militant suffragettes – whose militancy is now so completely concentrated on the desire to help the country in the war – visited Sheffield last night and addressed a recruiting meeting under the auspices of the Women's Social and Political Union. The gathering which assembled to hear her was one of the most remarkable held in the city since the commencement of the war. The Victoria Hall, which had been engaged, proved all too small to accommodate all who wished to attend. After every available seat and much of the standing room had been occupied, there were still about a thousand people unable to gain admission, and an overflow meeting had to be held in Nether Chapel […]

Mrs Pankhurst's address was an appeal to everyone to come to the service of the country in every possible way […] As to the Women's Social and Political Union, they had decided at the outset that it was unthinkable that they could embarrass the people who were responsible for maintaining the honour of the country and the safety of the nation. They were the first to declare a truce with regard to internal warfare, and as the days went on they felt that that was not enough, and they must do more [… The war] could only be satisfactorily settled by complete victory over Germany.

She dwelt on the ways in which women had shown themselves capable of doing work hitherto done by men, and appealed to employers to consider whether they could not employ women and so release men to do their duty to the country […] She appealed forcibly to the young men to take their courage in both hands, join the colours, and experience the joy of battle.

Sheffield's resolve was boosted by a visit from King George in September 1915, and motivational speeches in the city included more than one by Suffragette Emmeline Pankhurst who had previously been an implacable opponent of the government (see Display Box 6.3)[209]. Throughout much of the war, military bands gave concerts in several of the city's parks and public support was reinforced by War Emergency Concerts held in Sheffield's Albert Hall. More generally, fundraising efforts for war-related causes were publicized every week in the press and elsewhere.

Picture postcards also had a patriotic theme, for example urging people to 'Remember Edith Cavell' (above). Music-hall sketches showed incompetent German soldiers or a bumbling Kaiser, and newly written popular songs with a military theme became familiar through social get-togethers, concert parties and music-hall shows. In the autumn of 1914 a commercially-produced recruiting song included:

Oh, we don't want to lose you,
But we think you ought to go,
For your King and your Country
Both need you so.
We shall want you and miss you,
But with all our might and main,
We shall thank you, cheer you, kiss you,
When you come back again![210]

In this and other ways, the government was far from the only source of propaganda. The community itself sent out very similar messages.

Conscription and military tribunals

Britain's long reliance on a volunteer army had been made possible by maintaining only a small number of soldiers. However, as the Great War gradually needed more and more men, voluntary recruiting became less and less adequate. The years 1915 and 1916 saw a steady slide from free choice by individuals into compulsory conscription.

During the early months of war, volunteer recruits were sought to 'defend the British way of life' and to 'preserve our great and glorious heritage'. In addition, advertisements were aimed at particular types of skilled men needed in specific branches. The Royal Flying Corps 'urgently require[d]' carpenters, tailors, watchmakers, welders and others; advertisements in the city by the Army Service Corps sought experienced

G.  R.

WEST RIDING DIVISIONAL ROYAL ENGINEERS (T.), SHEFFIELD.

Lieut. Col. A. E. BINGHAM, V.D. Commanding.

MORE RECRUITS WANTED!

GOOD MEN and TRUE of the following trades and qualifications:—Blacksmiths, Bricklayers, Carpenters, Masons, Plumbers, Plate Layers, &c. and MEN WHO CAN RIDE. Saddlers, Shoeing Smiths and Wheelwrights SPECIALLY REQUIRED.

FULL ARMY PAY AND ALLOWANCES.

APPLY any week-day from 8.0 a.m. to 5.0 p.m., SATURDAYS from 9.0 a.m. to 12 noon.

Major L. E. COLLEY, T.D.,
O.C. Depot,
Headquarters, Glossop Road Drill Hall,
SHEFFIELD.

In February 1915, the Royal Engineers still needed to recruit Sheffield men with specialized skills.

drivers of motor cars and steam lorries for 'supplying the troops in action'; and the Royal Engineers advertised for 'blacksmiths, bricklayers, carpenters, masons, plumbers, plate-layers, etc'. Military units and their bands regularly marched through the city to encourage volunteers, and formal drills could be viewed in Hillsborough and other parks.

'On War Service' badges provided some indication that a civilian wearer was contributing to the national effort by making essential munitions rather than by enlisting in the army. Badges had initially been granted rather liberally, and allocations were repeatedly reviewed and restricted from mid-1915. The local military recruiting office became increasingly involved in discussions about particular cases, and in order to improve the information available a National Registration Act of July 1915 required households to provide details of every occupant aged between 15 and 65. The parish of Dore reported 115 single men and 126 married men between 17 and 39.

Britain retained voluntary enlistment throughout 1915 but recruit numbers became increasingly inadequate for military needs. Discussions in the press and more widely came to focus on the desirability of compulsory call-up, and a final voluntary effort was made in the Derby Scheme, named after the new director-general of recruiting, Lord Derby[211]. Special committees were set up in each of Sheffield's five parliamentary divisions, and several hundred canvassers were recruited to call at homes and factories. Special attention was paid to the city's 37,000 'unstarred' men of military age ('starred' men were protected as munition workers), as well as seeking to move individuals out of their starred status. Disputes about the starred or unstarred status of individual men became very common, and an appeal process was introduced with local tribunals established in Sheffield and elsewhere.

The Derby Scheme did not deliver enough troops to meet the need, and from January 1916 a sharp change in policy was announced. In that month a first Military Service Act ordered compulsory enlistment of unmarried men between 18 and 41, and a second Act in May 1916 extended conscription to married men also[212]. Individuals no longer had a free choice in the *laissez-faire* tradition. Instead, decisions about a man's fate were taken by the government. Families under threat of losing a wage-earner (although a dependants' allowance was paid) sought ways for him to avoid call-up, and the recently-established military tribunals acquired considerable power. These examined claims for exemption on grounds of occupational or personal need or because of conscientious objection. Sheffield's military tribunal met several times a week, often in an evening, and discussions and decisions were summarized in the city's newspapers.

By the end of 1916, pressure for more men had become intense and the pool of available conscripts had shrunk to a small number of workers mainly in protected jobs. Recruiting staff combed through one factory after

The city's recruiting office acquired a large staff. In the centre of the front row here are Captain Barnsley and Major Firth.

another, assessing all possible conscripts and enlisting many who had previously been badged as indispensable. Decisions about conscription became increasingly controversial and industrial disputes in the city included one that resulted in a countrywide strike by engineers[213].

A public round-up without warning on a Sunday afternoon in October 1916 started by shutting the gates of the botanical gardens. Soldiers required all young men inside to prove their ineligibility for military service, and around forty possible conscripts were taken to the recruiting office for further investigation. The office's staff grew to around 100 civilian clerks (mainly women) under the supervision of military officers[214]. For a year until mid-1916, the area recruiting officer was Major S. Firth, previously from Scarborough, and he was followed by Captain (promoted to Major) George Barnsley of local toolmakers George Barnsley and Sons. In 1916, the recruiting office acquired a 'substitution officer', charged to identify potential conscripts in local factories and to locate substitutes (women as well as men) who were ineligible or unfit for call-up. The 1917 *Sheffield Yearbook* tells us that this work was 'assisted by a considerable number of gentlemen who are ineligible for military service' – probably company managers with local knowledge. By the end of 1917, recruiting staff were administratively transferred from the War

Office into a new Ministry of National Service, and Major Barnsley was re-titled as an Assistant Director of National Service.

Aeroplanes, Zeppelins and government insurance

Prior to the Great War, Sheffielders could not envisage being attacked from the sky. However, by 1915, German airships were for the first time threatening the country and raids from the air had become a worrying possibility. In January of that year the lord mayor issued the city's first air-raid regulations. Lacking previous experience these were rather simple. For example: 'Take cover immediately; the nearest basement would be the safest. Remain under cover until the raid is over; drivers will get their horses under cover, or stand by their heads [...] Keep away from the vicinity of gas works; avoid broken electric wires.'

However, by February 1916, the chief constable issued to all policemen, firemen, doctors and others assisting with air-raids fifteen pages of detailed instruction. Lamplighters were required to extinguish street lamps and later relight them; vehicle, factory and other internal lights had to be reduced; and men of the Royal Army Medical Corps stationed at Hillsborough Barracks were to be despatched to main hospitals and police stations. Also called into action were voluntary groups such as St John's Ambulance Brigade, the Ambulance Section of Sheffield Volunteer Defence Corps, special constables, volunteer firemen and volunteer motor drivers.

Companies sought insurance against war damage. In June 1915, James Dixon and Sons took out a policy with Lloyds of London to protect its buildings and stock from damage 'caused by Aerial Craft including bombs, shells, and/or missiles dropped or thrown therefrom'. In July of that year, the Board of Trade introduced a standard government policy to protect against aircraft and bombardment. This could be purchased through approved insurance companies and was taken up by companies, churches, hospitals and other organizations. The Cutlers' Hall was in that way insured against bombing for £26,000, and insurance cover for its contents included clothing for hospital patients that had been gathered by the Mistress Cutler's charity (see Chapter Seven).

In December 1914, an Anti-Aircraft Corps was formed in the city. Like units elsewhere, this was initially part of the Royal Naval Reserve within the Admiralty (naval uniforms were worn), and members were on call day and night. Originally two guns, each with a petrol-engine-powered searchlight some 200 yards away, were provided for separate stations at Wincobank. By 1916, management of the corps had been taken over by the army, and additional stations were placed in Manor Lane and at High Storrs in Ecclesall. Some reports also mention Intake. The corps was at first only partially funded and donations had to be requested from the Sheffield public. From these were purchased furniture, utensils, rifles and ammunition.

Around half-a-dozen air-raid warnings were sounded during the second half of 1915, in the form of a buzzer in the city centre and in more than twenty other locations[215]. The following year, warnings became more common (some reports suggest twenty-three), and people became used to taking cover in cellars or similar places, sometimes feeling safer in fields, woods or parks[216]. Factory work had to cease as lights and machines were switched off, so night-workers had to spend long periods in the dark – perhaps snatching a little sleep.

Originally developed by Count von Zeppelin in the 1890s, German airships became increasingly effective, but often inaccurate, in night-time attacks on Britain. During 1915, bombs were dropped mainly near the East coast in Kent, East Anglia, Tyneside and particularly on London. The following year, attacks were directed at industrial towns away from the coast, and Sheffield's munition factories became a potential target. By late September, Zeppelin attacks had reached Retford and Nottingham to the south of Sheffield, and in the evening of 25 September 1916, a fleet of seven airships set out to bomb inland towns, including Sheffield. Alarms were sounded in the city and just before midnight a single airship was heard. This met no opposition from searchlights or guns[217]. It flew over the city as if seeking its target, and then headed in the direction of east-end munition works.

This Zeppelin bombed Sheffield on 25 September 1916, but missed the munition works.

In practice, its bombs all fell away from factories, instead landing on or near houses, a pub and a chapel across Burngreave, Grimesthorpe and Darnall. The entire chapel was destroyed except for one wall displaying what now was the ironic commandment 'that ye love one another'. Among the fatalities was 57-year-old Elizabeth Bellamy, who was looking after her 11-month-old granddaughter Marjorie at home in Writtle Street.

Elizabeth Bellamy of Writtle Street was killed by a Zeppelin bomb while looking after her baby granddaughter.

Some of the damage from September's Zeppelin raid on Sheffield.

Passing a window near the baby's cot, Elizabeth was hit by shrapnel from an explosion outside and later died. Luckily baby Marjorie survived. The bombs killed a further twenty-seven people and around nineteen more were injured. Eighty houses were seriously damaged and more than 100 others also needed repairs[218].

The raid was mentioned in local and national newspapers, but not in a way that directly identified Sheffield. On 27 September 1916, the *Sheffield Daily Independent* carried details of an attack 'in the early hours of yesterday' on 'a Midland town' and the *Telegraph* referred to 'a town in the Midlands'. Both papers described damage and injury, and the *Independent* included the report shown in Display Box 6.4.

Display Box 6.4
GOOD NEWS AND PRAISE TO GOD
From *Sheffield Daily Independent* 27 September 1916

TOUCHING INCIDENT

A touching incident was witnessed in a smoke-grimed street in a Midland town during the afternoon *[of 26 September 1916]*, when a golden-haired, blue-eyed little fellow was rescued from a cellar after ceaseless work. He was carried aloft, quite a ray of sunshine in the dark street, to a friend's house. A dense crowd followed, clapping and cheering.

Then a sweet voice rang out with 'Praise God from whom all blessings flow', and the whole crowd joined in the hymn, singing with deep feeling. A Salvation Army lassie mounted a doorstep, and immediately conducted a service of thanksgiving, impressive in its simplicity. The crowd packed the street, but was very quiet, and only the mechanical clamour of industry joined with the young voice.

By 1917, the design and manufacture of aeroplanes had been greatly improved and, although Zeppelin attacks on Britain did continue, bombing by plane became more likely, especially on London. As a result of the 1916 airship raid, Sheffield's defences were strengthened by additional searchlights and guns on local hills, but German planes were unable to reach Sheffield and the city experienced no more raids from the air until the Second World War[219].

Hospitals throughout the city

Across the Great War's four-and-a-half years British deaths came to number about 750,000, and more than 2,000,000 others required medical attention. Many injured soldiers later returned to active or reduced service, but almost all first required treatment. Initial care was provided near the front line, but more serious and long-term problems demanded a period in hospital. For that purpose, large numbers of men were shipped back to England.

The scale of this operation was enormous. Between 1914 and 1918 almost 2,500,000 soldiers were returned to this country for hospital treatment[220]. It is important to note that around half of these were formally defined as sick rather than wounded. Although press reports and everyday conversations referred (and still refer) to 'wounded soldiers' or 'casualties' in the city and elsewhere, many patients (although ill because of war service) had not been injured by German weapons.

Whatever the cause of their ill-health, hospitalization in Britain was required, and more buildings and staff became essential[221]. Almost immediately in August 1914, the War Office mobilized the territorial forces of its Royal Army Medical Corps (RAMC). Plans had been prepared, and very soon twenty-three (later twenty-five) general military hospitals were opened around the country. One of these territorial hospitals was in Sheffield – the Third Northern General Hospital[222]. In addition to a central 'base', this came to include more than fifty associated units. Many of its medical officers were civilian doctors, sometimes already in the territorial RAMC, who were now commissioned as officers. They were previously in private medical practice and/or attached to hospitals such as the city's Royal Infirmary and Royal Hospital.

A second new category of provision came from already-established facilities that became converted and designated as war hospitals. Ultimately numbering about eighty, these were set up in asylums and similar buildings administered by county councils and other public bodies after current occupants had been transferred elsewhere. Their superintendents and many staff continued in post, and officers and men from the RAMC were brought in to provide essential military services. Locally in this category, the Wadsley Asylum became the Wharncliffe War Hospital.

In a very short period of time these two Sheffield hospitals were able to provide more than 6,000 beds for military patients. Around a fifth of Sheffield's patients came from within the UK and a number were Belgian.

Although many men were seriously ill, requiring intensive and possibly long-term treatment, a large number soon reached the convalescent stage. These were placed in convalescent units and might be allowed to spend time outside their hospitals. Some were granted 'sick furlough' until fit for service. Those could live at home or perhaps with a host family in the neighbourhood, usually continuing as a hospital out-patient. Invalid soldiers became a common sight around Sheffield. Patients received free travel on the city's trams and seats were provided in convenient locations in many streets. Away from their hospitals the men wore going-out uniforms of light-blue cloth with white lapels. Across all the war years, Sheffield's military hospitals received in excess of 70,000 men.They were transported from the railway station by ambulance or car, in many cases by volunteer car drivers from the city who together contributed many hundreds of hours to this work.

Concerts for patients took place in each hospital throughout the war, sometimes with professional artistes but mainly provided by amateur singers, dancers, instrumentalists, jugglers, comedians and so on. For instance, in one afternoon in March 1916, patients in the Ecclesall Road base of the Third Northern General Hospital were entertained by Caitlin's Royal Pierrots and enjoyed songs like *Chicken dinner*, *That little bit of cucumber* and *How ashamed I was*. On the same afternoon, at the Wharncliffe War Hospital the band of the Hallamshire Regiment was joined in a concert by a local violinist and a soprano, Lydgate School

One of the ambulances serving the city's military hospitals.

Hospital had a variety performance by Mr P. Depledge and friends, and patients at Hillsborough Barracks Hospital were entertained by St Vincent's Young Men's Society.

Christmas Day each year received particular attention, with special concerts and carol services and many gifts of clothes, food and cigarettes[223]. In addition, medical requirements, such as bandages and splints, were delivered from the university and from the Cutlers' Company[224], and ambulances, wheelchairs and other equipment were donated by a large number of individuals and groups.

Volunteers were also important in the provision of nursing. In addition to having fully-qualified nurses, Sheffield's military hospitals depended on work by part-qualified members of a local 'voluntary aid detachment' (VAD). These were linked to the British Red Cross Society or the Order of St John, and are described below.

The Third Northern General Hospital This had been established by the Royal Army Medical Corps as a territorial unit in 1913. Soon after war was declared, the corps, with headquarters in Gell Street, requisitioned the Teachers' Training College located in Ecclesall Road and Collegiate Crescent. The College's three principal and other buildings were refurbished and equipped with operating theatres, an X-ray unit and other facilities[225], and on 3 September 1914 the first patients arrived from the Western Front.

Initial medical staff came mainly from hospitals in the city, with Mr (now Lieutenant-Colonel) Arthur Connell as commanding officer. He was an honorary surgeon at the Royal Infirmary with his own consulting rooms in Glossop Road[226]. It was usual in peacetime for hospital medical staff to hold honorary part-time appointments in voluntary institutions, and to earn their income from independent civilian activities. Also from the Royal Infirmary, Dr A. G. Yates was appointed as registrar with the rank of major, and staff drawn from the Royal Hospital included Drs (now Lieutenant-Colonels) J. Sinclair White and W. S. Porter[227]. Among the hospital's

Lieutenant-Colonel Arthur Connell was commanding officer of the Third Northern General Hospital for much of the war.

BASE HOSPITAL FOR WOUNDED SOLDIERS. SHEFFIELD. 3834.

The base of the Third Northern General Hospital was in Collegiate Crescent and Ecclesall Road.

clinical staff were eight professors or lecturers from Sheffield University, and the Ecclesall Road annexe came to employ around twenty-five doctors and more than 200 nurses. Matrons were drawn at different times from the Royal Hospital or Royal Infirmary[228]. About sixty volunteer auxiliary nurses also worked there, and two local clergymen served as visiting chaplains in addition to a resident army chaplain. RAMC staff numbered around 200 and several dozen support workers were employed for cooking, cleaning, maintenance and similar jobs.

As the number of patients increased during 1915 and 1916, the Base in Ecclesall Road expanded within its large grounds. Huts containing additional wards and recreation facilities were partly financed by voluntary contributions; in the summer of 1916, Colonel Connell and the Master Cutler jointly raised more than £3,500 for equipping and staffing 350 extra beds[229]. In addition, as shown in Display Box 6.5, the Third Northern General Hospital included around fifty treatment units located throughout the city and neighbourhood. More serious cases were treated in Ecclesall Road, the Royal Hospital and the Royal Infirmary, and other patients were placed in auxiliary and convalescent hospitals elsewhere. Patients came and went throughout the war and ambulances travelling from the station, between hospitals and to other centres, became part of Sheffield life[230].

This recreation hut in the hospital's grounds was financed by donations from people in the city.

The mascot on this 1916 card had lived in the hospital grounds since at least the early days of the war. 'S.C.T.' on the sentry box refers to Sheffield Corporation Tramways. It was previously a street shelter for 'points boys' who adjusted the track's points for approaching trams.

Display Box 6.5
UNITS OF THE THIRD NORTHERN GENERAL HOSPITAL

This large military hospital was centred on a 'Base' in Ecclesall Road and also occupied buildings across the city and nearby. Details changed slightly from year to year, but enlargement meant that around 4,600 beds were available in all sections by 1918. (Bramall Lane Hospital – last in the list below – started work in that year.) Principal locations and sizes of units in 1918 are listed in the sequence of their opening:

Primary units (2,602 beds in total)
    Ecclesall Road Base, 438 beds
    Royal Infirmary, 87 beds
    Royal Hospital, 80 beds
    Winter Street Hospital, 134 beds
    Firvale Hospital, 462 beds
    Carterknowle School, 115 beds
    Lydgate Lane School, 130 beds
    Ranmoor School, 110 beds
    Greystones School, 150 beds
    Shiregreen School, 145 beds
    Firshill School, 150 beds
    Western Road School, 70 beds
    Ecclesall Infirmary, 200 beds
    Endcliffe Hall, 130 beds
    Oakbrook Officers' Hospital, 51 beds
    Bramall Lane Cricket Pavilion, 150 beds

Auxiliary and convalescent hospitals
In addition to the hospitals listed above, around thirty affiliated institutions provided about 2,000 beds for less serious cases. Within Sheffield were St John's Hospital at Dore and the Woofindin Convalescent Home in Whiteley Wood, and outside the city were (for example) Longshaw Lodge at Grindleford, Aston Hall in Derby, Loversall Hall in Doncaster, and the Devonshire Hospital in Buxton.

The Royal Hospital allocated its Fulwood Road annexe and three wards in its main building to military patients, and the Royal Infirmary offered 100 of its 350 beds. For three years both these voluntary hospitals treated military patients without charge to the government. Several Sheffield companies donated large sums to them specifically for miltary work, and subscriptions from individuals and groups were regularly listed in local newspapers[231]. However, financial problems became steadily worse as the cost of food and medical supplies continued to rise. The two hospitals' positions were improved from September 1917 when they accepted an offer from the War Office to pay 4 shillings (20p) a day for each serviceman they treated.

Medical staff were in great demand from the army and voluntary hospitals found it increasingly difficult to recruit qualified doctors. In 1915, the Board of the Royal Infirmary reported the appointment of women 'to fill some of the Resident Medical posts, and it is with pleasure that they [...] record the general excellence of the work done by these ladies'. In 1919 the Royal Infirmary and other principal hospitals received large certificates from 'the Army Council in the name of the nation', signed by the secretary of state for war, Winston Churchill, thanking the staff for their contributions.

Other units of the Third Northern General Hospital opened throughout the months of 1915 when seven of the city's schools became hospitals (see Display Box 6.5). In October, Carterknowle School was converted for patients from the Western Front and the Dardanelles, with a nursing sister, three nurses and two VAD helpers. Volunteer assistants undertook cooking and other tasks. Items such as a piano, gramophone and billiard table were all donated, as were chairs, kitchen equipment and hot water bottles. Lydgate School in Crosspool also opened as a hospital in October 1915 – with a sister-in-charge, five nurses, two VAD helpers and many volunteers. The large majority of the first year's patients in Lydgate Hospital suffered from dysentery and other intestinal complaints, with a smaller number being treated for gunshot or shrapnel wounds, shell-shock and other results of enemy action. Unfortunately, patient records for this and other Sheffield hospitals are no longer available, so it is not possible to determine the overall mix of conditions treated in the city. It is likely that different parts of the Third Northern General Hospital focused on different kinds of disorder, but details are lacking[232].

Of course, pupils had to be moved from these seven schools into nearby buildings. For example, Lydgate children were transferred into Wesley Hall and Crookes Baptist Church. A description of Ranmoor's move in the *Sheffield Daily Independent* illustrates the style of the times (see Display Box 6.6)[233]. Throughout the war, children and teachers from a

Some of the patients and nursing staff at Ranmoor Military Hospital after the schoolchildren had moved out.

transferred school cared particularly for 'their' hospitalized soldiers, visiting them, presenting concerts, and providing gifts at Christmas and other times. More generally, children and parents across the city collected eggs, fruit, vegetables and other items, and worked throughout the war to help soldiers in their neighbourhood hospital.

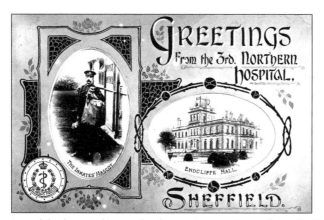

This version of the hospital's standard greetings card was from the Endcliffe Hall unit.

Display Box 6.6
RANMOOR SCHOOL MAKES WAY FOR TROOPS
An excerpt from *Sheffield Daily Independent* 15 October 1915

There was considerable excitement at Nether Green yesterday afternoon. About a quarter past four two long processions of children emerged from the Ranmoor Council School, one of boys, the other of girls. Hundreds of them there were, many carrying parcels containing their books and apparatus. At the end of Storth Lane they formed up into a compact mass, and at the suggestion of the Headmaster gave a final glance at the school, which they were handing over to be transformed into a hospital for wounded soldiers. Then they sang 'God save the King'.

This concluded, the Master suggested that, if they were willing and glad to give up their beautiful school and to take up less convenient quarters in order to help the wounded fighters, they should give three cheers for the brave men who were to occupy their classrooms. These were given with a will, and followed by cheers for the old school.

Then the girls marched off up Storth Lane, the boys giving them a cheer as they went. The lads then proceeded in fours to the Ranmoor Parish Room, which is to be their quarters for the term of the war. The girls are to occupy the Ranmoor Wesleyan Schoolroom.

Among the other units in Display Box 6.5, Firvale and Ecclesall Hospitals were located in the two workhouse infirmaries. Overall, Sheffield Guardians' Firvale Hospital treated almost 10,000 wounded and sick soldiers and carried out around 1,000 operations[234]. Endcliffe Hall in Ranmoor, headquarters of the territorial Hallamshires since January 1914, was converted to provide eight military wards, including one of thirty-two beds in the Hall's ball-room. Its large glass conservatory was used as an open-air ward after the roof had been removed. The new hospital was staffed by a nursing sister, four nurses, two VADs and supporting workers. Next door to Endcliffe Hall was (and is) Oakbrook, which in the spring of 1917 became a hospital for around fifty officers. It had been offered rent-free to the War Office, and furniture and equipment were funded through a special appeal by the lord mayor to local firms and individual businessmen[235].

Many convalescent units of the Third Northern Hospital were outside

The long conservatory in Endcliffe Hall was used as an open-air ward.

Sheffield, but one was located in Dore. This was St John's Hospital, improvised in October 1914 in the Church Institute on Abbbeydale Road South. Created to help wounded Belgian soldiers arriving in the city, it was at first staffed entirely by volunteers: Red Cross[236] nurses, cooks, cleaners and other helpers. Furniture, food and money were provided by local people both at the outset and through subsequent fundraising events. St John's Hospital became a convalescent unit within the Third Northern General Hospital and cared for British and empire troops. In at least the early days a local general practitioner doctor visited regularly and was on call as needed.

Just outside the city was Longshaw Lodge convalescent hospital. This was made available in early 1915 by the Duke of Rutland – it was his shooting lodge – and came to accommodate around sixty men, including many (referred to as colonials) from dominions of the empire. In addition to a small number of RAMC soldiers, staff included two nursing sisters within the Third Northern General Hospital and three VAD nursing assistants, supported by a laundress and other workers. The government paid a fee for each patient, initially 2 shillings (10p) a day but that figure was increased for more complex cases. Running costs at Longshaw were greater than the allowance available and, as in other cases, Sheffield's lord mayor appealed for donations from the public. In addition to that fund, many gifts of money, food and other items were received directly from individuals and groups throughout the war.

It was common for the non-medical administration of convalescent hospitals to be supported by a committee of volunteers chaired by a middle-class lady of some standing in local society. Mrs Edith Peech

Wharncliffe War Hospital had previously been the South Yorkshire Asylum at Wadsley, and in 1948 it became Middlewood Hospital.

officer, Lieutenant-Colonel William Vincent (previously and subsequently director of the asylum), and the registrar, Major D. Gillespie, were assisted by a total of around twenty-five resident or visiting doctors. The hospital's matron, sisters and nurses were accommodated in their own buildings on the site and previous asylum staff were appointed as assistants. Five chaplains were available for patients of Church of England, Nonconformist and Roman Catholic religions.

As in other cases, Wharncliffe War Hospital received help from many volunteers. These organized ambulance or car transport for arrivals from the station and on other needed journeys, and additional food and other supplies were provided by the Soldiers' Personal Comforts Department (next chapter) and by many individuals and groups. Handicraft activities were developed to pass the time and restore skills, and items made by patients were offered for sale in the city and in London. As in other hospitals, concerts were held frequently.

Lapel badges were very popular in this period. This one is for helpers at the Wharncliffe War Hospital.

The overwhelming majority of military patients in Sheffield were treated in these two newly created hospitals, but a few were placed instead in the existing sixty-five-bed hospital within Hillsborough Barracks[239]. As in other cases, volunteers from the city

The privately-funded Edgar Allen Institute provided physiotherapy for injured soldiers as well as for patients from the city.

worked to make life better for those patients, providing furniture, extra food and other items and arranging visits to social and entertainment events. Another medical unit making a significant military contribution was the charity-based Edgar Allen Institute (see Chapter Three). Each year this provided out-patient physiotherapy treatment, 'founded on the Swedish system of physical exercises', for around 1,000 soldiers from the city's military hospitals in addition to its civilian patients [240].

Voluntary Aid Detachments (VADs) As in other parts of the country, Sheffield's qualified nurses were assisted by volunteers from a Voluntary Aid Detachment[241]. Detachments were part of the nation's territorial force and could cover a wide range of nursing and non-nursing activities[242] within and outside Britain. Volunteers' contracts were either mobile or immobile, with the latter usually in one's home neighbourhood, and many mobile volunteers serving on the Western and Eastern Fronts. VAD units were exclusively either male or female, with men often supporting troops as drivers, stretcher-bearers or in manual work. Women (the majority) served mainly as nurses, but female VADs (the term referred to individuals as well as their units) were also employed as drivers, cooks, store-keepers and in other needed roles.

VAD auxiliaries undertook less technical but necessary tasks in support of qualified staff. Before being accepted into the role, they had to attend lectures and obtain basic qualifications in first aid and nursing practice, and had to gain at least a month's practical ward experience. Although the organization had been established before the war, in 1910, VAD units expanded considerably as new military hospitals were created.

These volunteers were often from middle-class families. They had to pay for their initial instruction and buy their uniforms (in at least the first part of the war), cope without an income from employment and obtain a character reference from a doctor, priest or magistrate. Although wages were not paid until 1916, some expenses could be claimed for laundry, travel and other necessities. VADs were co-ordinated through local sections of the British Red Cross Society or St John's Ambulance Brigade. Most Sheffield VADs were attached to St John's, and for some time in this period Sheffield's VAD commandant was the Mistress Cutler, Mrs Lucy Ellis, who herself served as a volunteer in the brigade.

Voluntary Aid Detachments were made up of volunteers to assist military hospitals in this country and abroad.

Long-skirted uniforms were pale blue or grey with white apron, headgear and starched detachable collars and cuffs. There were some differences between regions and time periods, but in general VAD nurses linked to the Red Cross had a red cross on the front of their apron and those within St John's Ambulance Brigade wore a detachable arm-band above the left elbow[243]. By mid-1915, around eighty VAD nurses worked in Sheffield hospitals, and that number is thought to have doubled in later war years. More VADs served in other units of the Third Northern General Hospital outside the city. In addition to their general medical assistance, they helped with outings, played cards, joined in concert parties and helped patients write letters home. They were essential contributors to the positive atmosphere needed in a military hospital[244].

The Silver War Badge As well as many thousand sick and wounded patients in military hospitals, the city was also home to soldiers and sailors who had been discharged from military service because of incapacity or disability[245]. The contribution made

This VAD nurse's uniform includes a St John's Ambulance Brigade armband.

by these men was recognized by the award of a Silver War Badge, sometimes known informally as a discharge badge.

With an accompanying certificate, this new badge received royal authorization in July 1916 and the first awards were made in September. Badges were available to men who had served in the war at home or abroad and who had been discharged because of sickness, wounds or what was described as old age. Also entitled to the badge were discharged civilians, nurses and VAD members undertaking war service and meeting one of the criteria.

The Silver War Badge was inscribed 'For King and Empire: Services Rendered', and more than 1,000,000 were issued. Worthy Wigmore, a stationery engine driver at Kiveton Park Colliery serving with the Coldstream Guards on the Western Front, suffered a severe injury to his left foot in February 1915. He spent around nine months in hospital and was discharged in March 1916 as being (in the official terms) 'no longer physically fit for war service'. Sheffield-born William Hill received the badge

A Silver War Badge was awarded to those who had been discharged through incapacity or disability.

after being discharged from the Royal Garrison Artillery in September 1917, as did miner William Cross who was discharged from the West Yorkshire Regiment with head wounds in October 1916.

Other local holders of the badge included Captain Joseph Ryle Clarke of Hunter House Road, who served in the King's Own Yorkshire Light Infantry. In February 1915, Joseph received a major head wound and remained unconscious for two weeks. In due course he was transferred to the Third Northern General Hospital in Sheffield where a bullet was removed – leaving a 3-inch (8-centimetre) hole in his skull. A gold plate made in the city by Mappin and Webb to the hospital's specification was placed inside his head and, although Joseph's hearing was now impaired, he was able to return to the army. He was formally retired in early 1919 and the next year received a Silver War Badge. With the gold plate still in place he worked successfully in the city and lived for more than sixty additional years, dying in 1983.

As was the case for hospital patients, a high proportion of Silver War Badge holders had been discharged as invalids because of sickness rather than being wounded in battle. By the end of 1916, the number of disabled ex-troops in the city had become considerable, and several national and local organizations were set up to work on their behalf[246].

CHAPTER 7

Giving and Doing: The City's Voluntary Work

We will never know how many Sheffield people volunteered to help during the Great War, but the number was huge. In some cases help may have been no more than donating to a worthy cause, but for a large number of individuals daily life revolved around unpaid activities responding to the needs and pains of war.

The city's first concern in August 1914 was for families likely to be pushed into poverty by unemployment. The lord mayor immediately set up a Sheffield Distress Committee, which sought cash from the public for a local War Relief Fund to help in times of economic hardship[247]. However, the country's need for war materials soon created so many new manufacturing orders that trade boomed rather than collapsed. The city's relief fund was rarely called upon. It continued in existence, but many other groups provided their own forms of support.

Contributing clothes, food and vehicles
Rapid expansion of the army created a shortage of materials and equipment, and the public was soon asked to contribute. The War Office immediately issued an urgent request for blankets for the troops, and following publicity in Sheffield's newspapers as many as 15,000 were quickly donated from the city. The newspapers also published requests for more clothes, some of which could be made by women at home. These requests were addressed firmly to 'our lady readers', often in articles written by the paper's 'lady editor'. For example, on 27 August 1914 the *Sheffield Daily Independent* wrote:

Thanks to the energy and promptitude displayed by the women

readers of the *Sheffield Daily Independent*, the Lady Editor has been able in less than three weeks to despatch to her Majesty the Queen at St James's Palace no fewer than 6,000 comforts for the brave boys who are fighting the cause of the Allied Nations on Belgian soil. This handsome total has included over 650 pairs of socks.

Now that we have got sewing parties at work all over Sheffield and the surrounding districts [...] we can suggest another direction in which the unfailing sympathy and industry of women can be employed.

Not every woman can knit socks. But a neck scarf or a pair of mittens would be within the capabilities of any women [...] Think of the agonies of frost-bitten fingers and feet inflamed with chilblains [...] To keep the wrists warm nothing is better to wear than woollen mittens or muffs.

The paper then gave instructions about the appropriate type of knitting needles and wool for mittens or muffs, so that women could make them and deliver them to the paper's office[248].

The queen, mentioned by the *Independent* above, took an active interest in helping the troops through her own Queen Mary's Needlework Guild. This was formed from an earlier group on 8 August 1914 to co-ordinate the making and collection of soldiers' clothing and other items from across the country. With headquarters in St James's Palace, it came to have more than 500 associated groups in Britain and almost 100 in Allied countries.

Members of Queen Mary's Needlework Guild provided clothes and other items for serving troops.

On another day the *Independent*'s women readers were encouraged to 'share with us the pleasure' resulting from letters 'sent by command of her Majesty the Queen' ('the highest lady in the land') for garments provided. Weekly despatches had included 2,000 sleeping helmets using patterns previously published in the paper. By the end of 1915, the *Independent* could report that nearly 50,000 articles had been subscribed by 'our lady readers'. In the autumn of 1914, the local Red Cross Association asked for bed jackets, hospital shirts, nurses' aprons, surgeons' overalls and other items for use in military hospitals, and soldiers' 'comforts' came to receive an enormous amount of attention in the coming years. Many church and other ladies' groups worked throughout the war to provide an unknown but huge number of items[249].

As the number of sick and wounded soldiers in the city increased sharply from the later months of 1914, the people of Sheffield set about providing help of a non-medical kind in local military hospitals. Ladies' working parties were set up all over the city, producing a steady supply of clothes, food and other items, sometimes sent directly to a particular hospital but often co-ordinated through the city's recently-established Soldiers' Personal Comforts Depot. This started work in September 1914 in Leopold Street[250], and came to employ around fifty unpaid workers.

Display Box 7.1
COMFORTS FOR SOLDIERS IN HOSPITAL:
CHRISTMAS 1914

The *Sheffield Daily Independent* of 24 December 1914 reported under the headline (in quotation marks) 'Personal Comforts':

Yesterday that part of the ground-floor showroom which Messrs Johnson and Appleyards have set apart as a receiving depot was a cheering picture. Tiers and tiers of shelves and rows of broad tables were piled with Christmas fare, not higgledy-piggledy but artistically arranged and divided in sections for the various hospitals. There were plump turkeys and gorgeous pheasants, countless plum cakes, some iced and some otherwise, a great array of mince pies, masses of fruit, hampers of vegetables, and underneath the tables stacks of Christmas puddings and other seasonable foodstuffs. Two 'surprise' hampers, one collected entirely by a lady and her maid, contained a well-packed medley of good things for invalids, and included such delicacies as calves-feet jelly and pineapple […]

Some of the most interesting gifts again came from children. Greystones School, Standard 1, sent three boxes of dates, a box of figs, and several cakes; Bow Street Standard 1 contributed potatoes, a bag of fruit and three shillings in coppers; Huntsman's Gardens School (Infants) gave up a treat to buy cakes; Darnall Road School (Girls) contributed fruit; two puddings were sent by 18 of the bigger girls from Hunters Bar School; and two other puddings made in the dinner hour by and from materials brought in by the bigger girls of Pomona Street School.

The Personal Comforts Depot supplied a colossal number of meals and other items to the city's military hospitals. Many patients were provided with three breakfasts[251] and three teas every week – more than 500,000 of each in the depot's peak year of 1916. Pork pies, sausages, eggs, cakes, ham, bacon, oranges and apples were channelled through the depot in enormous quantity, as were cigarettes, clothing, chairs and other items. This huge number of deliveries required detailed planning and considerable personal commitment[252].

The depot's unceasing workload also included gathering supplies and money from individuals and companies across the city. Public interest was maintained by regular articles in Sheffield's newspapers, providing the opportunity to seek additional contributions. In January 1915, one article urgently requested 'eggs, vegetables, sausages, cakes and dried fruits', and in May 1915, the depot's special requirements were potted meat and polony, a type of sausage. The next month readers were asked to provide, in addition to food, handkerchiefs, nail brushes, toothbrushes, carpet slippers, crutches ('urgent') and rubber tips for crutches (which, readers were told, could be bought locally). Later in the year, requests were made for hot-water bottles, books, slippers, sacks to hold vegetables, and zinc baths for storing eggs. Deliveries and some collections from donors were initially made by a single van provided by an Ecclesfield family, but in 1915 a second vehicle was also donated by well-wishers. In addition, the depot co-ordinated a range of other activities. Its Arts and Crafts

Volunteers from the city's Personal Comforts Depot supplied a huge number of meals to local military hospitals.

Committee helped military patients to develop skills and interests in practical handiwork.

The principal organizer of the Soldiers' Personal Comforts Depot was Miss Edith Sorby, who lived in Peel Terrace. She was also active in many other helping projects. A large number of ladies set up their own schemes to provide materials. Mrs Gilmour of Sandygate worked to help Canadian soldiers in this country by collecting socks, shirts, scarves and comforts of all kinds. In August 1914, the Mistress Cutler formed an Army and Navy Aid Committee of ladies to collect, make and distribute mufflers, mittens and other garments. A workroom was established in the Cutlers' Hall and by the end of 1915, as many as 85,000 items had been distributed, with around a quarter of those going to hospitals in the city. In addition to items made in the Cutlers' Hall itself, individuals and groups from all over Sheffield (including more than sixty churches) brought in tens of thousands of garments for onward transmission[253]. In 1917, the committee became part of a nationwide organization and was renamed the Sheffield Voluntary Aid Association – often known simply as the Sheffield Voluntary Association. It delivered more than 200,000 articles during the war.

Consistent with the nation's hierarchical society, it was normal for principal positions in city-wide voluntary groups to be taken by ladies who were distinguished by their marriage to prominent men. Men were occasionally present on committees of this kind, but almost always in roles viewed as requiring business expertise. For example, the Mistress Cutler's committee contained sixteen women and a single man, who served as the honorary treasurer. For Britain's women, the war created many opportunities for unpaid as well as paid work.

The city's newspapers vied with each other to persuade readers to send in items for onward transmission to serving troops, war hospitals or to British prisoners-of-war. 'Smokes' were given great prominence, with papers offering different-priced packages of cigarettes both for individuals and as bulk purchases. Advertisements in the *Sheffield Daily Independent* asked for money 'in sending cigarettes, tobacco and other comforts to the Sons of Britannia whose glories will be sung right through the coming ages' (in April 1916), and cried 'SOS' – 'Send out Smokes' (in January 1916). The paper's Christmas boxes, to be paid for and sent to troops at the end of 1916, contained either fifty or 100 cigarettes as well as 'one box quinine and phosphorous tablets, one box peppermints, one box Meloids for the throat, one box tea tablets, one box Oxo Cubes, and one stick of shaving soap'.

Sir Joseph Jonas donated and converted this car for use as an ambulance in the city.

Sheffielders were also keen to assist in the supply of vehicles. Ambulances for the battle zone or for transporting injured soldiers around the city were financed and provided by, for instance, Mr and Mrs T. W. Ward, Mr Brook Shaw, Countess Fitzwilliam, Sir Joseph Jonas, Pickford Trowne and Company, William Cooke and Company, Stocksbridge Works Distress Fund, Vickers Employees' War Relief Fund, local publicans and their staff, fairground workers, and the city's two Co-operative Societies. In May 1915, the lady mayoress established a fund within a national scheme through which the public could contribute to an ambulance named 'Sheffield' on the Western Front, and by the end of 1916, the Sheffield Military Hospitals Motor Ambulance Fund had raised around £2,500. Separately, children at local council schools raised enough money for four ambulances by November 1917.

Cash was acquired in many ways. Schools and firms[254] had regular collections and events to raise cash, artistes and orchestras from local theatres performed unpaid in fundraising matinees, and boxes to receive donations were provided in the city's trams and picture houses. Local boy scouts carried out paid tasks and donated their earnings to the Ambulance

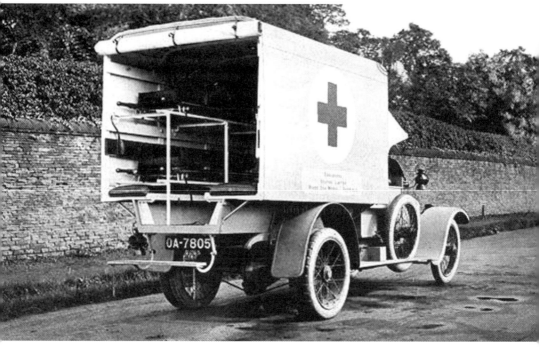

Vickers Employees' War Relief Fund assisted in many ways, for instance by funding this and other ambulances.

This recreation hut at Redmires Camp was important throughout the war. It was initially financed by a local family and then operated by the YMCA.

Fund, and the Girls' Friendly Society in Dore raised money through a Patriotic Social Evening and other events. Mrs Machon of Abbeydale Road took an unusual approach by requesting that unwanted silver items be deposited with the Personal Comforts Depot. They would be melted down to purchase an ambulance. In addition to these local activities, large amounts of money were paid directly to national schemes.

Other gifts from the city included an entire 100-bed hospital for British soldiers and officers in France (in December 1914, by Sir Robert and Lady Hadfield[255]), and several motor field kitchens for the Front (from Sheffield motorist groups and others). Facilities for relaxation in newly created military camps were inevitably limited, and a YMCA-operated social institute for the Sheffield City Battalion and other troops at Redmires Camp was financed by Mr and Mrs Meggitt-Johnson. Similarly, the Master Cutler co-ordinated money-raising for a Sheffield recreation hut at Ripon military camp. On a smaller scale, books and magazines were collected through local libraries for onward transmission to serving soldiers. In May 1916, the *Sheffield Daily Independent* sought money to buy books for troops in military hospitals near the Front. In October 1915, a group of soldiers 'who are on a lonely post and have no kind of entertainment' asked through local newspapers for an old gramophone and records, and patients in Winter Street Hospital made the same request a year later. Many letters of this kind were published in the city's papers throughout the war. It became usual at Christmas for churches to send presents to serving men from their parish.

A different set of soldiers received help through the Sheffield Prisoners of War Help Committee, which was formed in September 1915. By 1918, more than 1,500 local men were held as prisoners-of-war in Germany and elsewhere, and the Sheffield committee sent a steady stream of parcels – food, clothes, tobacco and other items – from its headquarters in Holly Street. Hospitals in this country and abroad were assisted by the Hospital Supply Depot established by Sheffield University to prepare bandages and other medical requirements. Other wartime requests were for waste paper, collected by the city's newspapers, churches and Salvation Army, and for field-glasses and telescopes for military and naval use.

Providing a service
In parallel with the provision of materials and giving money, many Sheffield people devoted hours of their time to war-related help. Thousands and thousands of activities are, of course, unrecorded. Of the

ones that are still known about, many were in aid of sick and wounded soldiers now based in the city.

Helping soldiers A large number of amateur groups provided concerts in the Third Northern Hospital, either in its base in Ecclesall Road or in one of the outstations. Newspapers of the period describe a succession of 'pianoforte solos', 'cheery songs', 'comic contributions', 'quaint juggling', 'clever recitals', 'comedy and simultaneous dancing', 'melodramatic monologues', 'humorous recitations', 'funny stories' and generally 'capital entertainment' for the patients. In addition, professional artistes from local theatres sometimes provided afternoon performances in a hospital, perhaps with the added attraction of free cigarettes for all[256]. Songs ranged from *I like your old French bonnet* and *Sunshine and butterflies* to the extremely popular *Tipperary*. In all cases concerts finished with the National Anthem, in which the patients were regularly said to have 'joined in heartily'.

Convalescent military patients were sometimes invited to 'smoker sing-songs' in their hospital or offered activities elsewhere in the city or nearby. In August 1916, the Original Thursday (angling) Club entertained soldiers to lunch and three hours fishing at Brigg, and in September patients from Longshaw Lodge Hospital were taken on a tour of the offices and printing facilities of the *Sheffield Daily Telegraph*, followed by tea in the office canteen. Another 'substantial tea was heartily appreciated' by Longshaw patients after their visit to Haddon Hall, financed by Miss Catherine Firth of Hope. In October 1916, the Ladies B Team of Hillsborough Park Bowling Club competed against men from local hospitals. Other groups of ladies devoted many hours and much effort to helping hospitalized men acquire skills in handiwork, with products sometimes sold to aid hospital finances.

A large number of other outings were arranged by local well-wishers and motoring groups. On 18 August 1916, the *Sheffield Daily Telegraph* described how around sixty patients from military hospitals 'were conveyed by motors to the green at the Stag Inn, Psalter Lane. Games of Clock Golf, Target Bowls and Doubles were indulged in with evident delight, prizes being given to winners in each event.' As on other occasions, that outing finished with 'a capital tea'. On the same day, another fifty soldiers played bowls after being invited by the Ladies' Section of the Crookesmoor Bowls Club. Many other contributions were made by local churches, including in the summer of 1916 the ladies of St Peter's Mission Church, Heeley, entertaining convalescent soldiers at a garden party.

Volunteers staffed an Invalid Soldiers' Rest Room in premises (previously the Black Rock Hotel) in Castle Street[257], and a separate Sailors' and Soldiers' Rest Room and Buffet for troops in transit was operated by unpaid helpers on a platform of the Midland Station[258]. Volunteers also assisted in the Sheffield Soldiers' Home, founded in 1907 opposite the Barracks in Langsett Road[259], and worked in the YMCA canteens for local munitions workers and at Redmires Camp (see Display Box 7.2). In August 1915, Totley Union Church and the Women's Total Abstinence Society made available Totley Brook Hall as a soldiers' club between 4 pm and 9 pm daily for troops stationed at Totley Rifle Range.

Thousands of troops spent time in the buffet and rest room run by volunteers at Sheffield Station.

Many families with men serving in the war were helped by volunteers from the Sheffield division of the Soldiers' and Sailors' Families Association. During 1915 almost 15,000 Sheffield women and children were granted financial assistance when their breadwinner was in the forces or had been wounded or killed. The city also had a War Club for the wives of serving soldiers and sailors. This used rooms in Pond

Sheffield Soldiers' Home, opposite these Barracks in Hillsborough, also depended on donations from the public.

Display Box 7.2
SHEFFIELD YMCA IS VERY BUSY

The Young Men's Christian Association in Sheffield occupied substantial premises above retail shops in Fargate, with a restaurant, a lounge, rooms for reading, writing, relaxing and playing billiards, a gymnasium (including 'Swedish apparatus'), a library, a lecture room and other facilities. There was also a branch in Crookes. Despite its primary membership (the 'young men' in its title), the Association was greatly assisted by women, and its number of female volunteers increased substantially as new services were created by the war.

Free access to Sheffield YMCA services and buildings was offered to all serving troops, and many thousands of teas were provided in the city centre. The association opened additional centres for troops in Bow Street, at the end of Leopold Street, including sleeping accommodation and bathrooms, and in Pomona Street, for patients and orderlies from the base hospital. The local YMCA also made arrangements at Christmas for some military patients to spend time with local families.

By the end of 1914, the association had become responsible for the social institute built at Redmires Camp for the Sheffield City Battalion. Staffed by volunteer women and some men, this served refreshments at cost price and provided books, games and facilities for relaxation. Writing materials were free of charge for letters and postcards – around 3,000 a month were posted in 1916 – and a savings bank was installed. Small bibles were presented to men of the battalion, and the institute also issued several hundred anti-alcohol temperance pledges. Church services on a Sunday were separately conducted for different religious groups, and briefly at the end of each day, and the popular sing-songs and concerts, including minstrel events, were able to make use of the piano and song-books provided.

As munition factories expanded in the city's east end, refreshment facilities for the many thousands of additional workers were increasingly inadequate. Within a national YMCA policy, two volunteer-operated canteens and a coffee stall were opened from late 1915 onwards near major Sheffield works, serving refreshments and many thousands of low-priced meals. These were staffed by more than 100 women volunteers from within the city.

Street, which included a nursery where children could be briefly left. The families of local German and Austrian men who had been interned were aided by a different group – the Sheffield Committee for Assisting Aliens in Distress. Munition workers in the city also received volunteers' attention. A group from St Vincent's Church gave early morning and evening concerts in works canteens. Communal kitchens opened in 1917 to provide low-price meals – by the Salvation Army near the Moor and by the City Council in Gibraltar Street – and these were almost entirely staffed by unpaid volunteers.

Other work by volunteers included a 1917 Christmas concert and party at Firth's National Projectile Factory for 150 men from the city's military hospitals as well as about 600 children of workers from the factory. Performances for adults were by the works' Choral Society and other artistes, and children were entertained by a Punch and Judy Show from Professor and Miss De Lyle – in fact Arthur Fox and his daughter from Ecclesall Road using a name drawn from tins of syrup.

Helping the city A different kind of unpaid contribution was made by members of the Sheffield Volunteer Defence Corps. This had been established in the autumn of 1914 as the Chief Constable's Civilian Corps (see Chapter Four), and by late 1915 described itself as the oldest Volunteer Defence Corps in the country. Membership was open to men who were not eligible for military service because of their age, health limitations or employment on government work, and call-up would only happen if an invasion of the country was imminent. The Sheffield Corps was largely self-financing and members were required to pay a monthly subscription[260].

At the end of 1915, the Sheffield Volunteer Corps had around 1,800 volunteer members in two battalions[261] who met for training and drill practice several times a week, including Sundays, initially in the Jungle building at the bottom of Hawley Street but, from late 1916, in new headquarters in what had been the Olympia Skating Rink in Bramall Lane. The Corps held parades in several of the city's parks and football grounds, and different sections received training for motorcycle, motor-vehicle, ambulance, signalling and other types of work. A camp was held annually, in later years jointly with a regular unit. When exempting men from call-up into the services, the city's military appeals tribunal frequently required that individuals instead join the Volunteer Corps. Members assisted with crowd control during public events and at night they guarded important sites and communication lines, also manning barriers on main roads into the city that had been erected soon after war broke out. (Some training exercises at the time involved imaginary attacks on Sheffield by German troops.) They were also called into action whenever air-raids were threatened, visiting homes and ensuring that darkness was maintained. The corps' ambulance section was required at those times to stand ready for action.

The Sheffield Volunteer Defence Corps was formed in 1914 and eventually had around 2,000 members.

Also created early in the war, in February 1915, and receiving support from the chief constable was a Sheffield branch of the Women's Defence Relief Corps, with headquarters at 14 Broad Lane. This paraded in school yards and military drill halls, and sometimes in the Jungle building. The corps prepared women to take over men's activities if those men became required for war, and by the middle of 1915 it had around 200 members. As an additional incentive to joining, they were granted half-price admission to Glossop Road Ladies' Plunge Bath on Fridays.

A small number of other female volunteers, probably fewer than twenty, provided women's patrols to protect women in public places, for example after work in the late evening. Patrol members checked streets in which men were likely to be intrusive or where morally inappropriate behaviour seemed possible. They patrolled in pairs with identifying armbands and initiated several court cases against men accosting women. Girls were encouraged to join a church or voluntary organization and the patrols also monitored young boys in city streets during the day.

Part-time volunteers served as special police constables throughout the war.

Some militarily-ineligible men provided unpaid service as special police constables, usually in addition to a paid job. They accompanied regular policemen on routine patrols and other activities to maintain public order and were granted the same powers as those policemen. Whenever an air-raid was threatened, they had to report for duty at the central police station. The number of 'specials' increased substantially in this period, as regular Sheffield policemen joined the armed services and the city's population grew through an influx of munition workers. Initially, special constables were identified only by armbands, but some uniforms became available later. Display Box 7.3 illustrates how they went about their job.

Display Box 7.3
SHEFFIELD'S VOLUNTEER POLICEMEN

The duties and activities of Sheffield's Special Constabulary were specified by the chief constable. The 1919 regulations (reference MP946M in Sheffield Local Studies Library) include these sections:

PARADE FOR DUTY: At Divisional Headquarters, or where otherwise detailed, with Warrant Card, Truncheon, Whistle and Armlet.
DUTIES: (a) Protection of life and property.
  (b) Prevention and detection of crime.
  (c) Maintenance of peace and good order.
  (d) Report all unusual occurrences to Sergeant or Inspector.
    Examine list prepared at Divisional Stations showing situation of vulnerable points in City, and make notes of same.
USE OF TRUNCHEON: The truncheon must never be drawn unless personal injury of Constable is either apprehended or has been inflicted. When acting in a body its use is prohibited except by order of the person in command who may be called upon to justify his actions.
BRIDGES (LINES OF COMMUNICATION) ETC.: Watch carefully to prevent destruction.
EXPLOSIONS: Render what assistance possible. Divert traffic if necessary. Acquaint authorities concerned or affected.
LETTER BOXES: Examine pillar boxes and private boxes. Arrest persons placing fire, dangerous substances, etc. therein.
ROYAL MAIL VANS: Facilitate the passage of His Majesty's Mails.
TELEGRAPHS AND TELEPHONES: Report breakages of wires. Prevent wilful damage to posts, insulators, etc. If witnessed, arrest offenders.
  In all cases Special Constables will be accompanied in their duty by a member or members of the City Police Force.

Men also offered themselves for the Sheffield Motor Volunteers. By June 1918 this had more than 200 members and the group was affiliated through the West Riding Volunteers to the Motor Transport section of the Army Service Corps. Volunteers also served in the city's fire brigade. By 1916, the brigade's working strength had been substantially reduced as men left to join the armed forces, and part-time helpers were called upon to help with both fire-fighting and ambulance duties. Like other volunteers, they had to report for duty whenever an air-raid warning was sounded. Another form of unpaid service was invaluable in the summer of 1915, as the city had to respond to the recently-passed National Registration Act. This aimed to obtain details of every adult in the country in order to produce a complete record of possible workers or troops. In Sheffield it was volunteers who distributed the registration papers to every house in the city, explained what was needed, collected completed papers, and subsequently collated and classified the responses. Everyone undertaking this work was unpaid – more than 1,000 of them.

Giving money
A third way to help was to contribute some money. This could be done either by adding to the government's funds or by directly helping people in need.

Money for the nation The government needed to borrow millions of pounds to pay for its conduct of the war. Some was borrowed overseas, and in this country three separate war loans were promoted, from November 1914, June 1915 and January 1917. Individuals and organizations could commit money for fixed periods at a favourable rate of interest. For instance, the first issue, with a target of £332 million, offered annual interest at 3½ percent until redemption between 1925 and 1928, and later issues (repayable in the 1940s) paid either 4½ or 5 per cent.

Many people lent money to the nation in this way and a number of Sheffield companies took the opportunity to invest some of their wartime profits. Commercial banks also helped by lending money to individuals which they could then use by taking out government loans[262]. During the war loan issue of January 1917, Sheffield newspapers carried large advertisements asking people not to spend their money on clothes, amusements or food. Instead: 'Lend money to the nation. Wear old clothes, old boots, old dresses. Ask your bank or your employer to make you an advance to help you purchase War Loan.' Other advertized investments included interest-bearing exchequer bonds, which could be bought from post offices and other places. Among government attempts to arouse interest in those was the advertisement shown in Display Box 7.4.

Display Box 7.4
EXCHEQUER BONDS FOR WOMEN

During April 1916, large advertisements appeared in Sheffield newspapers headed 'To the Women of Great Britain and Ireland'. In large typeface, these read:

The Women of England, Scotland, Ireland and Wales have nobly helped the War in a thousand ways. They have given their husbands and their sons to fight for their Country; they have nursed the wounded; organized relief; helped recruiting; manufactured munitions of war; and taken men's places in business offices, on farms, and in trades innumerable.

They are now asked to help by lending their money to the Nation. A long purse means a shorter war. Money is the mainspring of all our warlike energies and enterprises. It buys ships, shells and aeroplanes; and clothes, feeds and pays our soldiers and sailors.

The simplest and safest investment in the world is the 5% Exchequer Bond of the British Government. No higher interest on money can be obtained with the same security in any other way.

The advertisements then provided details of different ways in which women could make purchases.

To complement these high-profile fundraising procedures, steps were taken to mobilize local efforts. A network of around 40,000 war savings associations was created across the country, each of which sponsored its own activities to persuade local people to buy war savings certificates[263]. Sheffield's Central War Savings Committee, established in March 1916 and based in Church Street, was chaired by the lord mayor and brought together representatives of local employers, trade unions, the city council, friendly societies, banks, schools, churches, women's organizations and other groups. Linked to that Sheffield-wide committee, about fourteen Ward Savings Committees were set up in different parts of the city.

Those ward committees in turn formed about 500 War Savings Associations in the city's churches, factories, schools and other settings. Workers were encouraged to save regularly through weekly deductions from their wages, sometimes with competitions between departments to save the most, collections took place in schools and families were asked to make regular contributions. The local associations signed up more than 15,000 members across Sheffield, each person buying and, it was hoped, encouraging others to buy certificates. As well as its co-ordination activities, Sheffield's central savings committee sponsored a large number of lectures and local campaigns. During 1917 and 1918, the committee also contributed to the National Welfare and Economy Campaign and mounted a Tank Week, a Cruiser Week, a War Weapons Week, a Gun Week and a Feed the Guns campaign. Each of those raised substantially more than £1,000,000 and overall in this period the city provided tens of millions of pounds in loans to the government.

Money for people in need In addition to lending money to the nation, Sheffielders were keen to help with cash for people suffering from the war. Thousands of fundraising projects in the city financed support for soldiers

A Tank Week in December 1917 provided a tank bank in Fitzalan Square from which war bonds could be bought.

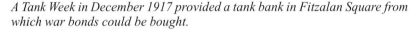

in local hospitals and assistance to Belgian refugees or contributed to country-wide schemes like the Prince of Wales' National Relief Fund.

Money came from individuals, employee and church groups, local communities, business organizations and many others. Schoolteachers organized fundraising events and collections by their pupils, and schemes in Sheffield factories yielded thousands of pounds. For instance, in 1917 the girls of Hunter's Bar Council School paid for five invalid chairs and four wheelchairs for the Third Northern General Hospital, and in 1915 pupils of the Boys' Charity School in Psalter Lane managed to provide 9 shillings (45p) together with some eggs, ham and soap for soldiers in the Ecclesall and Fir Vale (Workhouse) hospitals. The employees of Thomas Firth and Sons raised nearly £3,000 during 1915, with more than £700 passed to the Sheffield lord mayor's fund, £500 going to the Serbian relief fund and £450 being given to local Belgian refuges. On a smaller scale, the Sheffield Branch of the Empire Shakespeare Society raised £80 for the local Belgian Relief Fund by performing *Much Ado about Nothing*, and the grounds of many large houses were made available for fundraising garden parties.

Military hospitals in the city received money, food and other gifts throughout the war. Thousands of pounds came from individuals' and companies' contributions to the Sheffield Military Hospitals Motor Ambulance Fund and a separate scheme was run for Colonel Connell's Fund. Colonel Arthur Connell was commanding officer of the city's main military hospital, and his private fund paid for patients' families to visit from afar and stay in the city, as well as for Sheffield families to travel to a military hospital in other parts of the country. In 1917, as many as 6,000 grants were made. Money came from direct gifts from individuals and groups, social events, bazaars, concerts, garden parties and flag days.

The groups working for the military hospitals included one with the abbreviated name PIPS, and the full title of the Picnickers' Imperial Parties Society. This was formed in late 1914 to take patients from the Third Northern General Hospital for picnics and to provide other forms of relaxation and entertainment. It developed into a very active society of around sixty members raising money from bazaars, social events, raffles, whist drives and concerts in order to assist the hospital and to provide activities for patients. For example, in the summer of 1917 PIPS' members organized an open-to-the-public gymkhana in the hospital grounds with comic sports for staff and mobile patients (blindfold races, wrestling in

The 'Picnickers' Imperial Parties Society' (PIPS) delivered Christmas presents to patients in the Third Northern General Hospital, here in 1916.

An open-air theatre in the grounds of the Third Northern General Hospital, here shown in June 1915, was entirely financed by the public.

sacks, etc), band performances, and stalls selling refreshments, flowers and other items. Also in 1917 they provided a substantial tea for patients and staff, numbering around 700, which included a whist drive and musical contributions. Members provided Christmas presents, and several donations were made to Colonel Connell's Fund.

PIPS members paid for and part-furnished an open-air ward in the Base hospital (the 'PIPS ward'), provided an open-air theatre, and in July 1916 converted a hut in the grounds into a recreation room for patients. This contained two billiard tables, a piano, tables for writing letters and playing dominoes and cards, and a library of books, and was maintained by the society throughout the war. Some PIPS events were also held at the auxiliary hospitals in Endcliffe Hall and Longshaw Lodge.

Another set of volunteers with an abbreviated name was the ECs – Ecclesall Comforts and Entertainment Committee – who worked to help military patients in the Ecclesall Workhouse Infirmary. In addition to the usual concerts, events and supplies of comforts, in 1917 the ECs raised money by the production and sale of golliwogs. Several other groups joined in, as well as some Ecclesall patients, and around 15,000 of the black-faced dolls were expected for Golliwog Day on 27 October.

Also on that day Sheffield's Blighty Bungalow [264] found an owner. Auctioneer Frank Bush had personally organized sales of raffle tickets, offering the winner a bungalow in Totley. Substantial advertising in the

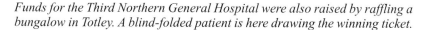

Funds for the Third Northern General Hospital were also raised by raffling a bungalow in Totley. A blind-folded patient is here drawing the winning ticket.

previous weeks and much work by many people had sold as many as 32,760 tickets, and the winning number was drawn with appropriate ceremony at the base hospital. This raised £800 from ticket sales – £600 for the hospital, £100 for St John's Hospital at Dore and £100 for the local Belgian Refugee Committee.

Local newspapers regularly published lists of contributors to major funds. In each case donors were named and each amount given was cited. These lists make it clear that the range of contributors was very wide, including prominent citizens and employers but also a very large number of ordinary citizens, workers in factory departments, public houses, social and sports clubs, schoolchildren, churches, restaurants, and organizers of concerts and many other events. In addition, newspaper items of the period sought money or listed donors for the Prisoners of War Aid Committee, St John's Ambulance Brigade Hospital Fund, the Lord Mayor's Russian Fund, Help Serbia Fund, several war casualties funds, the Montenegrin Fund, the YMCA Redmires camp fund, the Incorporated Soldiers' and Sailors' Help Society, the Fund for Starving Belgians, the RSPCA Fund for Sick and Wounded Horses, the YMCA Yorkshire Fund, and many others.

Display Box 7.5
HER LAST SHILLING

Under the headline HER LAST SHILLING, the *Sheffield Daily Independent* of 11 November 1914 reported as follows. (A shilling was twelve pence, a twentieth of a pound.)

A deeply pathetic story is related of a dying Sheffield crippled girl sending her last shilling to Princess Mary's Sailors' and Soldiers' Christmas Fund. She had been paralysed for seven years, but earned a little money by rug-making. Accompanying her contribution was the following note:

6, Wostenholme Place, Powell Street, Sheffield
Dear Princess Mary,
This is the last money I will earn, and as the doctor says I will not be here at Christmas I would like it to go to the Sailors' Christmas Box.
      Respectfully yours, Gertie Melson.

The paper added that Princess Mary wrote with thanks, but the letter 'arrived after the child's death, which took place on Wednesday last'.

Socks Day in October 1914 was the first of many flag days and street collections in the city.

Considerable sums were also obtained through donation boxes on the city's trams, with recipients changed on a regular basis. Street collections in the city centre became common. Early in the war, on 19 October 1914, a Socks for Soldiers Day saw around 300 boy scouts sell 50,000 floral favours – flowers in the British and Belgian colours – many of which had been donated by Atkinson's department store on the Moor. Scouts were in action again a couple of weeks later with a repeat event. On that occasion, the number of floral emblems was raised to 100,000[265], and as the war progressed the city's scouts gave practical help as required in many public activities and fundraising efforts.

In subsequent months flag days were held almost weekly. In April 1915, Primrose Day for the Red Cross and the St John's Ambulance Society was marked by women selling over 2,500 bunches of primroses

Here are some of Weston Park Museum's collection of lapel flags used in street collections in the city during the war.

at a penny each. Other collections (sometimes repeated) included those for Colonel Connell's Fund, Sheffield Soldiers' Comforts Fund, the University Hospital Supply Depot, the Sheffield Military Hospitals Motor Ambulance Fund, the YMCA and the Russian Relief Fund. Others were for the Sheffield Soldiers' Home, Sheffield Prisoners of War Help Committee, the British and Foreign Sailors' Society, the Salvation Army, Dr Barnado's Homes and the RSPCA, as well as in an Italian Flag Day, a Serbian Flag Day[266] and a French Red Cross Flag Day. Typically more than 2,000 helpers came forward, and early in the war dogs sometimes served as carriers of collection boxes. The use of animals was prohibited from 1916[267], as it still is. Fundraising for non-military purposes continued throughout the war, for example an annual Alexandra Rose Day[268] for local hospitals and Daisy Day for the National Children's Home.

Under the headline 'Daughters of Vulcan Play Football', the *Sheffield Daily Independent* at the end of December 1916 described a charity match between two teams of 'lady footballers' drawn from Vickers' South and East Projectile shops. Around 10,000 spectators paid their entrance fee in aid of sick and wounded soldiers in the city's hospitals, and the tone of the *Independent*'s report would cause problems today:

The matronly goalie […] was a formidable obstacle […] of magnificent physique.

The floundering and slipping about was done with a subtle grace which mere man could never hope to emulate.

The winning goal came after 'little Fattie' passed the backs who 'made sure their hair was all right'. Several other charity matches – by men as well as by women, but never together – took place subsequently.

Throughout the Great War, people in Sheffield worked hard and generously in these ways to organize projects and to raise substantial amounts of money for the nation and for individuals and families in need. In the words of the 1919 *Sheffield Yearbook*, 'they have never wearied in well-doing'. Before the welfare state became established, it was expected that support for people in need would come largely from the community, and caring for others was a central part of life in First World War Sheffield.

Display Box 7.6
HELP FOR HORSES

Among the many requests for wartime donations was this *Sheffield Daily Telegraph* advertisement in the autumn of 1914, which recognized that sufferers in battle were not all human:

'WILL YOU HELP THE BRITISH ARMY HORSES?
RSPCA FUND FOR SICK AND WOUNDED HORSES
(Approved by the Army Council)

What we want:
2,000 shelters for horses before and after treatment
20 horse ambulances and motor lorries
5,000 rugs, old or new
5,000 woollen bandages
5,000 ordinary head collars
5,000 halters
What will you give?'

CHAPTER 8

Industry Responds
to War

As Britain's armed forces expanded, the extra men required weapons and ammunition, and before long manufacturers in Sheffield and elsewhere were receiving more government orders than they could cope with. So began a sequence of events that transformed working life in the city and reshaped much of its industry.

Before the war, the country had obtained its armaments from three government-owned factories – the Royal Arsenal at Woolwich, the Royal Small Arms Factory at Enfield and the Royal Gunpowder Factory at Waltham Abbey – together with a few private companies appointed by the government as official suppliers. These included Cammell Lairds, Firths, Hadfields and Vickers in Sheffield, all of which were well-equipped and effective but soon unable to meet the ever-growing demand.

In May 1915, supply problems hit the headlines in what became known as the 'shell scandal'. The war correspondent of *The Times* learned from a high-ranking officer on the Western Front that recent British attacks had failed because the troops lacked high-explosive shells to dislodge the enemy. His article told readers that 'the want of an unlimited supply of high explosives was a fatal bar to our success'. It caused uproar, especially after the complaints were elaborated as a 'tragic blunder' by the widely-read *Daily Mail*[269].

Discussions had recently started between politicians and trade union officials about possible changes to some traditional industrial practices, and these were soon followed by the creation of an entirely new government department – the Ministry of Munitions. Officially established on 9 June 1915, this was charged with organizing the munitions of war, taking over many aspects of work from the Admiralty and the War Office. The first minister of munitions was Liberal David Lloyd George, previously the chancellor of the exchequer, and his four-man advisory team included Dr Christopher Addison MP, who had been a lecturer in anatomy in Sheffield Medical School between 1897 and 1901. The new ministry included among its top executives around a hundred company directors and managers, and those transferred from Sheffield included Charles Ellis from John Brown and Company, who was appointed as the ministry's deputy director.

Despite many false starts and failed initiatives, this new government department gradually persuaded factories all over the country to work within an overall programme to deliver a hugely increased supply of armaments and equipment. As well as organizing more workers and factories, the department had to ensure that supplies of previously-imported raw materials were maintained. In 1914, about a third of the ore converted by British manufacturers into pig-iron came from abroad and special efforts were now needed to obtain deliveries from Sweden, Spain and the United States. In addition, in 1917 Sheffield University unveiled new procedures to use British-sourced alternatives instead of high-grade imports[270].

The government also had to improve the movement of materials between companies and find ways to restrain price rises. In these and other respects, detailed intervention by officials became the norm. The country's railways had been taken over as soon as the war started, and the entire coal-mining industry gradually became controlled by the government. Acids, fuel oils and other essential materials, including sacking for sand-bags, were soon exclusively channelled through the government at centrally-determined prices, and standard purchasing procedures and/or maximum prices were introduced for many metals, armament components and part-completed products. Allocations to each manufacturer of essential materials were fixed either centrally[271] or by the establishment of a directing committee representing key producers.

Display Box 8.1
THE GOVERNMENT'S NATIONAL FACTORIES

From September 1915, the government financed more than 200 new factories to produce armaments and materials. These 'national factories' were owned by the government but most were managed by local companies in accordance with detailed regulations from the Ministry of Munitions.

National Explosives Factories produced TNT and other explosives or components of explosives: thirty-one factories of this kind were opened around the country, none in Sheffield.

National Shell Factories made smaller varieties of unfilled artillery shell: forty-eight factories, including two in Barnsley and one in Rotherham.

National Projectile Factories produced medium and heavier types of shell: fifteen factories, including two in Sheffield (managed by Firths and by Hadfields) and one in Nottingham managed by Sheffield-based Cammell Laird.

National Filling Factories packed empty shells with explosives or chemicals: twenty-seven factories, recognized to be particularly dangerous working environments. None were in Sheffield.

National Cartridge Factories manufactured small arms ammunition: six factories.

National Ordnance Factories repaired artillery weapons: four factories, including one in Sheffield (Hadfields) and one in Nottingham (Sheffield's Cammell Lairds), both of which had previously operated as National Projectile Factories.

National Aircraft Production Factories made aeroplanes and some balloons: eight factories.

Other National Factories repaired equipment and manufactured gauges, boxes, optical instruments, anti-gas apparatus, specialized ammunition, etc: around seventy-five factories, including two small ones in Sheffield in 1918.

In addition, the country's established ordnance suppliers were expanded: the Royal Arsenal at Woolwich (formed around 1695); the Royal Gunpowder Factory at Waltham Abbey (from 1787); the Royal Small Arms Factory at Enfield (from 1804); and the recently established Royal Aircraft Establishment at Farnborough (from 1905).

National factories

In a particularly important development, the Ministry of Munitions created and controlled around 215 'national factories'[272]. These included the established armament producers at Woolwich, Waltham Abbey and Enfield, but were otherwise entirely new establishments spread across the country (see Display Box 8.1).

The factories' construction and equipment were almost entirely financed by the government, but everyday management was typically in the hands of a manufacturer from the area who acted as agent for the ministry and received a fee for the work[273]. Managing companies had to follow government rules for staffing, purchasing, accounting and other activities, and a factory's output had to be delivered to the government at fixed prices. Although these companies did not own the factories they managed, they worked for profits that depended on their effectiveness in keeping costs low.

Increased resources and standardized procedures gave rise to clear benefits. The ministry arranged for centralized buying of raw materials and sold those to factories at prices below free-market levels. Economies were created by imposing the same accounting systems in all government-owned factories and requiring each one to submit detailed costings for comparison with national benchmarks. Improvements were demanded when a factory appeared inefficient. New methods of scrap utilization were introduced nationally, as were modern procedures for what we now call human resource management. Research into steel and other materials was expanded, and recommendations were disseminated widely throughout industry.

Controlled establishments

The national factories were invaluable, with each one producing its own kind of product. But they necessarily took several months to start work and the country's need was immediate and wide-ranging. What about already established companies – ones that had never before produced munitions? Could their experiences and equipment be directed instead to war work?

In casting its net widely, the government decided to introduce legally backed regulations about company operation. The Munitions of War Act became law on 2 July 1915 and required sacrifices from employees as well as employers. The original focus was narrowly on armament-makers themselves, but it soon became clear that companies making other articles for use in war (uniforms, tools, eating utensils, etc) also needed inclusion. The government took powers through the Ministry of Munitions to declare any firm engaged on munition-related work to be a 'controlled establishment', in which certain rights of workers were removed and owners' profits and freedom were limited for the duration of the war. The number of controlled firms increased steadily in the following months.

No overall list of controlled organizations has survived and historians have differed in their estimated total. Nationally the number of controlled establishments certainly exceeded 5,000 and may have reached 6,000. Sheffield had around 350 (estimates vary, up to a maximum of 450). It was explicitly stated that the Act would be in force only for the duration of the conflict, and that unions' and employers' rights would be restored without change at the war's end.

The 1915 Munitions of War Act also made it illegal for workers to strike, and trade union restrictive practices and rules were to be suspended. As a parallel restraint, controlled employers were forbidden to lock-out workers in a dispute and companies breaking the new law became subject to a large fine. Owners of controlled companies were required to provide regular details of employees, equipment and jobs undertaken, and any excess profits (above 20 percent of pre-war net levels) were taxed.

Disputes about applying the new regulations were to be settled by newly established munition tribunals. Around sixty relatively informal courts were established around the country, each comprising an independent adjudicator[274] who was advised by one member each from an employers' and a workmen's panel. Proceedings of the Sheffield Munition Tribunal were reported in the local press and ranged widely across behaviours falling within the Act. Workers were able to appeal to the tribunal about an employer's action, and employers themselves brought complaints against individual workers for drunkenness, disobeying orders or absence from a job.

War service badges

The 1915 Munitions of War Act also empowered the ministry to issue badges that could be worn by workers in munition factories and shipyards to show they were contributing to the nation 'On War Service'. It was hoped that these badges would help dissuade munition employees from offering themselves for military

Unofficial 'On War Service' badges included this one from Cammell Lairds, which was worn by William Ray who lived in Cartmell Road in Woodseats.

service[275], and in the war's opening period some munitions companies created their own badge. However, by late December 1914 the Admiralty thought it better to issue its own official version to dockyards and suppliers and in March 1915 the War Office followed with its own badge.

So far so good, but soon after the Ministry of Munitions was formed in mid-1915 it decided to issue a single badge to replace both the Admiralty and War Office versions. In a huge nationwide administrative task, up to 500,000 previously-issued badges had to be called in and assessments were made of a similar number of men in potentially appropriate jobs. This process was carried

Steelmakers Edgar Allen issued this 'On War Service' badge to its workers in early 1915.

out in Sheffield by the city's Committee on Munitions of War, and more than 10,000 new badges and accompanying certificates were issued to local men after recommendations from the committee. The nation was now in an era of debadging and rebadging.

After the introduction of non-voluntary conscription in early 1916, exemptions from call-up were possible for workers on war-essential jobs, and authorized possession of a war service badge and accompanying certificate became essential to avoid being sent to war. Several government departments and committees struggled at different times to determine the national importance of particular jobs and to reduce contradictions between policies, and across the years decisions about which types of worker were eligible for a Scheduled Occupation Certificate gradually became more systematic and centrally determined. Badging and debadging became based on detailed nationwide schedules of protected occupations rather than on the needs of particular companies.

This is an early version of the war service badge issued by John Brown and Company.

Arguments about badging and debadging had mainly concerned men of military age, but other men also sought badges to demonstrate their own contribution – for example, munition workers above military age and younger ones who had volunteered but been rejected as medically unfit. Women munition workers also wanted

This is the standard badge authorized by the Ministry of Munitions in 1915.

a badge. Until late in the war women could not volunteer for military service and regulations about the issue of war service badges did not apply to them. In the early days of single-company badges, firms could issue their own version to female as well as male staff. During 1915, as company badges became replaced by a standard issue and the number of munition companies employing women increased, public recognition through a badge became widely demanded. The government was concerned about the high financial and administrative cost but in May 1916 agreed to introduce the women's version. On the reverse this had a pin for attaching to clothes and was in effect a brooch rather than a badge. As well as workers directly making munitions, women employed as clerks, canteen assistants and similar jobs could receive a brooch, the issue of which was left entirely to employers without close government supervision. Many thousand women received this version of a war service badge.

This brooch for women munition workers was worn in Sheffield by Hannah Roberts. She had to find care for her 4-year-old son during the working day. Her husband was in the navy.

Dilution and women workers

As more and more men moved into military service, Sheffield and the rest of Britain experienced a gradual 'dilution' of its labour force. This process placed a wider range of people in jobs that had previously been reserved only for men who were designated as skilled. Time-served tradesmen and their unions had long dominated engineering and related industries and these groups fought hard to protect their privileged position[276]. However, by 1915 national union officials accepted the nation's need for more armaments and in the spring of that year joined with the government to find a way forward. They broadly supported the Munitions of War Act of July 1915 and in a national agreement of 19 September 1915 several unions agreed to 'assist in the re-organization of the skilled labour employed in government arsenals and controlled

Several different posters encouraged women to become munition workers.

establishments, in order that semi-skilled or unskilled labour may be employed on a much more extensive scale'. That process was strongly encouraged by the Ministry of Munitions, and it gradually became widespread.

Through dilution, skilled men became released for call-up or for more important munition work on the basis that all or part of their job could be assigned to less-qualified individuals. Initially, the focus was on the wider employment of men not eligible for military service or boys below 18, but gradually the introduction of women became more common. These were at first widely considered to be unsuited for most jobs, certainly those requiring more than a minimum of skill and physical effort, but as men left for military service in ever-increasing numbers, less-skilled workers of either sex gradually became drawn in as replacements. By 1917 and 1918, the process had advanced so

Another romanticized poster urging women to move into munition work.

much that men and women from outside a trade could move into jobs or parts of jobs at a relatively high level of skill. In Britain at the time that was a very remarkable change.

Female tram conductors were appointed for the first time. They eventually numbered more than 600 in the city.

Nationally, between 1914 and 1918, the number of women workers in all occupations grew by more than half, with greatest increases during 1915 and 1916. A few industries, such as textiles and clothing, saw a reduction in female workers as their export trade declined, and the number of domestic servants also went down. On the other hand, the metals industry and the civil service both came to employ more than three times as many women as before the war and the transport sector also took on large numbers [277]. In Sheffield, reports in the period covered women munition workers, bank clerks, brickmakers, car drivers, carriage cleaners, crane operators, factory police, farm workers, gardeners, letter sorters, mail deliverers, materials inspectors, porters, toolmakers, tram conductors, tram ticket inspectors and window cleaners. In addition, the number of female schoolteachers increased substantially. And we should not forget the expansion of nursing roles, women's contribution as non-combatant troops[278], and the vast amount of voluntary work undertaken by women of all kinds.

The introduction of dilution – both male and female – was not trouble-free. As well as inevitable unease about change and many false starts, established workers' objections led to frequent conflicts. The Munitions of War Act of July 1915 made strikes in controlled establishments illegal, and for senior trade union officials it was important to work only within the law. However, that was not always the case at company level and some locally elected shopstewards chose to take strike action despite that being opposed by their own leaders. Major stoppages occurred in the South

Postwomen were recruited in large numbers to deliver mail around the city.

Wales coalfield, Clydeside shipyards and Lancashire engineering works as well as in the Sheffield area. For the nation as a whole, the number of days lost through strikes, which had declined after August 1914, rose steadilyfrom mid-1915 – and so did the number of dilutees.

Working conditions and health
As the government struggled to provide a steady supply of armaments and equipment, an underlying set of issues came to the fore – how to maintain the health and effectiveness of the workforce. The Ministry of Munitions promoted investigations to learn about and reduce the harmful effects of long working hours and poor working conditions. Sixty or seventy hours a week were widely regarded as normal, and workers were sometimes at their job for longer than that. Systematic overtime was usual and Sunday working was widespread. In some munition factories women as well as men were present for twelve-hour shifts as well as coping

Nineteen-year-old Edith Ashley (to the left) lived in Burton Road and worked for Cammell Laird.

with tram or other journeys before and after those times. (A meal break was taken within a shift.) By 1916, new government research showed that a shorter working week could cut down absenteeism and lateness with no loss of output, and from then onwards hours in munition factories were gradually reduced – but still to levels far above those we now consider acceptable.

The Ministry of Munitions also sought to improve other aspects of factory life. Over the next three years it campaigned actively for the establishment of factory canteens, the employment of medical staff within companies, the provision of women's rest rooms and 'welfare supervisors'[279].

The city's factories
Life in Sheffield was dominated by a massive expansion of the city's armaments trade. Tens of thousands of workers and their families found themselves part of a huge mobilization of effort and skill. Already at the end of 1914, the *Sheffield Daily Telegraph* saw it like this:

With the exception of clothing for the men and saddlery for their horses, there seems scarcely a requirement of the war which Britain and her Allies are not looking to Sheffield to supply in some form or another […] From a bayonet to an officer's sword, from a rifle barrel to the largest calibre gun, from the finished parts of a dashing scout boat to those of a super-Dreadnought, from an aeroplane dart to a shell weighing – never mind how much. Sheffield makes them all, besides many other things, from military workshops on wheels to camp kitchens, from thin bullet-proof hut steel to armour-plate many inches thick, from torpedo-net wire to net for big guns, from transport waggons to armoured motor-cars, from stretchers to ambulance carriages, and from hoop iron for military packages to horse-shoe iron. Sheffield makes the razor placed in the soldier's kit, the knife, fork and spoon he carries with him into the trenches, and the combination pocket-knife without which he would be at a complete loss, and also provides similar articles for the blue-jacket and marine. The Allied governments are coming here for entrenching tools. And the high-speed steel so essential in the production of much of the heavy war material is, of course, a well-known speciality of this district. For these things the nation has looked to Sheffield, and has not looked in vain.

Bending armour plate at Cammell Laird's Cyclops Works in 1918.

Heavy shell production at Cammell Laird's Grimesthorpe Works.

The city's established manufacturers of armaments – John Brown and Company, Cammell Lairds, Thomas Firth and Sons, Hadfields, Vickers – all saw enormous expansion during the war. For example, John Brown turned out huge quantities of steel, forgings, crankshafts and armour plate for military use in shipyards and companies around the country[280]; and substantial deliveries were made to British and other countries' railway systems (crucial in wartime) by producing wheels, axles, springs, buffers and other products. Like other Sheffield manufacturers, John Brown repeatedly extended its works and installed a range of new equipment.

Cammell Laird and Company also greatly expanded its production and by the end of the war employed twice its earlier number of workers, including many women. The city's largest armament firm was Vickers, with more than 10,000 Sheffield employees by 1916. The company was also one of the country's biggest employers, and across the war years it delivered from all its sites around seventy ships and fifty submarines, 2,500 artillery guns, 100,000 machine-guns and 5,500 aeroplanes. The company's River Don Works and Holme Lane (Hillsborough) site produced hundreds of thousands of shrapnel and high-explosive shells.

From January 1916 a National Projectile Factory, erected by Thomas Firth and Sons on open ground at Templeborough, made artillery shells of many kinds, turning out more than 2,500,000 in the next three years. The

Thomas Firth and Sons built and operated this National Projectile Factory on a greenfield site at Templeborough.

factory came to employ around 5,700 workers, of which nearly 90 percent were women.

Government work was spread far beyond the traditional armament producers, and the city's wartime products ranged across munitions and equipment of many kinds. J. A. Chapman and Company and Sanderson Brothers and Newbould turned out bayonets, high-speed steel created by Jonas and Colver was in demand for aircraft engines, and James Neill and Company responded to the need for those engines' magnetos by developing its production of magnet steel. J. H. Andrew and Company already produced cast steel for shells and rifle barrels, and now greatly expanded its output. So too did Ambrose Shardlow and Company, whose crankshafts were urgently required for aircraft and tank engines. The company also started to make micrometers in place of imports, which were no longer available. Marsh Brothers increased production of twist drills to 30,000 a week, wire-drawers J. Stead and Company extended their range to produce springs for artillery guns, and James Dixon and Sons, previously specializing in silver and electroplated goods, adapted their Cornish Place works to produce cupro-nickel, 100,000 pairs of piston rings for aeroplane engines, and many thousands of parts for mines and depth charges.

Firth's National Projectile Factory at Templeborough used an 'NPF' version of the women's war service brooch.

That company also devoted itself to delivering a million steel helmets. Steel sheets made by Hadfields and other Sheffield manufacturers, were pressed and fitted with a liner in Dixons and around half-a-dozen other firms. Also in great demand were table knives, forks and spoons for the

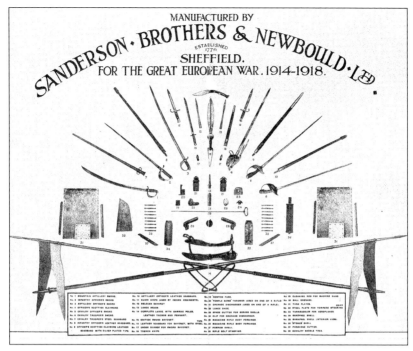

Wartime items produced in the city by Sanderson Brothers and Newbould.

James Dixon and Sons of Cornish Place was a major supplier of steel helmets.

troops and more than 3,000,000 were ordered from Sheffield firms. The nation's manufacturers had great difficulty turning out enough razors, and the Cutlers' Company organized voluntary donations of second-hand items for refurbishment in the city[281]. Tin openers, cooks' knives, pocket knives, surgical scissors, water bottles, metal mirrors, axes, spades and saws were ordered in large quantity. Many tiny firms were also busy. Henry Pickin provided his horse and cart for transporting shells and other items around the city.

These were hectic, sometimes stressful, years during which Sheffield and Sheffield people made a major contribution to the country's eventual wartime success.

For trench warfare on the Western Front the army needed tools as well as weapons.

CHAPTER 9

Sheffield in 1917 and 1918

The last two years of war were increasingly difficult for Britain and its allies. Despite some significant victories, overall military progress was poor, and by the spring of 1918 a German victory seemed very possible. At home, conditions were steadily getting worse and the public, dulled by deaths and disablement, was becoming weary of war. Food, fuel and other essentials were increasingly scarce, some rationing had to be introduced, and military conscription took more and more men away from their families. Adding to the pain, in 1918 Britain was hit by a major epidemic of influenza.

By late-1917, long queues outside food shops were common and supplies often ran out. Lighting regulations were firmly enforced as policemen ensured the black-out of houses and other buildings, retail shop displays were darkened, illumination was reduced in churches and public buildings, and most street lamps were extinguished. Petrol shortages prevented travel by car, and passenger journeys by train were difficult as military and goods transport took priority. The Budget in April 1918 once more increased taxes on income, alcohol, sugar, tobacco and matches, as well as raising postal and other charges. Across all the war years the cost of living more than doubled, with greatest increases in the price of food – particularly affecting poorer families. Furthermore, by mid-1917, even people in work were finding it difficult to pay for what they needed and industrial disputes were common. The number and intensity of factory disputes and strikes increased throughout 1917 and into 1918.

British troop losses in 1917 were even worse than in previous years and casualties from Sheffield mirrored the national pattern. The city suffered around 1,500 and 1,700 military deaths in each of 1917 and 1918, up from about 800 and 1,250 in the two previous years respectively, and the high number of disabling injuries increased in the same way. All neighbourhoods knew some families' grief. Furthermore, the city was now home to many hospitalized soldiers and men discharged from the services as disabled. These hundreds of invalids filled the city's streets and public buildings[282], and societies like the National Federation of Discharged Soldiers and Sailors and the Comrades of the Great War were prominent through regular meetings and fundraising campaigns. The human cost of war was by now very obvious.

Support for the national effort was boosted by many public meetings and church activities. Religious services regularly contained prayers for the troops and often included sermons praising the nation's cause. Encouragement from outside the city included several more visits from suffragette Emmeline Pankhurst. In April 1918, her Sheffield speeches praised women munition workers and boosted the government's substitution campaign by urging older men to offer themselves in place of called-up workers. As elsewhere in the country, by May 1917 the council had established a National Service Committee to channel volunteers into factory work.

Fundraising activities were hard to avoid. Many companies encouraged weekly deductions from workers' pay or requested extra donations to special relief causes. Flag days were held almost every week. Special campaigns like Tank Week, Cruiser Week, War Weapons Week and Gun Week included displays, bands and speeches in Fitzalan Square and around the city. And schoolteachers were persistent in encouraging children (through their parents, presumably) to buy still more war savings certificates.

Conscription, tribunals and conscientious objectors

By late 1915 the flow of volunteers into the army was too low to meet the army's need and Military Service Acts in January and May 1916 took away personal choice by introducing compulsory conscription. Men between 18 and 41 were now called up to fight, and by 1918 that upper age-limit had (with some variations) been increased to 50.

To cope with the additional administration Sheffield's recruiting office, now installed in the Corn Exchange, took on more civilian staff under the supervision of military officers. However, even with compulsory call-up,

Display Box 9.1
CONKERS AND MOSS

Sheffield played two unlikely roles in the country's war effort – collecting horse chestnuts from the city's trees and processing moss gathered from local moors and around the country.

Horse chestnuts – the conkers of children's games – became important in the autumn of 1917. The country needed large amounts of acetone for the manufacture of cordite – a propellant for shells and bullets. However, imported wood, the traditional basis of acetone, was becoming scarce and a replacement was needed. In 1915, scientists at Manchester University developed a chemical alternative using grain or maize, and two factories were built that successfully provided acetone in sufficient quantity for military needs.

By 1917 grain and maize were also in short supply and the Manchester scientists were asked to find an alternative source. They discovered that conkers – abundant from British trees in the autumn – were suitable, and factories were converted to turn those into acetone. In July 1917, schools and clubs around the country were offered a conkers bounty by the director of propellant supplies, and several thousand tonnes were obtained through children's efforts – more than could be carried in the available trains. Unfortunately, their impact was not great. Teething problems held back production until the spring of 1918, and even then yields were poor. Production soon ceased.

More successful was the city's work with **sphagnum moss**. This was widely available on Derbyshire moors and elsewhere in the country and could form very effective sterile dressings for soldiers' wounds. In August 1916, the university's Hospital Supply Depot responded to a request from the director-general of voluntary organizations by organizing teams of ladies to supply sphagnum moss dressings to military hospitals. Newly picked moss was received from local volunteers and from other parts of the country, hard pieces were removed, and standard-size muslin bags were filled and then sterilized at the base hospital before dispatch. This work continued right through the war, and as many as 34,000 moss dressings were sent from Sheffield to military hospitals.

From 1916 the city's recruiting office was based in the Corn Exchange in Sheaf Street.

the number of new soldiers remained below military needs, in part because many were rejected through poor physical condition. Nationally, only around half the men examined in 1917 and 1918 were passed as immediately fit for full combat service. Some were considered suitable for hardening by route-marches and other physical activity, and others were rejected entirely. Early in the war most medical examinations were carried out by civilian practitioners on a part-time basis and some variability between doctors and regions was found. By the middle of 1916, assessments had become more standardized and were now explicitly linked to different military needs. From then on, men were placed in one of thirteen medical categories, each of which defined a person's physical suitability for particular kinds of military role. Many of those called-up served in a valuable capacity but were not themselves active in battle.

The period saw many comb-outs of entire firms, as recruiting authorities trawled through complete workforces to locate more men who could be enlisted[283]. In these ever-tightening conditions, many workers objected to a decision that they should be called up and lodged a request for exemption. The Military Service Act of January 1916 allowed for this possibility by establishing military service and appeal tribunals around the country. Sheffield's military service tribunal (sometimes referred to as the Sheffield recruiting tribunal, the Sheffield military tribunal or simply

Sheffield local tribunal) became extremely busy and operated as two parallel courts. These often met several times a week, starting at five o'clock, and they handled almost 35,000 cases in more than 250 sessions before closing in November 1918[284]. An objector's case was sometimes presented by a local solicitor, and a representative from the city's recruiting office was also present – almost always urging conscription. He was not himself a member of the tribunal.

Most conscripted men accepted their position and joined the services so that only a minority came before a tribunal to request exemption. Court sittings were described in the local newspapers, and reports reveal that the most frequent outcome was a temporary delay of conscription – usually for between three and six months conditional on circumstances not changing[285]. A small number of applicants received a complete exemption without an expectation of call-up, but the military representative might later request that this be changed. It is also clear from newspaper reports that in only very few Sheffield tribunal cases was immediate call-up required.

On what bases did men claim exemption? Three general arguments were used: family need; business requirements; and conflicts with conscience[286]. In the first case some men pleaded that their assistance and income were essential for an elderly parent or family members in difficulty. For example, in 1916 a 19-year-old carter was temporarily exempted from call-up so that he could continue giving wages to his widowed mother and two younger brothers and two sisters. However, claims of this kind were concentrated in the first year of conscription, as financial allowances for dependants subsequently became more widely known.

A second basis for objection was in terms of business requirements. Some claimants argued that their call-up would destroy a company engaged on nationally-important work or would throw people into unemployment. On that basis, three-month exemptions were awarded in Sheffield to a builder constructing new houses for the city's workers and to decorators painting munition factories. Several single-person coal merchants were also deferred for three months. As national frameworks of protected occupations gradually became established, the tribunal was increasingly required to assess whether or not a particular job fitted into an exempted category.

In the absence of published overall figures and in view of the fact that an unknown number of men applied again at the end of current exemption, it is not possible to cite total numbers of men exempted versus called up. However, it is clear that very few tribunal applicants in Sheffield were immediately required to join the services and that complete exemption from conscription was also rare. Similarly, only a minority of applications to the Sheffield military tribunal were totally rejected. Most claimants were conditionally deferred for a few months, and presumably a large number of these subsequently became troops.

However, men exempted from military service were not freed from all responsibilities. They were required by the tribunal to undertake military drill and musketry training with the city's Volunteer Defence Corps and were instructed to undertake work of national importance. Such work, perhaps arranged through the labour exchange, could be (for example) in a munition factory, on a farm, or in a hospital or asylum. Other possibilities included taking non-combatant military service or working with the Friends' Ambulance Unit.

Conscientious objection was the third possible basis of a claim for exemption. There was no requirement that an exemption claim should be based on religious belief, and at least one person appealing to the Sheffield military tribunal argued that socialism was his religion. Conscientious objectors were only a minority of tribunal applicants and, like others, exemption required that they contribute to the war effort in a non-fighting role. Nationally, around 3,300 such men joined the army's Non-Combatant Corps (NCC), which was created in March 1916. Its members (uniformed private soldiers) were subject to military discipline and were supervised by army officers, but they were not required to carry rifles or take part in combat. Instead, they worked to repair or construct roads, railways and army buildings and assisted in other practical ways.

Although many conscientious objectors found this an acceptable alternative to serving in combat, others refused to be 'part of the war machine'. Instead the Sheffield military tribunal offered these men work with a medical service, for example with the Red Cross or in one of the local hospitals. Several agreed to join the Friends' Ambulance Unit (FAU), a national organization set up in September 1914 by volunteers from the Quaker religious group (the Society of Friends)[287]. The FAU transported wounded men in its own ambulances and administered a number of hospitals near the Western Front as well as providing orphanages for children who had lost their parents. Its uniformed members worked in semi-military units alongside army units but not under military control. Members of the unit (eventually around 1,200) received no wages, and funds and equipment were raised from public donations. Although most FAU work was in France and Belgium, a few hundred members served in Britain and several dozen were in hospital ships.

More generally, although Quakers had always argued for non-violent pacifism and continued to do so, they also advocated individual freedom of conscience. As a result, Friends were free to respond to the war in their own way. A minority, perhaps about a third of those eligible, accepted the need to fight in one of the services, often with considerable distinction. In Sheffield, Herbert Barber, Master Cutler in 1909, lost two sons who were serving as army officers. Other Quakers worked during the war in non-military ways, for example helping British families of German men who had been interned as enemy aliens.

The sanctity of life was often stressed by other men seeking exemption from conscription, not always with links to religious belief. National protest groups included the No Conscription Fellowship (NCF), founded in December 1914 and open to all men of military age who were not prepared to take a combatant's role. The NCF contained many Quakers and other religious pacifists, but most of its members had secular or socialist objections. The fellowship produced thousands of libertarian and anti-war leaflets, with some authors being prosecuted under the Defence of the Realm Act, and its local branches included one in Sheffield. Several objectors before the city's military service tribunal, both religious and non-religious, declared that they were NCF members.

Shortages and rationing

The country had long needed to import much of its food (for instance, around two-thirds of its sugar and four-fifths of its wheat), and German submarines were now sinking thousands of tons of food on its way to Britain. During 1916, the authorities tried to improve production and reduce consumption in several ways. A Regulation of Meals Order set limits on some servings in restaurants and hotels, a Milling Order required the extraction of more flour from the available wheat, and the public was urged to have one meatless day in each week. Those were by now obligatory in public eating-places. Fines were introduced for wasting food by feeding it to pigeons or stray animals.

In October the government took control of all wheat purchases from abroad, and its Corn Production Act of April 1917 guaranteed farmers minimum prices for wheat and oats, hoping to increase the country's own output. A national food controller was appointed with (eventually) a large staff. His department urged restraint through advertisements and posters by publicizing ways to avoid waste[288], and by encouraging voluntary self-rationing in terms of maximum amounts to be eaten each week. Food economy was included in school lessons and it was forbidden to throw rice at weddings. A food economy department was set up within the Ministry of Food and this bombarded the country with advice and organized many economy-oriented events around the country. In May 1917, Sheffield's Cutlers' Hall housed a two-week National Economy and Welfare Exhibition, which provided lectures and demonstrations about how to save and produce more food and gave detailed advice about growing vegetables. For a week in January 1918, the Cutlers' Hall housed an SOS exhibition – Save or Starve. This had a rather single-minded focus on potatoes, since those were readily available. It promoted cookery with potatoes rather than flour or other material – demonstrating (with free samples)

By 1917 the country was desperately short of previously-imported wheat, and posters like this were widely displayed.

the use of potato bread, potato soup, potato scones, potato butter, potato and apple pudding, savoury potato roll, and meat and potato pie with a crust made of flour and (surprise, surprise) potato.

The government's Cultivation of Land Orders included new authority for councils to take possession of land for allotments. The city, with its own Land Cultivation Committee, took over several sites and released additional areas it already owned. Many Sheffielders took this opportunity to grow food, paying a monthly rent for their plot, and in the course of the war the number of allotments in the city, some from a private landlord, increased from about 1,600 to around 10,000.

In August 1917, Sheffield established its own food control committee, and this and its sub-committees of councillors and suppliers worked to fix prices for all the city's retailers, often on a weekly basis[289]. Much of the committee's effort went into improving supplies to the city and controlling local allocations so that individual retailers were granted amounts that matched their estimated customers. From September it introduced schemes to allocate fixed amounts of sugar to families of different sizes. The city's meat sub-committee checked that all retailers displayed a notice of their prices. Rabbits were in great demand, with butchers' prices determined by

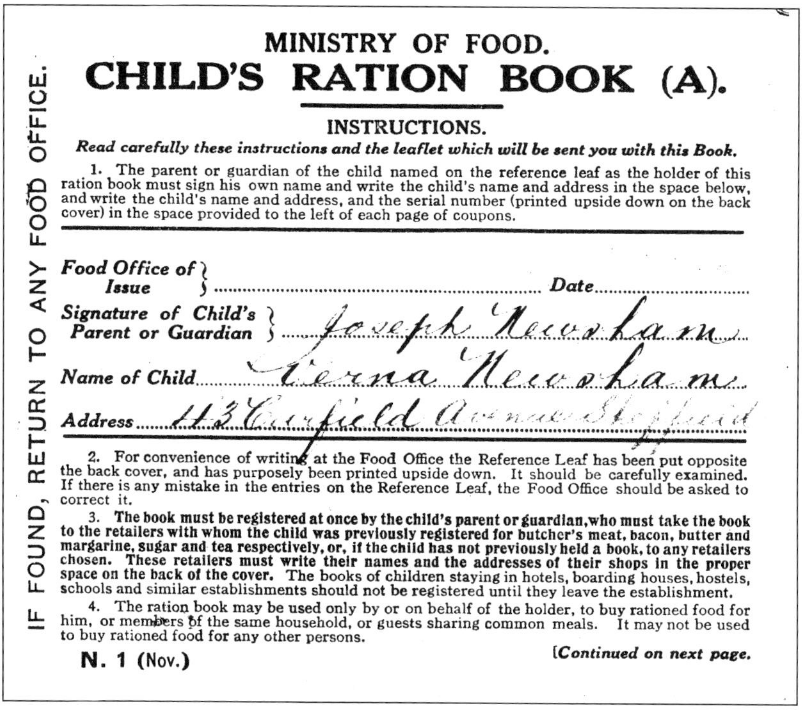

IF FOUND, RETURN TO ANY FOOD OFFICE.

MINISTRY OF FOOD.

CHILD'S RATION BOOK (A).

INSTRUCTIONS.

Read carefully these instructions and the leaflet which will be sent you with this Book.

1. The parent or guardian of the child named on the reference leaf as the holder of this ration book must sign his own name and write the child's name and address in the space below, and write the child's name and address, and the serial number (printed upside down on the back cover) in the space provided to the left of each page of coupons.

Food Office of Issue .... ***Date***..........................

Signature of Child's Parent or Guardian ....Joseph Newsham....

Name of Child....Verna Newsham....

Address....113 Carfield Avenue Sheffield....

2. For convenience of writing at the Food Office the Reference Leaf has been put opposite the back cover, and has purposely been printed upside down. It should be carefully examined. If there is any mistake in the entries on the Reference Leaf, the Food Office should be asked to correct it.

3. **The book must be registered at once by the child's parent or guardian, who must take the book to the retailers with whom the child was previously registered for butcher's meat, bacon, butter and margarine, sugar and tea respectively, or, if the child has not previously held a book, to any retailers chosen. These retailers must write their names and the addresses of their shops in the proper space on the back of the cover.** The books of children staying in hotels, boarding houses, hostels, schools and similar establishments should not be registered until they leave the establishment.

4. The ration book may be used only by or on behalf of the holder, to buy rationed food for him, or members of the same household, or guests sharing common meals. It may not be used to buy rationed food for any other persons.

N. 1 (Nov.)

[*Continued on next page.*

Some food rationing was introduced in 1918, requiring the issue of different ration books to adults and children.

the government's Wild Rabbits (Prices) Order. Even horse-flesh shops (around ten were flourishing in the city) had queues from time to time.

The year 1917 also saw the opening of communal kitchens in the city, providing at moderate prices prepared food that could be taken home to eat. First, in February, came a small outlet close to the Moor which was operated by the city's Salvation Army, and in May 1917 the council opened its own public kitchen in Gibraltar Street, run by volunteers and assisted by two paid cleaners. The scheme became very successful as the cost of food continued to rise and supplies became scarce. In the following spring other low-price outlets, now within a countrywide framework of 'national kitchens', opened in Burngreave and in Mowbray Street, and by November 1918 the city had a total of seven public kitchens within the scheme.

The government tried to equalize the amount available to everyone by rationing principal foods. Details changed slightly as experience led to improvements, but each household had to register for each type of rationed food with a retailer accepted by the local food control committee. Based on a family's size and membership, the control committee determined its weekly allocation of a particular food and worked to provide every retailer with the total amount required by all of its registered customers. Books of coupons were issued to each family[290], entitling every member to a specified quantity each week of butter, margarine, lard, sugar, tea, bacon (briefly) and jam (later). First within the scheme was sugar in January 1918, and the other items followed during the spring and summer. In the middle of the year the city also introduced meat coupons based on the value of a purchase. Bread was never rationed. After inevitable start-up problems, rationing worked smoothly and queues in the city and nationwide were gradually removed.

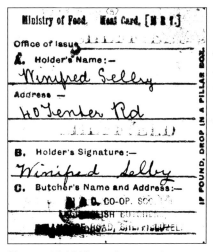

From mid-1918, each person's meat card had to be registered with a specific butcher to obtain a fixed quantity each week.

The government introduced controls of many other kinds. In the middle of 1918, domestic coal rationing was extended from London, where it had been introduced in October 1917, to Sheffield and the rest of the country. In July 1918, the city appointed its own coal controller and a fuel and lighting committee to ensure that permitted quantities were allocated to each house in terms of its number of rooms. Gas and electricity allowances were fixed similarly. As in the case of food, the price of each kind of coal was specified by the authorities and every household had to register with a particular supplier.

The city also suffered from the nation's lack of paper. Paper bags became scarce, newspapers and magazines were reduced in size, and books became less available and more expensive. Schools suffered and some postponed their annual prizegiving as no suitable books for prizes were available. Tobacco, glass containers and other items for household use were also scarce, and controls, committees and shortages extended even to the humble match. The government set up yet another control board and from 1917 maximum prices were set for a box or book of every variety of match.

Prisoners of war and influenza

As the war continued, both sides captured more and more enemy troops. By the end of 1918, around 150,000 German, Austrian and other prisoners of war (97 percent German) were held in more than 400 camps around Britain. Two of these camps were in Sheffield – at Coal Aston and at Redmires.

In February 1917 around 300 German prisoners arrived at Coal Aston airfield[291], and that number was probably increased later. Many of them were later put to work under military guard on construction projects at the camp and elsewhere, but little information is available about their activities. Redmires Camp also housed prisoners of war, but not until October 1918 when it received captured German officers and their orderlies. These were held at Redmires and other UK camps until the autumn of 1919.

Prisoners made a less dramatic impact on the city than did another arrival – an influenza virus. A world-wide epidemic, sometimes called a pandemic, of flu reached Sheffield in the summer of 1918. The illness killed millions of people around the world and at least 150,000 in Britain alone[292]. It caused nearly 3,000 deaths in Sheffield, often from linked bronchitis or pneumonia, after it reached the city in three main waves – in July 1918, November 1918 and with less intensity in the early months of 1919. For a period in the autumn of 1918 some 300 deaths were occurring in the city each week from influenza and associated pneumonia, and at its Sheffield peak in November the disease caused around 750 deaths in a single week[293].

Illness and death from the influenza epidemic darkened further the city's mood into the autumn of 1918. News from the battlefield was improving, but optimism was still in short supply. Nevertheless, the military worst was indeed over, and on the eleventh of November an Armistice was signed and the fighting stopped.

The Armistice and peace

During the first few days of November, newspapers reported events in Europe that at last pointed to an end to the struggle. When the Allies demanded Germany's acceptance of peace terms by Monday 11 November, that country could see no alternative, and signatures from both sides were placed on the document at ten minutes past five on that morning. Hostilities were to cease at eleven o'clock.

Sheffield and the rest of the nation were waiting for that signature. The city's newspaper offices received the news at around 10.30, just in time for the proposed ceasefire at 11.00. By then, in the words of next day's *Sheffield Daily Independent*: 'The city right out to the suburbs had undergone a remarkable transition from the grey of a November morning. Flags were unfurled, colours flying, and smiling faces and laughter bespoke the message – Peace. Bells that had been silent for the greater part of the war clanged in measured refrain, as they do on royal occasions; and the air-raid buzzers that had been wont to break in like a nightmare on the sleep of citizens told to all far and near the glad message of the hour.'

The city-centre bells of the cathedral and St Marie's rang in turn throughout the day, and thanksgiving services were held there, in the (Methodist) Victoria Hall and in churches around the city. Flags were suspended from windows and buildings, injured soldiers and others paraded around the city, and the Town Hall clock was again illuminated. The *Independent* noted that in the churches, 'perhaps better than anywhere else in public, one grasped in a fuller sense the mingling of joy in the hour of triumph and of pathos in the memory of those who had fallen. Hearts were full and tears were many.'

As 1918 passed into a new year Britain was still officially at war. It was assumed that the ceasefire agreed in the Armistice would become permanent, but as yet peace was only temporary. Some troops had been demobilized, but most remained impatiently in their units. Industry's war-work had almost disappeared, and employees – especially women – were losing their jobs in growing numbers. International discussions about peace arrangements were scheduled, but these, which did not start until mid-January, proved to be complex and lengthy.

At last on Saturday 28 June 1919, Germany and the Allies jointly signed the Treaty of Versailles and the Great War formally came to an end. Germany was required to accept harsh conditions and make substantial payments to its enemies. It had been clear for some days before the treaty date that signature was imminent, and Sheffield's morning papers on that Saturday suggested that signing would be at three o'clock. By then, the city centre had been decorated and around 20,000 people had gathered, jamming many streets. The news arrived by telegraph at 3.40 pm (signatures had been finalized at 3.12), and rockets were fired, buzzers and sirens were sounded and bells rang out from the cathedral and other churches. Speeches were made outside the Town Hall, hymns were sung, and cheers were raised for the king and prime minister. The lord mayor

Crowds fill Fargate as Sheffield celebrates peace on 19 July 1919.

then led a procession along Fargate to the Cathedral Yard, where around 15,000 people joined in a non-denominational service. Other services were held around the city including in Endcliffe Park, and many shops closed their doors for the day. The next day (Sunday) saw thanksgiving services in many churches and in open-air settings like Sheffield Wednesday's football ground. The following Sunday, 6 July, was declared Empire Thanksgiving Day, and church services were held throughout the country, including in the city's cathedral and churches. However, despite the positive mood, peace had come too late for many families. Grief and mourning for lost young men were also widespread.

The government sought fitting public tributes and celebrations for what was widely referred to as the Great Sacrifice or the Great Deliverance, and decided to mark the war's newly confirmed end with a national Peace Day on Saturday 19 July. Like other cities, Sheffield held a peace parade and celebrations on that day. Streets were decorated with flags and bunting, and many thousand spectators gathered in the city centre for a parade of bands and troops that marched past the lord mayor and other dignitaries at the Town Hall. A white memorial cross was placed at the junction opposite the cathedral, encircled by a Union Jack and surmounted by a

July 1919 Peace Celebrations in Amy Street, Crookes.

Preparing for Peace Celebrations in Summer Street, Netherthorpe.

laurel wreath. This was treated with great reverence by individual citizens and members of the passing parade. After the march-past, schoolchildren presented patriotic tableaux on platforms outside the Town Hall. Subsequently, more than a dozen bands played in parks, teas were served to around 5,000 widows and orphans of the war, and in the evening bonfires were lit at five of the city's highest points.

However, the mood of celebration was only short-lived. A fortnight after the Armistice in 1918, Prime Minister David Lloyd George had proclaimed the nation's task: 'To make Britain a country fit for heroes to live in.' But that was proving extremely difficult. After a brief economic boost, the nation's and Sheffield's industry fell into decline, personal disfigurement and loss from the war became all too evident, and poverty became widespread. Sheffield's unemployment reached previously unimaginable levels, street demonstrations were common and several riots took place in the city. Distress and disillusionment accompanied a widely felt need to commemorate the huge losses, and memorials were erected all over the city. These and other postwar events are described in *Sheffield's Great War and Beyond*[294].

The city's war memorial in Barker's Pool is dedicated here on 28 October 1925.

Notes

Chapter One: 'The war that will end war'

1 For example, within two weeks of war being declared the *Yorkshire Telegraph and Star* advertised its own special publication 'The Great War', and within a month the *Sheffield Daily Independent* referred in articles to the 'Great European War'. More recently, the conflict has sometimes been described as the first 'industrial' war requiring the production of huge amounts of complex equipment capable of killing and mutilating on a large scale.

2 More than a hundred countries with some involvement in the war are listed at www.europeanhistory.about.com/od/worldwar1/a/ww1countriesint.htm. In addition to a large number of books about the war, websites with an emphasis on Britain and its allies include www.1914-1918.net, www.bbc.co.uk/wwone, www.europeanhistory.about.com/od/worldwar1/p/ww1101.htm, www.firstworldwar.com, www.historylearningsite.co.uk/ww1.htm, www.spartacus.schoolnet.co.uk /FWW.htm, with additional photographs at www.gwpda.org/photos and (including original song recordings) www.ww1photos.com. Some films are at http://www.britishpathe.com/workspaces/show/jhoyle/GfYgqoxq/thumb.

3 A few writers did use the term 'First World War' from around 1918, aiming to contrast the conflict's world-wide spread against earlier wars' restrictions to a few countries.

4 His article headlined 'THE WAR THAT WILL END WAR' was carried by the *Sheffield Daily Independent* on 14 August 1914. Wells' optimism was based partly on his plans to treat the defeated enemy in a generous manner and to establish a multinational Peace League. He declared that 'this war […] is quite a different war from any that have gone before it', and elsewhere stressed: 'this is already the vastest war in history. It is war not of nations but of mankind.' Furthermore, 'this, the greatest of all wars, is not just another war – it is the last war!'. See pages 12 and 14 of *The War That will End War* (New York: Duffield and Company, 1914).

5 These figures indicate the total across four years of war. Fewer men were, of course, involved at any one time. For example, 5,000,000 Britons served on the Western Front overall, but the maximum number there simultaneously was nearer 2,000,000.

6 For example, early assaults overran German colonies in the Pacific region, a naval base in China, and possessions in West Africa. German East Africa was not finally conquered until November 1918.

7 It is sometimes disputed by historians whether Britain was legally required to assist Belgium or merely had a moral obligation to do that.

8 Apart from its small regular force, Britain had for years relied on part-time volunteer territorial soldiers available to serve in this country in the unlikely event of it being invaded. In contrast, both France and Germany had large, well-equipped armies of conscripted men.

9 Field Marshal Earl Kitchener was a long-serving soldier with a distinguished career. When appointed Secretary of State for War in August 1914 he energetically promoted a recruiting campaign, but was killed in June 1916 when his ship was sunk by a German mine in the North Sea.

10 More than 250,000 of the new soldiers were below the official recruitment age – birth certificates were at first not required. Despite being only 14, plasterer's labourer Fred Lindley of Sheffield was accepted in 1914 but was wounded in 1916 and then discharged, before being called up in 1918 when he became 18. Tom Dyson of Woodseats joined the York and Lancaster Regiment in September 1914 although he was only 16. He was killed in May 1918. Around thirty Sheffield youths under the age of 18 died as a result of the war.

11 For example, the 'Sheffield Pals' (the Twelfth Service Battalion of the York and Lancaster Regiment; see Chapter Four) served in Egypt for several months in 1915 and 1916 before moving to the Western Front.

12 See page 141 of G. A. B. Dewar, *The Great Munition Feat, 1914-1918* (London: Constable, 1921). Men who died were not always identifiable, and work to bury them was additionally distressing. See www.1914-1918.net/died.htm. However, soldiers on the Western Front served in enemy-facing trenches for only a few days at a time, for intervening periods remaining some distance behind the front line itself.

13 The word 'casualty' is sometimes used inappropriately to suggest the number of men killed. In official language, casualties are losses of several kinds – death, injury, being unaccounted for, desertions, and being taken prisoner. For example, of the approximately 60,000 British casualties on the first day of the Battle of the Somme, around 36,000 were wounded, 3,000 were missing and 600 taken prisoner, in addition to the thousands who were killed. Across the war as a whole, more than 80 percent of injured or sick British soldiers later returned to some duty, although around 7 percent of this group died of their wounds and about 8 percent were discharged as invalids.

14 Details of 543 soldiers from the city who lost their lives on that day are at www.sheffieldsoldierww1.co.uk/search5b.php.

15 The horror of this period was not only for the British. The French and German armies were engaged in lengthy battles along the front line, with several hundred thousand deaths in each case. Overall, both those countries suffered a wartime death-rate even higher than Britain.

16 The British army had for many initial months of the war suffered from shortages of armaments and ammunition, but by the middle of 1918 supplies were extremely good. The greatest twenty-four-hour British expenditure of shell during the entire war took place on 28 and 29 September 1918 – almost 1,000,000 rounds in a single day.

17 Up to that date, the US had remained neutral and had traded with both sides. Its change of policy followed German attempts to arrange an alliance with Mexico – clearly a threat to nearby USA. And from January 1917 Germany's unrestricted submarine warfare sank merchant ships as well as naval vessels, so that American trade and the lives of non-combatant citizens were now in immediate danger. By this time, Britain and France had accumulated huge debts in the US, and many American companies were earning large sums from business with those countries. The US was likely to suffer considerable financial losses if Germany won the war.

18 An armistice is an agreed temporary ceasefire in order to discuss peace terms. Although fighting stopped in November 1918, the countries were still formally at war until a peace treaty was signed on 28 June 1919.

19 The first controlled flight took place in the US in December 1903, and Britain's first successful aeroplane flew in 1908.

20 Air reconnaissance at first involved hand-drawn sketches made from the air, but gradually photographic procedures became usable.

21 Some estimates exceed 800,000. All agree that British deaths in the Great War were as high as double those in World War Two.

22 Details of most of these have been brought together at www.sheffieldsoldierww1.co.uk. The city's earlier Roll of Honour is available at www.sheffield.gov.uk/libraries/archives-and-local-studies/research-guides/world-war-one.html.

23 British figures have been collated by J. M. Winter in 'Britain's "lost generation" of the First World War', published in *Population Studies*, *31*, 449-466. Around 85 percent of British troops served in the army, 10 percent in the navy, and 5 percent in the air-force.

   Approximate overall military figures for other countries include: Austria-Hungary, 1.2 million dead and 3.2 million wounded; France, 1.4 million dead and 4.0 million wounded; Germany, 1.9 million dead and 5.2 million wounded; Italy, 500,000 dead and 1.0 million wounded; Russia, 1.8 million dead and 5.0 million wounded; United States 115,000 dead and 200,000 wounded. Approximate numbers of deaths from Empire countries were: Australia 59,000, Canada 61,000, India 54,000, New Zealand 17,000, Newfoundland 1,000 and South Africa 7,000. Estimates vary slightly between some publications. Comprehensive overviews are at http://europeanhistory.about.com/cs/worldwar1/ a/blww1casualties.htm and http://www.1914-1918.net/faq.htm. Note that not all deaths were directly at the hands of the enemy. As in all wars, a proportion of deceased troops had been 'sick' rather than 'wounded'. Their illnesses and deaths could be due to the war but not identifiably caused by a physical assault by the enemy. The influenza epidemic of 1918 also killed many troops – possibly 10,000 from Britain.

24 Other British soldiers found guilty of serious offences were also sentenced to death by shooting, but most sentences were later reduced to a period of imprisonment. The French and Italian armies each executed around 700 soldiers between 1914 and 1918, but the German total is thought to have been less than fifty.

25 Details are provided at www.chrishobbs.com/sheffieldsoldiersfww.htm. All these executions took place in France or Belgium. Four of the seven were as late as 1918, despite increased recognition by then of emotional pressures in the front line.

26 Around 850,000 troops subsequently received disability pensions, but in addition an unknown number of non-pensioned men were also impaired. Of those receiving disability pensions, almost 40 percent had amputations or serious wounds and nearly 10 percent had cardiac illness of some kind. Details are provided by T. J. Mitchell and G. M. Smith in *Medical Services, Casualties and Medical Statistics of the Great War* (originally 1931, republished by the Imperial War Museum in 1997).

27 A single pair of rats could produce more than 800 others in a year. Apart from the nastiness of their unavoidable presence (for example, crawling over sleeping soldiers), they carried fleas, which could cause serious bacterial infections. Soldiers' health in the trenches was threatened overall by an accumulation of stressors – rats, lice, cold, damp, gas, chemicals, inadequate diet, poor sleep, constant noise, and exposure to danger, death and mutilation.

28 The official *History of the Great War* makes it clear that just over half of the troops sent back to UK hospitals were classed as 'sick' rather than 'wounded'; see *Medical Services: General History*, volume 1, page 390 (London: HMSO, 1921). For those in hospitals near the front line, 'it is probable that in the war 50 percent of the admissions to hospital from troops in the field armies were attributable to lack of personal cleanliness and to vermin.' See page 387 of *Medical Services: Hygiene in the Great War*, volume 2 (London: HMSO, 1923).

29 Others have drawn attention to the heavy greatcoats and other clothing necessary to keep warm, especially when drenched in rain-water or soaked by snow.

30 The *History of the Great War: Medical Services* (London: HMSO, 1923) reports that 'after every one of the larger battles there occurred a rush of patients suffering from a psychoneurosis of one form or another [...] the maximum number of cases is related to periods of active fighting' (volume 1, page 15).

31 Books about shell-shock include Fiona Reid's *Broken Men: Shell Shock, Treatment and Recovery in Britain 1914-1930 (*London: Continuum, 2010) and Wendy Holden's *Shell Shock* (London: Channel Four Books, 1998). The 1922 *Report of the War Office Committee of Enquiry into 'Shell-Shock'* was republished by the Imperial War Museum in 2004. See also Jay Winter's Chapter 13 in volume 3 of *The Cambridge History of the Great War*, edited by him (Cambridge University Press, 2014).

32 In part, disagreements about numbers hinge on the threshold used for diagnosis: how severe must symptoms be before they are defined as 'shell-shock'? During the 1920s, the number of ex-servicemen receiving pensions for all psychological complaints was between 50,000 and 65,000, nearly 10 percent of all war pensions. (Figures vary between years and diagnostic definitions.) In addition, non-pensionable cases of emotional distress were no doubt also numerous.

33 See the *Sheffield Daily Telegraph* of 15 February 1916. For the information about George England we are indebted to Jonathan England.

34 See also http://www.britishpathe.com/gallery/war-animals, and http://archiver.rootsweb.ancestry.com/th/read/GREATWAR/2002-01/1011069963.

35 Of external debt at the war's end, around £1,200 million was owed in the US and Canada, and about £200 million in other empire countries. Further details are available in Hew Strachan's *Financing the First World War*, published by Oxford University Press in 2004.

36 Different indicators of change in the value of money provide different estimates of its decline (see for instance www.measuringworth.com). For example, the retail price index (RPI) covers only goods and services purchased by individual citizens, whereas figures for the gross domestic product (GDP) extend to everything produced in the country. The two indexes are appropriate for different items and comparisons.

Furthermore, although government-cited expenditure figures are available for the war years, these exclude the many subsequent costs – lost company production, property rebuilding, invalidity pensions and so on, as well as colossal post-war debt repayments.

Chapter Two: What sort of a place was Britain?
37 Edward was noted for his love of parties, entertaining, gambling and horse-racing, and his several extra-marital affairs were reported with enthusiasm by the popular press. Some critics, drawing on a predecessor's label as 'Edward the Confessor' chose to refer to him as 'Edward the Caresser'. Others noted his 'passions for girls, gambling and gluttony'.
38 In that year, Wesley College (in Glossop Road) and Sheffield Grammar School (on Ecclesall Road) were merged and given the new name of 'King Edward VII School'. The combined school remained on the Glossop Road site.
39 The Rivelin Valley institution treated young people with tuberculosis, rickets, poliomyelitis and other physical problems until 1948, when it became the King Edward VII Orthopaedic Hospital within the new National Health Service. It closed in 1992, and was later converted into residential apartments.
40 Profits from Empire Day ticket sales were passed to children's charities. The history of the day has been reviewed by Jim English in 'Empire Day in Britain, 1904-1958' in *The Historical Journal*, 2006, *49*, 247-276. Several programmes of the city's early pageants are held by Sheffield Local Studies Library.
41 The 1911 census revealed a national population of around 45,000,000 people – around 22,000,000 males and 23,000,000 females.
42 By the end of the previous century, women householders and wives of householders had been given the vote in *local* elections.
43 Hunger strikes in prison were made legal by the Prisoners (Temporary Discharge for Ill-Health) Act of April 1913, popularly known as the 'Cat and Mouse Act'. Hunger-striking prisoners had previously been force-fed when they became extremely weak, but after the Act they were released and remained liable to re-arrest when healthy. Re-imprisonments and negative press publicity were accompanied by a growing opposition to the procedure.
44 Details of Suffragette campaigns in Sheffield are in Chapter Ten of *Rebel Girls* by Jill Liddington (London: Virago, 2006) and Chapter Nine of *Sheffield Troublemakers* by David Price (Stroud: Phillimore, 2008).
45 The 1918 Representation of the People Act gave the parliamentary vote to all men over 21 and to women over 30. Later, in 1928, women aged between 21 and 30 were also enfranchised. Some plural voting (in which an elector was able to vote more than once) continued until 1948.
46 The Labour Representation Committee had been established in 1900 to co-ordinate the efforts of several worker-supporting groups. It was renamed the

Labour Party after the 1906 general election, when twenty-nine Labour members of parliament were elected. In 1910, that number was forty.

47 See, for instance, Simon Fowler's *Workhouse* published by the National Archives in 2007, *The Workhouse Encyclopedia* by Peter Higginbottom (History Press, 2012) and *The Victorian Workhouse* by Trevor May (Shire Publications, 2009). Websites include www.workhouses.org.uk and www.institutions.org.uk.

48 Contemporary documents about these Acts can be found at http://www.pension100.co.uk/historyofpensions/timeline.htm. Historical developments are described at www.pensionsarchive.org.uk/74.

49 The government proposed that the new tax increases should mainly target more wealthy individuals, for example through duties on land and a new 'super tax' for the very rich. In the pre-war period income tax was paid by only around 10 percent of working people, but everyone paid indirect taxes, such as excise duty on alcohol and tobacco. These were also increased in the 1909 budget.

50 These conflicts between the House of Commons and the House of Lords led to the government introducing a new Parliament Act, which was eventually accepted by the Lords and became law in 1911. The Lords' power to veto proposals from the Commons was removed. Instead, they could merely refer back for further consideration proposals of which they disapproved.

51 In this period the British Medical Association analyzed a large number of patent medicines, concluding that many were harmless but a waste of money and others were potentially damaging. Generally, medical advertisements were 'the most fraudulent quackery'. The Association's reports, in 1909 and 1912, are available for on-line reading at http://openlibrary.org/books/OL21854495M/secret_remedies and http://openlibrary.org/books/OL7132864M/more_secret_remedies.

52 If the navy were defeated, Britain would lose command of the seas and thus the ability to ensure imports of food and trade with other countries. In those circumstances, even a large army may be inadequate to avoid defeat.

Chapter Three: Sheffield before the war

53 See pages 6 and 7 of Stewart Dalton's *Crashing Steel, A Personal View* (Barnsley: Wharncliffe Publishing, 1999). Sylvia Pybus has reviewed Vulcan's place in the city in *Vulcan: From Mount Olympus to Sheffield*, published by Aetna Enterprises in Sheffield in 1997. This is available at 398.2S in the city's Local Studies Library.

54 For example, the 1914 *Sheffield Year Book* reported for the previous year 'huge contracts in connection with new battleships' and described how 12-inch shells made by the Hadfield Steel Company had met the highest requirements of the American Naval Department.

55 By 1914 the building was already too small for the city's administration. It was designed for 220 staff but by then held around 500. Extension work started in 1914.

56 The current population, after six more boundary changes, is around 553,000.

57 These houses have been described by Rupert Hebblethwaite in *Architectural History*, 1987, *30*, 143-161. That article ('The municipal housing programme in Sheffield before 1914') is available in Sheffield Local Studies Library at reference 331.833S.

58 The national Labour Party developed from a Labour Representation Committee formed by members of several trade unions in 1900. Sheffield's own Labour Representation Committee was created in 1903, and by 1908 a wide range of local Labour organizations came together as Sheffield Trades and Labour Council, which combined trade union branches and Labour Party groups.

59 These 'elder statesmen' were appointed for six years on the basis of their distinguished service as councillors. Appointments were made in proportion to council membership, and in 1914 were: Conservative eight, Liberal seven, and Liberal-Labour one.

60 In addition, parts of the city were within two neighbouring constituencies.

61 The 1884 Representation of the People Act restricted parliamentary voting to adult males who either owned property valued at £10 or more or paid annual rent at that level. In 1914 this covered around half the country's men and no women. However, women were allowed to vote in *local* elections on terms similar to men. At the outset of war, around 75,000 Sheffielders were eligible to vote in parliamentary elections and approximately 100,000 in local government elections.

62 It is perhaps no surprise that the presidents of the two last-mentioned societies were respectively Mrs Letitia Fisher (wife of the vice-chancellor of the university) and the Duke of Norfolk (hereditary lord of the manor).

63 The *Telegraph* (founded in 1855) is now published once a week as the *Sheffield Telegraph*, and the *Star* continues as a daily morning paper. The *Sheffield Independent* (founded in 1819 and as a daily paper in 1861) ceased publication in 1937. The short-lived *Sheffield Guardian* described itself as 'a weekly journal for the assertion of the rights of labour and the promotion of socialism'.

64 Some historical details have been brought together by Chris Hobbs at http://www.chrishobbs.com/sheffield/stpaulschurchsheffield.htm.

65 Developments in Sheffield have been detailed by E. R. Wickham in *Church and People in an Industrial City* (London: Lutterworth Press, 1957).

66 Granite setts were noisy and sometimes slippery for horses and motor vehicles. They were far from universally popular. The Sheffield Street Pitching Society was formed in 1893 to 'resist the indiscriminate use of granite and to generally improve the methods of paving' (i.e., road-surfacing).

67 For an account up to nationalization in 1949, see D. E. Roberts, *The Sheffield Gas Undertaking* (Leicester: East Midland Gas, c1979).

68 Electricity power stations were sited at Kelham Island, Neepsend and Sheaf Street.

69 In 1914, Sheffield had around 280 covered double-deck trams and about fifty single-deckers. A detailed historical review has been provided by Charles C. Hall in *Sheffield Transport* (Glossop: The Transport Publishing Company, 1977), and other accounts include *Sheffield Trams Remembered* by Graham Hague and Howard Turner (Sheffield: Sheaf Publishing, 1987) and *The Tramway Era in Sheffield* published by Sheffield Transport Committee in 1960 to mark the final closure of the system.

70 Other early bus routes were to Stocksbridge, Totley, Upper Heeley, Upperthorpe, Wincobank and along the new Rivelin Valley Road (opened in 1907).

71 A comprehensive account has been provided by Stephen Myers in *Cars from Sheffield* (Sheffield City Libraries, 1986). Simplex models are described at

http://www.uniquecarsandparts.com.au/lost_marques_sheffield_simplex.htm. See also www.wincocars.co.uk for information about Stringer and Company, and Chapter Four of Tony Vernon's *Yorkshire Engine Company* (Stroud: History Press, 2008) for that firm's car-making.

72 Unfortunately, early local records are no longer available. Drivers had to be older than 17, but there was no driving test. An annual driving licence had to be purchased and vehicle duty was payable each year. Cars were expensive to buy and maintain, and their maximum speed was restricted to 20mph, or 10mph in some areas. They had to display number plates, with Sheffield-registered cars being identified as 'W', Rotherham as 'ET', and Derbyshire as 'R'. Petrol was bought in cans (usually containing 2 gallons) before petrol stations as we know them were gradually introduced after about 1915.

73 Collieries were all privately owned and in competition with each other. A few 'horse-gins' were still used in coal mines and elsewhere, and the gin stables for horses employed in the Duke of Norfolk's mines have since been converted to residential properties in the Park district of the city.

74 The number of vehicles in this 1910 census was only about 5 percent of the early 1960s number on those roads (see page 165 of H. Keeble Hawson's *Sheffield: The Growth of a City 1893-1926*. Sheffield: J. W. Northend, 1968). The 1910 number was perhaps around only around 1 percent of today's level.

75 The city's first motor sweeper was introduced in 1914 – replacing as many as six horses.

76 These pubs were respectively the Yellow Lion, the Victoria Hotel, the Old Carbrook Hall, the Fox and Duck, the Plough, the Hammer and Pincers, and the Rising Sun.

77 The 1914 Dore Ploughing Match included a 'local class, open to all residents within five miles of Dore Church, who have not ploughed in a champion class', and the 'local Dore and Totley class, open to all residents of the parishes of Dore and Totley'.

78 The city council employed smoke inspectors to record emissions of black smoke from industrial chimneys in terms of minutes of emission per hour. In the years preceding 1914, the inspectors had annually recorded the output from around 7,500 Sheffield chimneys, and black smoke emission had been reduced to an average of 2.6 minutes an hour. But around that all-chimney average many would have been producing black smoke for much longer periods.

79 Lacking a rear door or windows, back-to-back houses have relatively poor ventilation and were thought, therefore, to cause ill-health. Victorian law-makers had been very concerned to reduce diseases supposedly caused by impure air.

80 Sheffield Council had acquired its water-supply facilities from the privately owned Sheffield Water Company in 1888.

81 From 1912, the corporation offered to reimburse one-third of the cost of installing domestic water-pipes and an internal tap. One-third payments were also made for 'converting privies and ash-pits into water closets and dry ash-pits'.

82 For example, the corporation's pool in Attercliffe Road had forty-three slipper baths in addition to its swimming bath. In some cases both 'first class' and 'second-class' slipper baths were available, priced accordingly.

83 The country's telephone system had been nationalized (except in Hull) in 1913.

In 1914, Sheffield had about thirty telegraph offices, a main post office in Fitzalan Square, and around seventy-five sub-offices.

84 Nationally the telegram service continued until 1982, by which time personal telephones were widely available.

85 The Post Office gave permission for pictures to be included on cards in 1894, and in 1902 they allowed both the address and a message to be written on a single side, freeing the whole of the other side for a picture. Britain thus became the first country to introduce 'divided back' postcards with pictures on the front, and in the period up to and including World War One these were published and sent in huge numbers.

86 An illustrated account of these and other local shops has been provided by Ruth Harman in *Sheffield Shops and Shopping* (Stroud: Tempus Publishing, 2007).

87 These societies were independent within the national co-operative movement, which had been founded in 1844 to provide low-price unadulterated grocery items to workers and their families. Dealing in cash rather than through credit, societies within the movement returned to their members any profits made in terms of a 'dividend'. Centralized purchasing and quality control and the development of effective packaging (with associated simplification of salespeople's jobs) helped to boost sales.The two Sheffield societies came to an end in 2008.

88 The Royal Infirmary and the Royal Hospital both closed in 1978, when the Hallamshire Hospital was opened. The original Infirmary building (1795) remains today, as does one part of the Royal Hospital – the façade of the former Zion Chapel in Westfield Terrace. Accounts of their early years have been provided by J. D. Leader and S. Snell in *Sheffield General Infirmary* (Sheffield: William Townsend, 1897) and by E. F. Skinner in *A Short History of the Sheffield Royal Hospital 1832-1932* (Sheffield: Greenup and Thompson, 1932).

89 In addition, the privately financed George Woofindin Convalescent Home in Whiteley Wood advertised that 'charges are very moderate' for its approximately seventy rooms. The level of payment depended partly on a person's financial situation. Motor ambulances were by now available, but it was only in 1914 that the city's last two horse-drawn ambulances were disposed of.

90 The historical account by Helen Mathers and Tania McIntosh (*Born in Sheffield*, published by Wharncliffe Books in 2000) tells us that in this period 'the financial situation of the [Jessop] hospital was precarious […] By 1920 things had reached crisis point' (p. 51); there were 'too many patients, not enough income' (p. 54).

91 The Children's Hospital also had an East End Branch near the Wicker. Its first hundred years up to 1976 were in that year described by Peter Harvey in *Up the Hill to Western Bank*, published by the hospital.

92 The Institute had been financed by steel-maker William Edgar Allen (1837-1915) in 1911 'for the benefit chiefly of the male and female wage-earning classes, to help them regain the use of their limbs after injury or illness'. By 1914, around 200 patients attended each day. It became part of the Hallamshire Hospital soon after that opened in 1978.

93 This had been founded as the Borough Hospital for Infectious Diseases in 1881. Its design and location in a built-up area were soon found unsuitable for the illnesses treated, for example contributing to the spread of smallpox through nearby houses. For that reason, and to cope with the rising number of cases,

Lodge Moor Hospital was built on the outer edge of the city in 1887.

94 Commonside Hospital was also known as Moor End Hospital. It is now a care home. A plaque on a gatepost of what was Crimicar Lane Hospital, near the top of the lane, indicates: 'These are the gates of the former Crimicar Lane Isolation Hospital, opened 1901, closed 1956.' Even beyond the middle of that century some Sheffielders described others as having 'a Crimicar Lane cough'.

95 The term 'asylum' was changed nationally to 'mental hospital' in 1920, but that formal change occurred only slowly in much everyday conversation. The South Yorkshire Asylum became Middlewood Hospital after formation of the National Health Service in 1948; some details are in F. T. Thorpe's *A History of Middlewood Psychiatric Hospital, 1872-1972*, published by the hospital in 1972. Middlewood was closed in 1998, giving rise to a residential development on the site, which retains the original building.

96 The Fir Vale hospital was sometimes referred to as 'Sheffield Union Hospital'. Aspects have been described by Lyn Howsam in *Memories of the Workhouse and Old Hospital at Fir Vale* (Sheffield: ALD, 2002). Margaret Drinkall's *Sheffield Workhouse* (Stroud: History Press, 2011) looks also at earlier institutions.

97 See *The Workhouse and the Hospital at Nether Edge* by Joan Flett, published by the Hospital's League of Friends in 1984. The eighteen Fulwood Cottage Homes were open from 1905 to 1960. The two Poor Law Unions – Sheffield and Ecclesall – amalgamated in 1925, and the Guardians' duties were subsequently taken over by the city council.

98 Other charities in 1914 Sheffield included the Aged Female Society, the Orphan Homes, Dr Barnado's Homes, the Country Homes Society (to provide holidays in the country), and a local branch of the National Society for the Prevention of Cruelty to Children.

99 During 1914, advertisements by Wilson Peck and Company of Leopold Street and Fargate promoted eighteen models of gramophone at prices from £3 10 0 (£3.50) to £50: 'a veritable home theatre […] everything in entertainment from Caruso to Lauder'.

100 The branch libraries were at Attercliffe, Brightside, Darnall, Highfield, Hillsborough, Park, Upperthorpe and Walkley. Evening reading rooms were at Brightside, Broomhill, Crookes, Hunter's Bar, Meersbrook, Ranmoor and Wincobank.

101 During the Great War the Temperance Hall served many purposes, and from 1918 it was used by the recently formed Comrades of the Great War. That group soon became part of the British Legion. The hall was taken over by the Sheffield Repertory Theatre in 1928 and was renamed as the Playhouse Theatre in 1938. After some rebuilding in 1953, this was closed in 1971 when the Crucible Theatre opened. The building was sold in 1973 and was demolished for the construction of commercial offices.

102 See W. S. Porter, *Sheffield Literary and Philosophical Society: A Centenary Retrospect 1822-1922* (Sheffield: J. W. Northend, 1922).

103 Presumably some of these were repeat users. Municipal bowling greens were provided in ten locations across the city. One Alderman claimed that their popularity was 'a great work for temperance', keeping people out of the pubs.

104 The lack of tarmacadam on country roads meant that drivers towards the rear of a convoy were sometimes blinded by the dust from earlier vehicles.

105 These were Crookes, Darnall, High Storrs, High Wincobank, Meersbrook, Middlewood Road, Norton Woodseats and Rivelin Valley.

106 The Albert Hall had 1,994 seats in its large hall, with space for more people in the balcony (230) and saloon (850). A separate small hall could accommodate a further 350.

107 See pages 459 and 460 of *The History of the City of Sheffield 1843-1993 (Society)*, edited by C. Binfield, D. Hey, R. Childs, D. Martin, R. Harper and G. Tweedale (Sheffield: Sheffield Academic Press, 1993). The quotation is from a chapter by E. D. Mackerness.

108 The city also had several smaller theatres, and entertainment was still provided by some public houses. The Alexandra Theatre (in Blonk Street) closed in 1914, and by then the Albert Hall (in Barker's Pool) was increasingly showing films rather than only presenting live performances. Historical details have been provided by Bryen Hillerby in *The Lost Theatres of Sheffield* (Barnsley: Wharncliffe Publishing, 1999) and by the Sheffield Theatre Group in *Georgian Theatre in Sheffield* (Sheffield: Pickard Communication, 2003).

109 In addition to many new buildings, several of the city's established halls (for instance the Central Hall in Norfolk Street) also became used mainly as cinemas. These developments have been reviewed by Clifford Shaw, on behalf of the Sheffield Cinema Society, in *Sheffield Cinemas* (Stroud: Tempus Publishing, 2001) and Clifford Shaw and Christopher Stacey in a chapter in *Aspects of Sheffield 2*, edited by Melvyn Jones (Barnsley: Wharncliffe Publishing, 1999).

110 The Jungle was acquired by the city council in July 1914 as a garage for its expanding fleet of motor-buses, but after war commenced it was instead made available for various military uses – as a recruiting office, a base for volunteer defence workers, a location for several forms of training. From late-1916 the council took steps to convert the building into a bus garage, and in later years it served as a store for scrap metal. It was demolished in 1970. Activities at the Jungle have been investigated and described by the National Fairground Archive at Sheffield University. Information and illustrations are at http://www.nfa.dept.shef.ac.uk/jungle/index.html, together with material about other animal shows in the period.

Chapter Four: Autumn 1914: British recruits and Belgian refugees

111 As well as books already mentioned, Sheffield City Council has published useful guides for investigating Sheffield in this period. These are listed at www.sheffield.gov.uk/libraries/archives-and-local-studies/research-guides/world-war-one.html.

112 This was the first of many national controls introduced throughout the war. Each railway company was guaranteed the same level of profits as in 1913, and the newly-formed Railway Executive Committee mainly comprised managers from within the companies.

113 More than 80 percent of the gold coins in circulation were returned to the Bank of England in this way. The country had traditionally based its finances on the Gold Standard, such that the amount of cash in circulation had to be backed up by available gold to an equivalent value. The Currency and Bank Notes Act of 6 August 1914 loosened that restriction so that a larger value of money could be issued.

114 The unfolding of military activities was likely to increase the demand for newspapers, and already by 8 August 1914 the *Sheffield Daily Independent* was forced to reduce its number of pages, blaming that on restricted paper supplies and increased readership. The local morning papers emphasized prominently that their news about the war was more up-to-date than in the national papers, because they went to press several hours later.

115 These remained in place for approximately a year. Whenever air-raids were threatened, each site was guarded by nominated drivers who ensured that no lights were used on incoming vehicles. See page 201 of H. Keeble Hawson, *Sheffield: The Growth of a City 1893-1926* (Sheffield: Northend, 1968) and pages 50 and 141 of Stewart Dalton's *Sheffield: Armourer to the Empire* (Barnsley: Wharncliffe Books, 2004). The barrier locations are listed in the latter book and in Sheffield City Police's 1916 document *Defence of the City against Hostile Aircraft* (Sheffield Archives reference SY295/1/2/5).

116 Harris Leon Brown (originally Braun) was an immigrant from Poland who was naturalized in 1900. He was prominent in Sheffield's Jewish community.

117 Most of these were short silent films provided by the government to cinemas around the country. They were extremely limited by today's standards. For example, we are nowadays unlikely to agree with the *Sheffield Independent*'s 'deeply interesting' label for a 'view of a German warship passing along the Kiel Canal' or 'pictures of Lord Roberts reviewing the London recruits'.

118 'Service' battalions were raised only for service in the war, to be called on when needed. They were allocated to a local county regiment.

119 Sheffield was not alone in this development. During the period some fifty Pals units were formed around the country. The estimated number varies, depending on which definition is used.

120 Consistent with the original thinking, the university's Officer Training Corps continued to be a primary route into the battalion.

121 This large building was demolished in 1964 when new roads were created at the bottom of Commercial Street.

122 Construction at Redmires was largely undertaken by city council contractors, with building costs later reimbursed by the War Office. Activities at the camp have been illustrated at www.pals.org.uk/sheffield/redmires.pdf, and later occupants included units of the Sherwood Foresters and Royal Engineers. Nearby for at least part of the war was a small military airfield.

123 A detailed history of the formation and operation of the unit has been provided by Ralph Gibson and Paul Oldfield in *Sheffield City Battalion*, published by Pen and Sword Books (Barnsley, 2010). The battalion was disbanded in 1918. See also www.pals.org.uk/sheffield. Overall, about 3,000 men served in the battalion, around 6 percent of the *c*52,000 Sheffield troops of all kinds.

124 For a period the recruiting office in St George's Terrace was also open on Sundays for 'those who desire to enlist without having to lose a day's work'. In addition to the main office, temporary or long-term recruiting centres were at 429 Attercliffe Road (the Vestry Hall), 534 Brightside, 609 London Road, and in East Parade. From early September 1914 the principal recruiting office was augmented by the Jungle, a large building at the bottom of Hawley Street, which was originally a roller-skating rink and had recently been used for a menagerie and

similar activities (see www.nfa.dept.shef.ac.uk/jungle/index.html). Recruiting also took place from time to time in large firms, and individual regiments accepted recruits in their own barracks or at other locations. For example, the local headquarters of the Royal Army Medical Corps was in Gell Street.

125 Standards were later adjusted slightly to increase the acceptance rate, with some variation between different branches. Men from the working-class were particularly likely to be unfit, with up to 30 percent judged unsuitable for active service. At this stage, medical examinations at a recruiting centre were conducted by local doctors on a part-time (paid) basis.

126 Agreement about price was not always easily reached. For instance, on 30 October 1914 the Sheffield and Ecclesall Co-operative Society claimed in Sheffield County Court against the War Office for £80 considered to have been underpaid for fourteen horses requisitioned by the army.

127 In addition to this local activity, a National Relief Fund sponsored by the Prince of Wales received donations from across the country, with contributions from Sheffield also being channelled through the Town Hall. Amounts received by both relief funds were regularly listed in local newspapers, citing each donor and the precise amount provided.

128 For instance, a letter to the *Sheffield Daily Independent* on 22 August 1914 from a hardware retailer in the city was concerned about the problems caused by customers who had previously required him to stock up with German goods but who now would not buy them.

129 On a national level, the January 1915 general meeting of Carreras Limited ('an entirely British firm' in Bristol) was told that 'many millions of cigarettes and many thousands of pounds of tobacco had been sent to our gallant soldiers and sailors'. Furthermore, in order to 'cement the bond between the Allies long after the war is over', all packets of Black Cat cigarettes now sent to the forces and to the Allies 'enclosed a small English-French dictionary of 600 words in common and military use'.

130 Atrocity stories were usually unverified, and it has since become clear that many were exaggerated or fabricated. See for instance *Keep the Home Fires Burning* by Cate Haste (London: Allen Lane, 1977).

131 Speaking at the end of August 1914, the president of the football league's management committee had no doubts. 'Any national sport which can minimise the grief, help the nation to bear its sorrows, relieve the oppression of continuous strain, and save the people at home from panic and undue depression is a great national asset, which can render lasting service to the people.' 'In so far as [people's] minds may be temporarily directed from the horrors of war and the intense strain of days and weeks of almost unrestricted fighting much will be done to give them fresh heart, fresh hopes, and a renewed vitality for work before them.'

132 Developments for the country as a whole have been outlined in the *Times History of the War* (see Chapter 78 in Part 51, volume 4, 10 August 1915). This is available in Sheffield Central Library. A general account has also been provided in pages 217 to 226 of David Bilton's *The Home Front in the Great War* (Barnsley: Pen and Sword Books, 2003). Events in Sheffield have been described by Diana Gascoyne in 'Belgian refugees in Sheffield in the First World War', pages 51 to 56 of the *Sheffield History Reporter Annual*, 1998.

133 Like other cities, Sheffield had part-time consuls or vice-consuls working to represent a foreign country's citizens and to provide additional links between the city and that country. In 1911, senior businessmen in the city represented twenty different countries around the world. That remained the case during the war years when a German consular service was provided by the United States consul in Sheffield. In addition to his Belgian role, Arthur Balfour was also Vice-Consul to Denmark.

134 The 'lecturette' (illustrated with lantern slides) was entitled 'The brave land of Belgium', and the concert included musical items and a performance by the Ranfall Pierrot Troupe. (Ranfall – in Ranmoor Park Road – was the home of Walter Walsh, who was treasurer of the Belgian Refugee Fund.) In addition, the Reverend E. Callebert had composed a patriotic song entitled 'Belgium', which he performed to great approval on several occasions.

135 Wounded Belgian soldiers had reached the city's military hospitals a few days earlier. Those were placed in one of the units of the newly formed Third Northern General Hospital.

136 For instance, Hill Turrets, at the bottom of Bents Road, was borrowed from executors of the late John Turton to accommodate around a dozen injured Belgian soldiers.

137 For example, during November 1914 donations of around £115 in coins included money raised from the sale of 'badges', 'colours', 'gollywogs', 'hair slides', 'mascots', 'painted cards' and 'sand drying'. Many gifts came from the children of particular schools, including from those who offered their personal savings or the contents of their money boxes. For the District War Refugees Committee as a whole, a long list of donations received was published in local papers every week, identifying individuals, companies, groups of workmen and the proceeds from particular events.

138 King Edward VII School waived fees and provided books for seven Belgian boys. The school's pupils (and no doubt their parents) undertook to assist with clothing and other needs. Other schools and colleges also helped in these ways.

139 In November 1915 it was agreed that each month twenty Belgian soldiers should spend their leave in the city.

140 Arthur Balfour (1873-1957) was Acting Belgian consul until February 1915, when he became consul after the death of the previous incumbent. He was managing director of Seebohm and Dieckstahl, which changed its name to Arthur Balfour and Company in 1915. He had been master cutler in 1911, and during the war was also active in the Sheffield Committee for Munitions of War and in several government roles, as well as the city's National Insurance Committee. In later years he served as president of the Association of British Chambers of Commerce (1923 and 1924) and of the British Council (from 1947 to 1950), and was chairman of the advisory council for Scientific and Industrial Research from 1937 to 1957. He was knighted in 1923, created a baronet in 1929, and became Lord Riverdale in 1935. Some details of his life in Sheffield have been described in his son's autobiography, *Nine Lives in One* by Lord Riverdale of Sheffield (Sheffield: Sheffield Academic Press, 1998).

141 Documents from the chapel's Belgian Refugees' Fund are held by Sheffield Archives under the general reference UCR216.

142 The end of the war is sometimes indicated as 1919 rather than 1918, since a peace treaty was not signed until 28 June 1919. An armistice, as signed on 11 November 1918, provides an agreed pause in fighting but does not formally end a war.

Chapter Five: Born in Germany, living in Sheffield

143 In addition, around 14,000 from Britain's other main enemy, Austria-Hungary, were also in the country.

144 Three years later, the British Nationality and Status of Aliens Act of 1914 (introduced just before the war) confirmed two kinds of British citizen – individuals who had been born within the British Empire or of a British father, and those who had been granted certificates of naturalization. To gain that certificate applicants had to have been resident within the empire for at least five years and intend to continue to do so. They had to be judged 'of good character' and have a good knowledge of the English language. References from respectable citizens had to be obtained, and these were sometimes checked by the local chief constable after a request from the Home Office. For example, Nils Johan Anders Soderberg, a steel manufacturer's clerk living in Psalter Lane (here known as Andrew Soderberg), applied for naturalization in May 1915. He was Swedish but had been born in Hamburg, Germany. The city's chief constable was asked to carry out checks on his application, including ascertaining 'his sentiments in relation to the war'.

   In all cases, a naturalization fee of £2 was required and an oath of allegiance to this country was taken. Married women acquired the nationality of their husband, and British wives of aliens who became widows remained aliens unless they obtained a 're-admission' certificate to become British citizens again. For example, in October 1917 Clara Helen Schuhmetzler, a British-born widow living in Sheffield's Chantrey Road, was granted a re-admission certificate. Presumably her German husband had died.

145 Britain's foreign-born population, of course, included people from a range of other countries. The 1911 census indicated that the total number of foreigners in Sheffield was close to 2,500, with almost 600 from Russia and 450 from the US. Some of the American-born Sheffielders were children of British parents who were temporarily in that country.

146 This material is based on a longer account by Roy Koerner, to whom thanks are due, including for publication permission. Related information can be found in http://boards.ancestry.com/topics.immigration.europe.gernamemig/147/mb.ashx. The local situation has been reviewed by Gerald Newton in 'Germans in Sheffield 1817-1918', published in *German Life and Letters,* 1993, *46*, 82-101.

147 During World War Two some members of the Funk family changed their surname to 'Ford' or 'Fenton'. However, a butcher in Middlewood Road is still called 'Funk'.

148 These national themes have been covered in more detail by Panikos Panayi in *The Enemy in Our Midst: Germans in Britain during the First World War* (New York and Oxford: Berg, 1991). See also that author's chapter 'An intolerant act by an intolerant society' in the book edited by David Cesarani and Tony Cushner *The Internment of Aliens in Twentieth-Century Britain* (London: Frank Cass, 1993),

and Chapter Six in Cate Haste's *Keep the Home Fires Burning* (London: Allen Lane, 1977).

149 Sheffield was included as one target for the imaginary attack. The novel was initially serialized in the *Daily Mail*, and care was taken to mention a large number of towns and cities in order to boost sales.

150 In subsequently proposing a new Aliens Restriction Act in April 1919, the Home Secretary described the way government policies had been developed from August 1914: 'At that time we had not had experience of war so near our own shores, we had not had experience of the imminent danger of alien invasion, and we had not had experience of the danger of having enemies in our midst […] All of that was new to us, and largely, therefore, we had to move in an experimental way.'

151 In addition to Germans, aliens submitting themselves for registration in Sheffield at this time included Austrian, Belgian, French, Italian and Russian citizens.

152 Many restrictions of this kind were also applied to British subjects, under the Defence of the Realm Act (DORA).

153 Its Current Topics section of 19 October 1914 included: 'Knowing what we do about German cunning, we should not be at all surprised if many of the Germans were paid agents, waiting for some signal to damage railways or cut telegraph wires'.

154 Ferdinand Gebhardt's wife and children were born in Sheffield. He had not been naturalized by the date of the 1911 census.

155 The label 'Gotha' was particularly hated at the time, as Germany had just unleashed new bombers in punishing daylight raids on London. Their name? Gotha.

156 Timing of the arrests were not a complete surprise. For example, the *Sheffield Daily Telegraph* on the morning of 22 October had announced that they would take place that day. A small number of Sheffield men, thought to be particularly dangerous, were apparently already in custody from previous arrests, but details have not been located.

157 Releases were authorized by the War Office after recommendations from local chief constables. Among the factors considered were a person's length of residence in Britain, family connections, apparent sympathies, and the likely impact of his internment on local employment. In addition, written references were obtained from established members of the community.

158 Adolf and Emile changed their name from Viener to Viner in November 1925. Willie (and possibly his brothers) was naturalized in April 1924. Their company's manufacture of helmets and other war items is described in *Sheffield's Great War and Beyond*, by Peter Warr (Pen and Sword Books, 2015).

159 The German chemical industry in 1914 was larger and more sophisticated than in Britain, and was soon able to manufacture sufficient gas and the means of its projection. The French and British armies wanted to retaliate, but it took more than a year before they were technically able to do so.

160 For example, the *Sheffield Daily Telegraph* of 6 May 1915 contained this description by an officer: 'We have a lot of men who have been gassed in our hospitals. Their moans are awful, and they sit up swaying about, fighting and

gasping for breath. Their faces and bodies are a muddy purple black, their eyes glazed, and foam comes from their mouths. Their lungs are turned to liquid, and the doctors say they have the appearance of men on the point of death from drowning [...] Will this convince people at home of what the Germans are capable of? No law or man will hold them in check.'

161 John Brown and Company had produced many of the ship's components in Sheffield and had constructed it (1907) in their Clydeside yard, so the sinking had a special resonance in the city.

162 Some of the rioters expanded their violence to attack and loot non-German property. Sometimes a shop's German name may have provoked attack, even though the owner was in fact a British subject.

163 Sheffield street directories of the time include more than 100 pork butchers with names suggesting possible German links. Details of the city's riots can be found in Gerald Newton's article 'Germans in Sheffield 1817-1918' in *German Life and Letters*, 1993, *46*, 82-101, and in his typewritten *German Studies at the University of Sheffield*, published by the Department of Germanic Studies at the university in 1988. See also 'Germans in Sheffield, 1914-1918: A national story on a local scale' by Panikos Panayi in *The History of the City of Sheffield 1843-1993*, edited by Clyde Binfield, Richard Childs, Roger Harper, David Hey, David Martin and Geoffrey Tweedale (Sheffield: Sheffield Academic Press, 1993).

A more general account is in Chapter Eight of Panikos Panayi's *The Enemy in Our Midst* (New York and Oxford: Berg, 1991), and national issues are presented in detail in his *Prisoners of Britain* (Manchester: Manchester University Press, 2012).

164 It is not clear how widespread was the hostile activity. Although some men were involved, the main Sheffield rioters were apparently women or girls. Local police estimated the number as around 5,000, but some of 'the crowds that collected were obviously animated only by curiosity, and did not manifest any particularly menacing disposition' (*Sheffield Daily Telegraph*, 14 May 1915). Sheffield press reports at the end of May 1915 describe how forty rioters were fined (twenty-nine women and a 17-year-old girl, and eight men and two boys above 16). Others may have been charged on different occasions. Separate reports indicate also the presence of children during the riots, but those would not have been prosecuted in an adult court. Sheffield insurance brokers soon advertised that their War Risk Policy 'covers damage from riots'.

In a different episode, local papers reported an 'anti-German strike' in 'an East End firm' on 11 May. This involved about fifty men and 'there is every probability of the trouble being speedily settled'. No other accounts of anti-German industrial action in Sheffield have been located, and this was probably a small localized incident rather than a widespread campaign.

165 For example, John Funk, a pork butcher in his (naturalized) father's shop in Harvest Lane served in the Machine Gun Corps, one of Sir Joseph Jonas's sons was an officer in the Royal Engineers, and William Zeiher, a pork butcher in the Wicker whose father had also been naturalized, was in a Labour Battalion of the Middlesex Regiment. Many other British-born sons of German fathers served as non-combatants in labour units of that regiment. Some earlier volunteer recruits with German fathers also became transferred to the Middlesex Regiment from

other parts of the army, although many continued in fighting regiments. See for instance www.1914-1918.net/msex_aliens.html.

166 The *Sheffield Daily Telegraph* of 26 June 1915 wrote: '[T]he Detective Department of the Sheffield police were busy yesterday rounding up a number of non-naturalized German residents in the city. Later in the day they were taken to the station and entrained for an internment camp. The aliens have been living in the city for some considerable time, and many of them are well known. The police had no difficulty, and their work was carried out in a quiet and uninterrupted manner.'

Few details of individual internees from Sheffield are available. A parliamentary question in July 1916 indicated that E. Gerbel Strover, previously a manager at the British Abrasive Wheel company at Tinsley, had been interned somewhere.

167 Departments administering different parts of the internment process included the War Office, the Home Office, the Foreign Office, the Admiralty, the Board of Trade, the Post Office, the Treasury, the Police Service and Military Intelligence.

168 It appears that, nationally, more than twenty-five sites were used for civilian internment, some for very short periods or for particular purposes only. Locally, a number of internees were placed for a period in Hillsborough Barracks, but no additional Sheffield buildings were taken over.

169 Internment camp guards were usually older or less-fit men serving in what became the Royal Defence Corps in either 1916 or 1917 (reports vary).

170 More details can be found in the illustrated book *Living with the Wire*, edited by Yvonne Cresswell and published in 1994 by the Manx National Museum; www.gov.im.mnh. See also Panikos Panayi's *The Enemy in our Midst* (New York and Oxford: Berg, 1991) and *Prisoners of Britain* (Manchester: Manchester University Press, 2012), and John Yarnall's *Barbed Wire Disease* (Stroud: History Press, 2011). Some information was published locally on page 5 of the *Sheffield Daily Independent* on 19 July 1916.

171 Three of the men sent to Sheffield were Austrian (Johann Bartuschek, Karl Gebauer and Max Rotschwar) and one (Oscar Barthel) was German. This information was kindly provided by the Manx National Museum.

172 In 1919 Julius Freund became a professor in Berlin.

173 Those figures include 301 and eighty-four in 1911 and 1921 respectively who were truly 'aliens' – after omitting people born in Germany who were British through their father's nationality (thirty-six and twelve respectively) or because they had subsequently been naturalized (fifty-three and sixty-eight). In addition, the total numbers of Austrians in the city were fifty-one and twenty in 1911 and 1921 respectively.

174 For example, during June 1915 a total of 123 certificates of British naturalization were granted nationally, including three for Sheffield residents.

175 Advertisements for a share offer in May 1917 emphasized that 'the Treasury […] raises no objection', and that 'the special provisions of the Board of Trade relating to the nationality of silversmiths are incorporated in the Memorandum of Association'.

176 A general account of legal and other national measures against German business interests is in Chapter Five of Panikos Panayi's *The Enemy in Our Midst* (New York and Oxford: Berg 1991).

177 During the anti-German riots in May 1915, a performance at the Sheffield
Hippodrome was delayed by a threatened protest directed at Mr Hahn, the
conductor of the orchestra. The manager succeeded in preventing trouble through
a speech pointing out that Mr Hahn was the British-born son of a German who
had long lived in Britain and had become naturalized as British.

178 At the outbreak of war he was Acting Austrian Consul in Sheffield. His
activities have been described by Geoffrey Tweedale in 'The razor blade king of
Sheffield: The forgotten career of Paul Kuehnrich', *Transactions of the Hunter
Archaeological Society*, 1991, *16*, 39-51. See also several chapters of that author's
Steel City (Oxford: Clarendon Press, 1995) and information at
http://www.chrishobbs.com/sheffield3/paulkuehnrich.htm.

179 At different times during 1915, he was suggested in parliament to be supporting
an interned alien and was named as a potential danger to the country.

180 In this period many hundreds of other Sheffielders were similarly fined for
black-out offences. (Names were published in the press, no doubt to encourage
others to obey the law.) Paul Kuehnrich and his family were not at all unusual in
this respect.

181 Among his innovations was a tungsten high-speed steel named 'Cobaltcrom'.
This was widely advertized in 1917 and 1918 as 'the New Steel' – 'a wonder of
simplicity, utility and economy' with a range of wartime uses. Produced and
marketed through his two companies, Darwin and Milner and Sybry, Searles Ltd,
by mid-1918 this was allegedly 'in regular use in more than 1,000 works in Great
Britain'.

182 After the war Paul Kuehnrich's business flourished and he purchased several
Sheffield companies and (in 1924) the property of the Simplex Motor Works.
However, after about 1930 his financial situation became difficult. By 1932 his
interests were wound up and his assets (including his art collection) were
scheduled for sale. He did not live to see that day, instead committing suicide in
Holly Court on 28 April 1932.

183 Joseph Jonas's life and background has been described by Gerald Newton in the
chapter 'Sir Joseph Jonas of Bingen: Lord Mayor of Sheffield, University
benefactor, German spy, hidden Jew?' in the book edited by R. J. Kavanagh,
Mutual Exchanges, Sheffield-Münster Colloquium I (Frankfurt am Main: Peter
Lang, 1999). See also reports of his trial in N. R. Ballin's booklet (Note 186) and
at www.chrishobbs.com/sheffield/josephjonas.htm.

184 On the same day a 'statement and declaration' was published from his colleague
and fellow company-director C. A. Hahn: 'My home has been in Sheffield since
1872, in 1877 I was by my own request denationalised for the purpose of
emigrating to England, and soon after I was naturalised *[in 1884]*. My wife is a
daughter of Sheffield and my children were born here. My elder son joined the
British Army about seven years ago, and my younger son offered his service for
the British Medical Corps soon after the outbreak of war. I declare that, for loyalty
to the King and country of my adoption I and my family stand second to none,
and I wish to express – as I have to numerous friends – my indignation and
abhorrence of the inhuman acts committed by men of the German Army and
Navy.'

185 Complaints about the activities of apparent Germans were often confused and

inaccurate in terms of their actual nationality. For example, the minister of munitions was asked in parliament on 22 July 1918 to investigate 'unnaturalised enemy aliens in charge of controlled establishments', including Charles William Kayser, a director of Kayser, Ellison and Company of Carlisle Street East, Sheffield. In fact, Charles Kayser was born in Sheffield, his mother was also Yorkshire-born, and his father had been a British subject by naturalization since 1864. More generally, published reports and personal attitudes often confused Germans in Britain who were not naturalized with those who had taken out British citizenship.

186 Consistent with a general intertwining of the British and German steel industries before the war, the German (Paul von Gontard) was a customer of Vickers as well as a competitor. In addition, his German firm held a licence to produce the Vickers-Maxim gun, and a director of Vickers was also a director of von Gontard's company. In practice, the rifle planned to be produced by Vickers was never made, being replaced by a different one before the war started. See Neville Ballin's *For King or Kaiser? The Life of Sir Joseph Jonas* (privately printed in 1998), classified 345.0231S in Sheffield Local Studies Library.

187 His company continued to be the target of critical parliamentary attention. In August 1918, an MP known for strong anti-German views claimed that the quality of the company's air-frame steel was now inadequate; there should be 'a full independent inquiry […] into the transactions of this firm since the war began'. After investigating the situation, the Minister of Munitions replied that Jonas and Colver's products were as good as other companies' and that no inquiry was necessary.

188 Anti-German attitudes were sustained in many small ways. For example, training exercises by the Sheffield Volunteer Defence Corps were sometimes based on imaginary crises caused by non-interned Germans cutting local communication lines.

Chapter Six: 1915 and 1916: Adapting to war

189 Some politicians and parts of the press opposed the trend away from laissez-faire as a slide towards a hated German style of allegedly overbearing bureaucracy, which was said to hold German citizens in a state of servility.

190 Hours were further restricted on Sundays and for selling drink which was consumed off the premises.

191 The Football League declared that all players be classed as amateurs, and the still-active teams were organized into three regional divisions of the League – London, Midland and Lancashire. Sheffield United and Wednesday played in the Midland Section.

192 Across all the years of war, more than 550 men left the Tramways Department, around 400 went from the City Surveyor's, 220 from the Education Department, 200 from the Cleansing Department, and almost 400 from other departments. The council paid an allowance to dependants.

193 The number of Sheffield's panel doctors declined from 161 to 102 between 1913 and 1918, despite an increase of 30,000 in the number of insured persons.

194 The Press Bureau had other means of persuasion, such as in future depriving unco-operative newspapers of important news items. As well as focusing on the

British public, the bureau was greatly concerned to prevent sensitive information reaching the enemy.

195 The person writing as 'Eye-Witness' in Sheffield papers and across the nation was a senior establishment figure – Lieutenant-Colonel Sir Ernest Swinton.

196 During March 1915, the *Sheffield Daily Telegraph* requested details from its readers. 'We are anxious that those who suffer or die for their country should receive the fullest possible recognition […] The public ought to know who are the men who have made these greatest of all sacrifices for the common good.'

197 The first day of the Battle of the Somme was worse than any other day of war before or since, with around 59,000 British casualties of which 19,000 were killed. Among many published accounts is Martin Middlebrook's *The First Day of the Somme* (London: Allen Lane, 1971). Sheffield City Battalion suffered particularly badly with more than 500 deaths on that first day. The battle continued for another four months, creating in total more than 500,000 casualties.

198 In addition to men who were killed, wounded or missing, many were taken as prisoners-of-war – around 35,000 from Britain by the end of 1916.

199 Grammatical errors have been retained. The original hand-written page can be seen in one of the later entries at www.sheffieldhistory.co.uk/forums/index.php/topic/12967-great-war-letter/?hl=%2Bletter.

200 In addition, the lord mayor wrote to a number of grieving Sheffield families and a formal message was routinely sent on behalf of the king. At different times the parents of Arthur Greensmith received a typewritten indication from the lord mayor that the Red Cross had reported the death of their son 'fighting so gallantly for his King and Country', and also a brief note signed by David Lloyd George, then the secretary of state for war, reporting that 'The King commands me to assure you of the true sympathy of His Majesty and the Queen in your sorrow'.

201 One spectacular set of lies claimed in 1917 that Germany was converting the bodies of dead soldiers into lubricating oil, pig food and manure. Presented in a pamphlet and then elaborated in many news stories, this tale was not completely discredited until 1925.

202 Many books about civilian life in the Great War include brief sections on propaganda within a wider coverage. More extended accounts have been provided by Cate Haste in *Keep the Home Fires Burning* (London: Allen Lane, 1977), Tania Rose in *Aspects of Political Censorship 1914-1918* (University of Hull Press, 1995), and Michael Sanders and Philip Taylor in *British Propaganda During the First World War 1914-1918* (London: Macmillan, 1982).

203 In the first year of the war more than 2,000,000 copies of 110 different posters were issued; see page 734 in Trevor Wilson's, *The Myriad Faces of War* (Cambridge: Polity Press, 1986). Overall, government agencies published more than 50,000,000 copies of around 200 designs. Recruiting posters were co-ordinated by the Parliamentary Recruiting Committee under supervision from the War Office. Many examples can be viewed at http://pw20c.mcmaster.ca/case-study/british-first-world-war-recruiting-posters and at www.world-war-pictures.com/british-war-posters.htm.

204 In March 1918 the department became a fully-fledged Ministry of Information, led by Canadian newspaper owner Lord Beaverbrook.

205 A three-hour film entitled 'Britain Prepared', issued in late 1915, achieved a world-wide commercial distribution. And a real-time coverage (with some re-enactments) of fighting in the initial days of the Battle of the Somme made a huge impact. This was released in August 1916 and was seen by more than 20,000,000 British cinema-goers in its first six weeks, as well as being distributed internationally.

206 War-related exhibitions were held frequently in the Mappin Art Gallery. At different periods in 1915 and 1916 the gallery showed several sets of war paintings or drawings. In the summer of 1917, 126 paintings by Muirhead Bone were immensely popular, and subsequent exhibitions included war photographs and lithographs and a photographic exhibition with samples of women's war-work.

Private galleries in the city also provided exhibitions about the war. For instance, at the beginning of 1917 Sheffield's Church Street Galleries showed 'munition drawings' by Joseph Pennell, including some from the city.

(The *Sheffield Daily Independent* of 16 January was pleased that 'the smoke of Sheffield was often beautiful when seen with the sun shining on it'.) These drawings appeared in a 1917 book published by William Heinemann, which can be viewed online at http://www.archive.org/stream/josephpenne00penniala#page/n7/mode/2up.

207 For instance, bereaved relatives and others became increasingly convinced that the many fatalities and injuries should not be allowed to occur in vain. Victory was essential.

208 This was just after the Germans had introduced poison gas on the Western Front.

209 During 1915 and possibly later Mrs Pankhurst received government funding for her campaigning activities.

210 Several songs of the period can be listened to in original recordings at http://www.ww1photos.com/WW1MusicIndex.html.

211 The Derby Scheme divided the eligible male population into forty-six categories based on age and marital status, and men were encouraged to 'attest' for service by joining the Army Reserve. Call-up (if it came) would first take unmarried and younger men.

212 Subsequent Military Service Acts were introduced in April 1917, January 1918 and April 1918. The last of these extended the age-range for conscription from 17 up to (with some variations) 50. By then the need for more men was truly desperate.

213 A skilled fitter at Vickers' Brightside Works (Leonard Hargreaves) had recently been debadged, and thus had been conscripted into the army. In November 1916, Sheffield Engineers' Shop Stewards' Committee objected that the authorities had promised not to call up skilled men and were 'attacking our members for military service'. The committee demanded that Mr Hargreaves be released from the army. The request was not immediately granted, and tens of thousands of engineers in the city and around the country quickly came out on strike. The stoppage lasted only a few days.

It later emerged that one government department had in fact authorized an exemption badge for Leonard Hargreaves on 26 October, but that this decision had not yet been formalized in other sections. See page 35 of Part 1 of Volume 6 of the *History of the Ministry of Munitions* published by His Majesty's Stationery Office in 1922.

214 By now the recruiting office was located in the Corn Exchange, with additional offices in (for instance) the Town Hall, Attercliffe Vestry Hall, Edmund Road Drill Hall and the Jungle building. Administration was also carried out in Channing Hall, Surrey Street. The Corn Exchange in Sheaf Street had been completed in 1881 with a large central hall surrounded by offices and shops. It was damaged by fire in 1947 and was demolished in 1964.

215 A 1918 report refers to 'steam sirens and klaxon horns' at twenty-eight sites in the city, three of which had been added since the spring of 1916. They were at three power stations, fourteen factories, five police stations, two laundries and two hospitals, as well as at Nunnery Colliery and on the *Telegraph* building in High Street. Warning was provided by three minutes of triple blasts, and the 'danger past' signal was a continuous blast for one minute.

216 The following month's anxiety in one area of the city was illustrated in the October 1916 diary of Septimus Bennett: 'Practically all Hillsborough, Malin Bridge and Wadsley turned out at the sound of the first buzzer and flocked to Hillsborough Park and the countryside roundabout, some only half-dressed, some in their night-gowns, even children in arms and perambulators [...] where they spent half the night, not returning till the safety buzzer was sounded.' See pages 141-142 of *Septimus Bennett, Artist in Arms* by Martin Phillips and John Potter (Edinburgh: Pentland Press, 2001). Nationally, around 1,400 people were killed by air-raids during the war and about 2,000 were injured.

  Eric Hardcastle was a young child in Firth Park during the Great War, and later wrote: 'At the top of the road were Riley's Fields, and in the middle was a huge hollow. Whenever the sirens sounded we were all awakened from our sleep, wrapped in blankets, and taken to this hollow where we would stay until the "all clear" was sounded. Sometimes my father [a steel worker] was on night shift when this happened, so Mrs Gregory [next-door neighbour] used to carry me. The reason we slept in the hollow was to escape from shrapnel if a bomb should explode nearby.'

217 In April 1940 a letter to the *Sheffield Daily Telegraph* from an original member of the city's Anti-Aircraft Corps claimed that no defence was possible 'due to the action of the City Fathers in asking the works to put up a smoke screen from chimneys' through which nothing could be seen. At a time of heightened concern about air-raids the Corps would certainly have been on duty, contrary to a later suggestion that they were all attending a formal dinner.

218 Damage was caused primarily in Danville Street, Petre Street, Cossey Road, Corby Street and Princess Road. Detailed reports were not published until after wartime censorship had ended, and a comprehensive account appeared on pages 1 and 3 of the *Sheffield Daily Independent* of 3 December 1918. Information can also be found at www.chrishobbs.com/sheffieldsfirstraid1916.htm and www.brigantian.force9.co.uk/index.html. A summary is in pages 51 to 53 of Stewart Dalton's *Sheffield, Armourer to the British Empire* (Barnsley: Wharncliffe Books, 2004), and some oral (partly inaccurate) eye-witness recollections are at http://www.youtube.com/watch?v=tO2WMi-GdDs and http://www.youtube.com/watch?v=WDj4-lfulpI.

219 Britain also operated airships, primarily on reconnaissance work, but they were gradually replaced by aeroplanes. In addition to reconnaissance work, aircraft

were used for bombing and in attacks on enemy airships and planes. Aircrew were either in the Royal Naval Air Service (RNAS) or Royal Flying Corps (RFC), for navy and army use respectively, until those two were combined into the Royal Air Force (RAF) in April 1918.

Sheffield provided two aircraft landing sites. The racecourse next to Redmires army camp had been used before the war for display flights (including by two chimpanzee passengers advertising the Jungle menagerie in 1912), and this became a military airfield until around 1917. At Meadowhead, Coal Aston airfield was established by the RFC in 1915 and was used for training and regular flights before becoming a repair depot after Zeppelin threats had declined. Some details are in *From Bailey to Bailey: A Short History of Military Buildings in Sheffield*, written and published in 1998 by Stephen Johnson. Pre-war flights at Redmires are illustrated in www.nfa.dept.shef.ac.uk/jungle/index4d5.html. Both camps housed German prisoners-of-war later in the war.

220 See Table 14 (p. 390) in Volume 1 of the *History of Medical Services, General*, published in London by His Majesty's Stationery Office in 1921. In addition, almost 200,000 more arrived in UK in the two years after the war, almost all of whom were defined as 'sick' rather than 'wounded'.

221 Existing military hospitals were available in Aldershot, London, Netley, Woolwich and elsewhere, together with small hospitals in military garrisons, such as Sheffield's barracks at Hillsborough. These could handle problems occurring in peace-time, but now required reinforcement to cope with greatly increased numbers.

222 'Northern' refers to the army's Northern Command, not to the north of the city, and the Third Northern General Hospital covered an area outside as well as within Sheffield. The First, Second, Fourth and Fifth Northern General Hospitals were in Newcastle, Leeds, Lincoln and Leicester respectively.

223 For example, in 1914 the large volunteer-made Christmas cake for soldiers in the Royal Infirmary was topped with a model of the king and decorated in wholeheartedly patriotic fashion.

224 A list in www.scarletfinders.co.uk cites five additional small suppliers working in private Sheffield homes. These probably concentrated on bandages and other simple items. Their number presumably varied from year to year and may overall have been considerably greater than five.

225 It is probable that detailed plans had previously been drawn up. Premises taken over by the Third Northern General Hospital included residential hostels in the Ecclesall Road and Clarkehouse Road area. By 1916 the previous men's hostel in Southbourne Road had become home to around 100 sisters, nurses and VAD staff. The college's training work was at first continued in several locations – Carver Street Wesleyan School, the Technical School of Art, and the university's Applied Science Department – but later entirely in the university. *A History of the City of Sheffield Training College* by Roy Millington, published by the college in 1955, reports on page 53: '[T]he military authorities were quite ruthless when it came to turn the place into a hospital. In Collegiate Hall, cupboards, lockers and wardrobes were to be seen sliding and crashing down the staircases; soft furnishings were ripped down and anything considered useless was thrown out of the windows. Some furniture was placed in the grounds, where it either rotted or was stolen for firewood.'

A large collection of photographs about the Third Northern General Hospital is available in the Picture Sheffield web-site (http://picturesheffield.com). These come mainly from a set of originals held by Colonel Connell.

226 Arthur Connell (1872-1945) was born in Barbados but trained in London. In addition to his honorary work at the Royal Infirmary and his private medical practice, he was in 1914 a lecturer in surgery at Sheffield University and a territorial soldier. After the war he continued in those roles (becoming professor in 1919) until his retirement in 1931. Following his retirement, subscriptions from many Sheffielders were used to endow a bed in his name for free treatment in the Infirmary. Between November 1915 and May 1916 his sister Mary was also at the Third Northern General Hospital, serving as a sister in the Territorial Force Nursing Service.

227 Lieutenant-Colonel Sinclair-White took over as commandant from Arthur Connell in December 1917, after the latter moved elsewhere in Northern Command – probably to Lincoln – with the rank of full colonel.

228 For a period in 1917 three American military surgeons also worked in the hospital.

229 Photographs of the ward interiors were published in the *Sheffield Daily Independent* of 22 July 1916 and 22 August 1916 (page 5 in both cases).

230 Ambulance travel in the city during the war has been estimated to exceed 35,000 miles. Most vehicles (perhaps all) had been donated by the people of Sheffield. Difficulties occasionally arose, for example when two 17-year-old ambulance drivers were prosecuted in 1917 for repeatedly racing each other at speed through Sandygate.

231 In addition to other donations and bequests, beds could be endowed in these charity-dependent hospitals for general use or to provide for specified groups of patients. For example, in 1916 Lady Bingham financed two beds at the Royal Hospital in memory of her late husband. In 1917 the War Works Fund of William Cooke and Company paid £1,000 to the Royal Infirmary to endow a bed 'at the donor's nomination'. And in 1918 Hadfield's Managers' and Foremen's Fraternity endowed a bed for its members at the Royal Hospital.

232 The records of Winter Street Hospital are still available in the city's archives (reference NHS37/7/2), revealing that almost 2,000 patients were treated for a wide range of problems. Men suffered from wounds, fractures, shrapnel injuries, shell-shock, gas attacks, dysentery, measles or trench fever, and ear, nose, throat and eye problems were also common. As in other military hospitals, Winter Street patients were often explicitly defined as 'sick' rather than 'wounded'.

233 In October 1917, Sister Nellie Gregory of Ranmoor School hospital married at Ecclesfield one of her previous military patients – James Sutherland from Wick in Scotland. Those two may be near the right-hand end of the back row in the accompanying photograph.

234 In Ecclesall Workhouse Hospital (and possibly also at Firvale) nurses and assistants were paid a wartime bonus of between £5 and £8 a year. See page 23 of Joan Flett's *The Story of the Workhouse and the Hospital at Nether Edge*, published by the Hospital's League of Friends in 1984.

235 Following the death of owner William S. Laycock in March 1916, Oakbrook was offered for sale. It was then described as being 'equipped on the most lavish

scale, with every appointment which comfort and luxury can suggest', and the grounds included 'a foreman's cottage, barn, loose box and stable, with accommodation for five cows, pigsties, dog kennels, etc.'. A brief history of both Oakbrook and Endcliffe Hall is in *The Growth of Ranmoor, Hangingwater and Nether Green* by Peter Warr (Sheffield: Northend, 2009).

236 In addition to a local section of the British Red Cross Society, Sheffield had two units of the St John Ambulance Brigade – the Sheffield Corps and (from 1917) the Heeley Division. These provided uniformed first-aid men for public events, and during the war the brigade helped in Winter Street and other hospitals by providing night-time cover. They were called out as a precaution whenever an air-raid was threatened, and a section of the Sheffield Corps was sent to Malta in 1915. Linked to the brigade was the St John Ambulance *Association*, which provided instruction and certification in first-aid and nursing. At a national level, the British Red Cross Society and the St John Ambulance Brigade worked together through a Joint War Committee, but it is not clear how the two were co-ordinated in Sheffield.

237 Josephine Hutton was the wife of Herbert Hutton, a director of William Hutton and Sons, established manufacturing silversmiths in West Street. Alice Clifford was the wife of Colonel Charles Clifford, the proprietor of Sir William Leng and Company, publishers of the *Sheffield Daily Telegraph* group of newspapers, who was currently on active military service. Both ladies were established members of upper-class social circles in the city. (As was customary at the time, they were typically referred to by their husband's first name – 'Mrs Herbert Hutton' and 'Mrs Charles Clifford'.) Holders of this voluntary position in small hospitals were sometimes referred to as a 'matron' or 'organizing matron', using that word in its general sense as a mature woman who supervises an institution rather than as a 'nursing matron'. The more specific meaning applied primarily in larger hospitals that also had sisters-in-charge and a substantial number of other nurses.

238 The asylum opened its doors in 1872. In 1948 it became Middlewood Hospital, which closed in 1996. See F. T. Thorpe's *A History of the Middlewood Psychiatric Hospital*, published by the hospital in 1972. (A copy of this is held by Sheffield Local Studies Library.)

239 The barracks were built between 1848 and 1854 over more than 20 acres in Hillsborough. They included accommodation for nearly 900 officers and men, stabling for more than 200 horses, schools, canteens, wash-houses and a detention unit. During World War One, they housed several different detachments including from the Royal Defence Corps and the Royal Army Service Corps.

240 A booklet from the Institute in 1915 indicated: 'the Staff is composed of a Medical Director, a *[male]* Secretary, four trained Swedish masseurs and an English masseuse, and four assistants. There are also four members of the R.A.M.C., kindly provided by the Military Authorities to assist in the treatment of the simpler cases.'

241 General accounts of Voluntary Aid Detachments have been provided by Neil Storey and Molly Housego in *Women in the First World War* (Oxford: Shire Publications, 2011) and the website www.scarletfinders.co.uk. Accounts of the life and work of VAD and qualified nurses on the Western and Eastern Fronts have been brought together by Anne Powell in *Women in the War Zone* (Stroud: History

Press, 2009). A 1917 (and therefore necessarily incomplete) description by Thekla Bowser was reprinted by the Imperial War Museum in 2003: *The Story of British VAD Work in the Great War*.
242 Although VAD units were primarily designed for nursing, a General Service Division was also created.
243 Other VAD nursing uniforms were of different colours – scarlet for a commandant, grey for quartermasters and pale brown for cooks. Some illustrations are available at www.scarletfinders.co.uk/157.html and at www.photodetective.co.uk/VAD.html. Outdoor uniforms were also available.
244 Like other nurses, VADs were open to infection during their service. Emily Hartman of Botanical Road, Sheffield, was transferred as a voluntary nurse to Bermondsey Military Hospital where she died on 20 October 1918 from influenza caught from a patient.
245 Many of the troops discharged because of injury or illness also subsequently spent time in one of the city's hospitals or attended as an out-patient.
246 Local developments are described in *Sheffield's Great War and Beyond* by Peter Warr, published by Pen and Sword Books in 2015.

Chapter Seven: Giving and doing: The city's voluntary work
247 This was part of a national programme of funds in several cities and towns. In addition to obtaining money from other activities, the Lord Mayor's Relief Fund was helped by the willingness of many local employers (including the city council) to arrange optional deductions from the wages of their workers.
248 What we nowadays term knitting 'patterns' were then sometimes referred to as 'recipes'.
249 As well as gifts from established Sheffield people, some Belgian refugees in the city made and donated shirts, socks, gloves and other items for British as well as Belgian soldiers.
250 The Depot opened on 25 September 1914 in a room provided in Leopold Street by Wilson Peck and Company. It soon needed larger premises, and was offered part of the groundfloor showroom of cabinet makers and interior designers Johnson and Appleyard Ltd on the corner with Barker's Pool. (That company's stone inscription is still above the frontage of the current H. L. Brown's shop: 'Cabinet makers to HRH the Prince of Wales'.)
251 The 'regulation' breakfast for military patients was bread and jam, but the Depot was keen to provide meals to be cooked. One hospital matron declared 'You should see their eyes light up when they see a sausage coming'.
252 Several smaller groups served their local hospital in a similar fashion. For instance, the Nether Green Soldiers' Breakfast Fund was created in December 1915 to provide for soldiers in the Ranmoor Council School hospital, and in the previous month the (separate) Nether Green Hospital Tobacco Fund had started work. Other groups providing assistance are listed in the Sheffield Register for the War Charities Act 1916, which is held in Sheffield Archives (SY/140/L6/1). This describes and names the officials of more than 180 groups formed during the war, including almost forty created for only a single event.
253 The lady editor of the *Sheffield Daily Telegraph* was pleased 'to hear that even between the intervals of a wholesome game of tennis at the tennis clubs women

immediately take up a piece of knitting or other work' (5 June 1915).

254 As well as contributions from dozens of manufacturing companies, money was received from city council departments and other institutions. An early donation was from the Admiralty Projectile Examiner's Patriotic Fund, based in Janson Street. The ambulance provided for local hospitals by William Cooke and Company was also driven and maintained by staff from there, and several other vehicle donations also included money for maintenance.

255 These two also financed the hospital's operation. In January 1919, the *Sheffield Daily Independent* succinctly noted that 'it has cost a fortune'. A report in March 1916 described a staff of sixty-three medical and other workers and five ambulances. Lady Hadfield served in the hospital herself as lady superintendent. She was American by birth and the hospital became known as the Anglo-American Hospital. Originally for ten officers and ninety other ranks, in 1917 it became used by officers only. Overall the hospital cared for 15,000 patients.

256 An article in the *Sheffield Daily Telegraph* in April 1915 indicates that at least four concerts a week took place at the Third Northern General Hospital. 'Besides the many concerts arranged by individuals, we have been entertained by pantomime stars, musical comedy artists, professional and amateur pierrot troupes, concert parties, opera societies, glee societies, church and chapel choirs, constables, schools, shops, hand-bell ringers, children's dancing classes (very popular these), and many others. And we have had a progressive whist-drive, and the Boy Scouts are coming! And now that the weather is warmer, I hope to have a series of open-air performances by military and other bands.'

257 This opened in August 1916 with a refreshment room, a games room and a reading/writing room. Paying a nominal rent to the corporation and operating with money from public donations, the centre was staffed by volunteer Sheffield ladies. It served free cups of tea and cakes and was soon dispensing around 3,000 teas each week.

258 This was set up by the city's Personal Comforts Depot and the National Services League in June 1916 for troops in transit who were required to wait overnight in Sheffield station. It initially operated between 11 pm and 6 am, but these hours were in February 1918 extended to provide round-the-clock provision except for two hours for cleaning from 7 am. Letter-writing paper was supplied and additional facilities from 1917 included twelve free sleeping bunks and a refreshment trolley for meeting trains paused at a platform. The Midland Railway Company installed a gas stove and provided free gas and coal as well as the rooms. Furniture came from public donations, and around fifty helpers worked in shifts to serve low-price tea, coffee, cocoa, cakes and sandwiches. The Rest Room and Buffet was used by more than 20,000 troops each year.

259 A *Sheffield Independent* report of 27 November 1916 tells us that soldiers could gain access to the soldiers' home at any time, and that 'there is a large recreation and reading room, refreshment bar (with tables for accommodation of about fifty men), bathrooms, lavatories, cycle room, and sleeping accommodation'. By the spring of 1918 the home was each month receiving more than 6,000 visits and serving more than 1,000 teas.

260 In March 1915 the Town Trustees provided £500 'towards uniforms, equipment, etc.', and in July of that year the city council granted the corps £1,000 'for the

common good and benefit of the city'. Members paid for their clothes, equipment and other essentials, contributing also from mid-1916 to the cost of a new headquarters. A booklet of 167 pages describing the corps' 1915 standing orders, membership and early history is available in the city's local studies library, reference 335.22SST.

261 From the middle of 1916, these were the 17th and 18th Battalions of the West Riding Volunteer Regiment. The corps' commanding officer was also the city's chief constable – Lieutenant-Colonel John Hall-Dallwood.

262 At this time, the banks held large amounts of money, and it has been estimated that more than a third of war loan purchases came from banks themselves.

263 These were specifically aimed at members of the general public. Certificates cost 15/6 (£0.78) with a guaranteed value of £1 in five years' time. Up to £100 of certificates could be bought in local post offices, banks and retail shops acting as agents, and larger applications were sent direct to a London office.

264 'Blighty' was, and is, a slang word for Britain. The term was powerful to troops abroad, and a 'blighty wound' was sometimes considered desirable – one that was not life-threatening but serious enough to require a return to Britain. A popular song among soldiers and civilians alike was *Take me back to dear old Blighty*.

265 The scout movement had been initiated in 1907 to encourage a manly courageous outlook on life with an emphasis on service to the country and empire. By 1918, Sheffield had around 100 different troops. Among the badges available was a War Service Badge, which was awarded for twenty-eight (later fifty) days of unpaid service to the country, and the annual scout diary included pictures of 'British and Hostile Aircraft' for use when on watch. From 1916, Sheffield also had companies of girl guides, whose aim was said to be 'to make women womanly' by providing a 'splendid base for character training'.

266 At the time of the flag days, Italy and Serbia were countries within the alliance against Germany.

267 The Police, Factories, etc. (Miscellaneous Provisions) Act of 1916 introduced restrictions on street collections. Permits were required from a local police authority, which defined an area and time and specified that collectors must be adults who remained stationary and were not accompanied by an animal.

268 Sheffield's 1916 Alexandra Rose Day involved around 4,000 collectors, some of whom started at 2 am to catch workers leaving or entering factories. The city's Tramways Committee made available some motor cars, the Third Northern General Hospital supplied ambulances, and individuals loaned their own vehicles. 'Pink favours' were sold, providing the fund with more than £2,000. In 1917, the day's income rose to £2,900.

Chapter Eight: Industry responds to war

269 Both the *Times* and the *Mail* were owned by Lord Northcliffe, who campaigned vigorously throughout the war for stronger anti-German measures. He was a strident critic of the secretary of state for war, Lord Kitchener, and on 21 May 1915 wrote: 'Lord Kitchener has starved the army in France of high-explosive shells […] He persisted in sending shrapnel – a useless weapon in trench warfare. He was warned repeatedly that the kind of shell required was a violently explosive bomb which would dynamite its way through the German trenches and

entanglements and enable our brave men to advance in safety. The kind of shell our poor soldiers have had has caused the death of thousands of them.' Shrapnel shells, containing around 250 pellets for explosion above enemy heads, were Britain's traditional ammunition, but they were ineffective in the novel conditions of trench warfare. After the shell scandal, the *Times* war correspondent was tried and found guilty of disclosing secret information; he received a fine.

270 The university made many other important contributions, for instance through lectures, courses and technical innovations from a wide range of departments. See *Sheffield's Great War and Beyond* by Peter Warr (Barnsley: Pen and Sword Books, 2015).

271 The *History of the Ministry of Munitions*, published by His Majesty's Stationery Office in 1922, reports that 'by the end of 1916 the Ministry was already the largest selling, as well as the largest purchasing, agency in the world' (volume 3, part 1, page 29).

272 The estimated total number varies slightly between reports. The figures in this chapter are from the detailed listing in the official *History of the Ministry of Munitions*, volume 8, part 2.

273 However, Sheffield's Cammell Laird declined to accept a fee for either the construction or the management of their Nottingham factory.

274 In Sheffield, this was William Edwin Clegg (1852-1932) who had been a Liberal councillor since 1886. He became an alderman in 1892, was lord mayor in 1898, served as a magistrate and a town trustee, and was knighted in 1906. He served from 1897 as a council member of the city's university college and later its university.

275 Without the badges, civilian workers might receive insults about alleged cowardice or lack of patriotism. By July 1915 it was estimated that around 20 percent of male munitions workers had voluntarily left their jobs to join the forces. Overall, 40 percent of metal-workers (first volunteers then conscripts) became servicemen. In total, British troops (around 5,600,000 in the wartime period to November 1918) accounted for around one-third of the pre-war male labour force. See P. E. Dewey's article 'Military recruiting and the British labour force during the First World War' in *The Historical Journal*, 1984, *27*, 199-223.

276 As well as objecting to the possible impact of dilution on their wages, members of the Amalgamated Society of Engineers and other craftsmen were determined to preserve their high status in relation to less skilled men. Attitudes in Sheffield have been detailed by James Hinton in *The First Shop Stewards Movement* (London: Allen and Unwin, 1973).

277 Estimated national numbers in different sectors vary slightly between reports but the general pattern is clear – an overall increase in women's employment of at least 50 percent. Despite this great increase, we should not imagine that all women job-seekers could easily find a position. On 26 August 1916 the *Sheffield Daily Independent* reported that 'there are about 5,000 women on the books of the Labour Exchange, ready to undertake munitions work'.

278 The Women's Army Auxiliary Corps (WAAC) and the Women's Royal Naval Service (WRNS) were created in March and November 1917 respectively, and the Women's Royal Auxiliary Air Force (WRAAF) was formed in April 1918. Female troops were employed in catering, driving, store-keeping, telegraphic and office

jobs, and numbered almost 100,000 by the end of the war. Local newspaper reports indicate that 'some hundreds' came from Sheffield. The Women's Army Auxiliary Corps was renamed as Queen Mary's Army Auxiliary Corps (QMAAC) in April 1918, with the queen as honorary commandant. It was wound down in the autumn of 1921.

279 These and other industrial developments in the city are described in *Sheffield's Great War and Beyond* by Peter Warr (Barnsley: Pen and Sword Books, 2015).

280 The firm's own Clydeside yard built no less than thirty-five destroyers and four battleships.

281 More than 300,000 were delivered to the War Office.

Chapter Nine: Sheffield in 1917 and 1918

282 In July 1918 a question in parliament revealed that two families of disabled ex-soldiers were forced to live in disused wooden pigsties near Tinsley Park Road.

283 By the spring of 1918 the situation was so desperate that a 'clean cut' of all men aged below 23 was taken, almost irrespective of the importance of a man's job.

284 Men wishing to challenge the decision of this legally lower court could apply to an appeals tribunal. Sheffield appeals were heard by the South Yorkshire Tribunal, which covered a wide area of the (then) West Riding, including Doncaster and Rotherham. Up to its closure in November 1918, the South Yorkshire Appeal Tribunal dealt with almost 6,000 cases from its area.

285 In some cases a man lodged a second claim against call-up at the end of his exemption period.

286 Although applicants to a tribunal are widely referred to as 'conscientious objectors', claims on the basis of personal conscience were in fact very much in the minority.

287 However, membership of the Friends' Ambulance Unit was not restricted to quakers, and recruits came from a variety of backgrounds, both religious and non-religious.

288 Published government advice included suggestions that crusts cut from toast should be re-used in puddings or to thicken soup and even an invitation to save breadcrumbs from cut loaves. The public was also advised 'Eat slowly; you will eat less food', and the grandly-titled director-general of food economy urged people, especially women, to 'look well on the loaf on your breakfast table and treat it as real gold, because the British loaf is going to beat the German'.

289 Local prices were based on a succession of nationwide Prices Orders from the Ministry of Food. Several Sheffield retailers were fined for exceeding the local committee's figure.

290 Initial schemes used separate cards for particular commodities rather than the comprehensive books that came later.

291 Coal Aston Airfield opened around the end of 1915, originally intended for the air defence of Sheffield. It was located at the south of Norton Lane, near Dyche Lane and what is now Bochum Parkway, and grew to cover a large area. In addition to a landing ground, it had hangars, workshops, stores, living quarters for men and for women, and a cinema, post office and church. The airfield also had its own light railway. It became mainly used for the Second Northern Aircraft Repair Depot, repairing or rebuilding over 200 planes in the course of the war.

292 Cited numbers differ between published accounts. The country's flu deaths included around 10,000 of its troops.

293 Sheffield Archives have produced a helpful list of *Sources for the Study of the Influenza Pandemic of 1918*. This is available at https://www.sheffield.gov.uk/libraries/archives-and-local-studies/research-guides/influenza-pandemic.html.

294 Written by Peter Warr and published by Pen and Sword Books in 2015.

Index

PEOPLE

Addison, Christopher, 201
Albert, Prince, 33
Allen, William Edgar, 239
Archdale, Helen, 38

Balfour, Arthur, 98–9, 104, 116, 244
Ballin, N.R., 249–50
Banner, E.H., 104
Barber, Herbert, 221
Barnsley, George, 155–6
Barthel, Oscar, 248
Bartuschek, Johann, 248
Beal, Arnold, 145
Beaverbrook, Lord, 251
Bellamy family, 158
Bennett, Septimus, 253
Bilton, David, 243
Binfield, C., 241, 247
Bingham, Lady, 255
Bone, Muirhead, 149, 252
Bostock, Frank, 78
Bottomley, Horatio, 127
Bowser, Thekla, 257
Brown, H.L., 64, 84, 92, 138, 242, 247, 257, 272
Bryce, Lord, 149
Buchan, John, 149
Bush, Frank, 195
Butt, Clara, 84
Butterill, Mary, 20

Callebert, Reverend, 244
Cave, Leslie, 143
Cavell, Edith, 149, 152
Cesarani, David, 245
Chaplin, Charlie, 149
Chief Constable (Sheffield),

97, 117, 156, 187–9, 245, 259
Childs, R., 241, 247
Clarke, Joseph Ryle, 175
Clegg, W.E., 260
Clifford, Alice, 171, 256
Clifford, Charles, 256
Colver, Robert, 130
Connell, Arthur, 105, 162–3, 193, 195, 198, 255
Connell, Mary, 255
Coward, Henry, 73
Cresswell, Yvonne, 248
Cross, William, 175
Cushner, Tony, 245

Dack, William Smith, 116
Dalton, Stewart, 50, 236, 242, 253
De Broeck, A., 102
De Lyle, Professor, 187
De Waele, Jean Baptiste, 104
Depledge, P., 162
Derby, Lord, 154, 252
Dewar, George A.B., 232
Dewey, P.E., 260
Dixon, James, 114
Dolan, Father Oswald, 150
Drinkall, Margaret, 240
Dyson, Tom, 232

Edward VII, King, 30–1, 235
Ellis, Charles, 201
Ellis, Lucy, 174
Emmerson, Lance-Corporal, 145

England, George, 23, 234
England, Jonathan, 234
English, Jim, 235

Firth, Catherine, 184
Firth, S., 155
Fisher, Herbert A.L., 85, 149
Fisher, Letitia, 237
Fisher, Pete, 51
Fitzwilliam, Countess, 181
Fitzwilliam, Earl, 58, 74
Flett, Joan, 240, 255
Fowler, Simon, 236
Fox, Arthur, 187
Freund, Julius, 126, 248
Fritz, Robert, 126
Funk family, 108–109, 126, 245, 247

Gascoyne, Diana, 243
Gebauer, Karl, 248
Gebhardt, Ferdinand, 114, 120, 246
George V, King, 31–4, 81, 115–16, 152
Gibson, Ralph, 242
Gillespie, D., 172
Gilmour Mrs, 180
Glauert, Edward Colver, 116
Gontard, Paul von, 250
Graves, Robert, 21
Greensmith, Arthur, 141, 251
Gregory, Mrs, 253
Gregory, Nellie, 255

Hadfield, Lady, 183, 258
Hadfield, Sir Robert, 183
Hague, Graham, 237
Hahn, Carl August (Charles Alfred), 115, 249
Hahn, Mr, 249
Hall, Charles C., 237
Hall-Dallwood, John, 259
    see also Chief Constable (Sheffield)
Hamm family, 109
Hardcastle, Eric, 253
Hargreaves, Leonard, 252
Harman, Ruth, 239
Harper, R., 241, 247
Hartman, Emily, 257
Harvey, Peter, 239
Haste, Cate, 243, 246, 251
Hawley, Cyril, 201
Haynes, James, 142–3
Hebblethwaite, Rupert, 236
Hewitt, J.P., 47
Hey, D., 241, 247
Higginbottom, Peter, 236
Hill, William, 175
Hillerby, Bryen, 241
Hinton, James, 260
Hobbs, Chris, 233, 237, 249, 253
Holden, Wendy, 234
Houdini, Harry, 77
Housego, Molly, 256
Howsam, Lyn, 240
Hutton, Herbert, 256
Hutton, Josephine, 171, 256

Jenkins, George, 141
Johnson, Stephen, 254
Jonas, Edward, 131, 247
Jonas, Sir Joseph, 115, 128–32, 181, 247, 249–50
Jones, Melvyn, 241

Kavanagh, R.J., 249
Kayser, Charles, 250
Keeble Hawson, H., 238, 242
Kitchener, Field Marshall Horatio, 15, 82–3, 122, 139, 232, 259
Knapp, Frances, 132

Koerner family, 109–10
Koerner, Roy, 245
Kuehnrich, Paul, 128–30

Lauder, Harry, 240, 272
Laycock, William S., 255
Leader, J.D., 239
Leonard, Charles, 109
Lewis, Wyndham, 149
Liddington, Jill, 235
Lindley, Fred, 232
Lloyd George, David, 43–4, 81, 201, 229, 251

Machon, Mrs, 183
Mackerness, E.D., 241
Manvell, Walter, 81
Martin, D., 241, 247
Mary, Princess, 196
Mary, Queen, 33, 177, 261
Mason, Cecil Stanley, 144
Master Cutler, 163, 221, 244
Mathers, Helen, 239
May, Trevor, 236
Mayor, Lord, 90, 130, 141, 156, 168–9, 176, 191, 193, 196, 226, 228, 249, 251, 257, 260
Mayoress, Lady, 181
McIntosh, Tania, 239
Meggitt-Johnson, Mr and Mrs, 183
Melson, Gertie, 196
Middlebrook, Martin, 251
Millington, Roy, 254
Milner, I., 104
Mistress Cutler, 156, 174, 180
Mitchell, T.J., 234
Morris, Molly, 38
Morrison, Thomas, 139
Mottershaw, Ernest, 20
Myers, Charles, 22
Myers, S.J., 46
Myers, Stephen, 237

Nash, Paul, 149
Nell family, 144
Newsham family, 223
Newton, Gerald, 245, 247, 249
Nicholas II, Tsar, 33
Norfolk, Duke of, 31, 237–8
Northcliffe, Lord, 259

Oldfield, Paul, 242

Panayi, Panikos, 245, 247–8
Pankhurst, Adela, 38–9
Pankhurst, Emmeline, 37, 39, 52, 151–2, 216, 252
Peech, Edith, 169
Pennell, Joseph, 252
Pennington, Frank, 143
Perkin, P.K., 145
Phillips, Martin, 253
Pickin, Henry, 214
Porter, W.S., 162, 240
Potter, John, 253
Powell, Anne, 256
Price, David, 235
Pybus, Sylvia, 236

Queen Alexandra, 171

Reid, Fiona, 234
Rich, Eva, 93
Riverdale, Lord, 244
Roberts, D.E., 237
Rose, Tania, 251
Rotschwar, Max, 248
Rutland, Duke of, 169

Sanders, Michael, 251
Sanderson, Fred, 20
Schonhut, Ferdinand, 119
Schonhut, Frederick Charles, 115
Schuhmetzler, Clara, 245
Selby, Winifred, 224
Shaw, Brook, 181
Shaw, Clifford, 241
Sheffield Theatre Group, 241
Siddall, Eleanor, 146
Siddall, Joseph, 145–6
Sinclair-White, J., 162, 255
Skinner, E.F., 239
Smith, G.M., 234
Smith, William, 116
Snell, S., 239
Soderberg, Andrew, 245
Sorby, Edith, 180
Stacey, Christopher, 241
Stokes, John, 24
Stones family, 144
Storey, Neil, 256

Strachan, Hew, 234
Strover, E. Gerbel, 248
Sutherland, James, 255
Swinton, Sir Ernest, 251

Taylor, Philip, 251
Thorpe, F.T., 240, 256
Toyne, Dorothy, 126
Tsar, Nicholas II, 33
Turner, Howard, 237
Tweedale, G., 241, 247, 249

Unwin, Edwin, 114

Van Bergen, Leo, 23
Van Roosbroeck, Mrs, 105

Vernon, Charles Alfred, 115
Vernon, Tony, 238
Victoria, Queen, 31, 33, 36
Viener family, 118, 128, 246
Vincent, William, 172
Von Gontard, Paul, 250
Vulcan, god of fire, 50–1,
    198, 236

Wales, Prince of, 30–1,
    193, 243, 257
Walsh, Walter, 244
Ward, S.H., 98
Ward, T.W., 181
Warr, Peter, 246, 256–7,
    260–2

Watkins, Edith, 105
Wells, H.G., 12–13, 231
Wickham, E.R., 237
Wigmore, Worthy, 175
Wilhelm II, Kaiser, 18, 33,
    80, 110, 113, 115, 129,
    152, 250
Wilson, Trevor, 251
Wilson, Woodrow, 13
Winter, Jay, 233–4
Womack, F.D., 121
Yarnall, John, 248
Yates, A.G., 162
Zeiher, William, 247

SUBJECT

Abbeydale Road, 58, 183
Abrasive Wheel Company,
    127–8, 248
Acorn Street, 32
Admiralty, 18, 116, 156,
    201, 205, 248, 258
Aeroplanes, 14, 131, 137,
    156–7, 159, 191, 202,
    210–12, 233, 242, 253–
    4, 259, 261
Airfields, 225, 242, 254, 261
Air-force see Royal Air
    Force, Royal Flying
    Corps, Royal Naval Air
    Service
Air-raids, 20, 118, 156–9,
    188, 190, 226, 242, 246,
    253, 256
Airships, 14, 18, 156–7,
    159, 253–4
    see also Zeppelin attacks
Albany Road, 99
Albert Hall, 76, 84, 103,
    105, 127, 150, 152, 241
Alexandra Rose Day, 67,
    198, 259
    see also Flag Days
Aliens Restriction Act, 111,
    246
Allotments, 75, 138, 222
Ambulances, 25, 150, 161–

3, 172, 181–3, 187, 193,
    199, 210, 220, 239, 255,
    258–9
America, 13, 17, 76, 126,
    130, 233, 236, 245, 255,
    258
Amy Street, 228
Andrew, J.H. and
    Company, 212
Animals, 19, 26–8, 57, 60–
    1, 78, 90, 198, 234
    see also Dogs, Horses,
    Pigeons
Anti-Aircraft Corps, 156,
    253
Aristocracy, 33, 41, 43, 236
Armament works, 80, 91,
    131, 200–14
    see also Factories,
    individual companies
Armistice, 18, 225–6, 229,
    233, 245
Army and Navy Aid
    Committee, 180
Army Service Corps, 25,
    152, 190, 256
Army Veterinary Service, 25
Atkinsons, 64–5, 92, 94,
    197
Attercliffe, 60–1, 74, 119,
    130, 240, 253

Attercliffe Road, 83, 238,
    242

Badges, 138, 244
    'On War Service', 153–5,
        204–206, 252, 260
    Silver War, 174–5
    Voluntary workers, 172,
        259
Balfour, Arthur and
    Company, 98, 115–16,
    129, 244
Barkers Pool, 65, 76, 78,
    84, 103, 150, 230, 241, 257
Barnsley, George and Sons,
    156
Barracks (Hillsborough),
    113, 156, 162, 172, 185,
    243, 248, 254, 256
Barriers, 81, 188, 242
Base hospital see Third
    Northern General Hospital
Baths, public, 63, 73, 95,
    102, 238
Bayonets, 212–13
Belbroid Lingerie, 103
Belgians, 80, 98–106, 160,
    169, 193, 196, 243–4,
    246, 257
Belgium, 14–16, 79, 80,
    84, 97–8, 103, 112, 149–

50, 177, 196–7, 221, 232–4
Bents Green, 60
Bents Road, 244
Birth certificates, 232
Blackbrook Road, 70
Blighty Bungalow, 195–6
Bohler Brothers, 127
Boots Chemists, 92
Botanical Gardens, 155
Botanical Road, 257
Bow Street, 186
Bow Street School, 178
Bowling, 74, 184, 240
Boys' Charity School, 193
Bramall Lane, 32–3, 35–6, 75, 87, 165, 187
Bread, 222, 224, 257, 261
Briar Road, 144
Brightside, 65, 71, 74, 240, 242, 252
Brightside Lane, 20, 83
Brincliffe, 138
British Abrasive Wheel Company, 127–8, 248
British Empire, 13–15, 30, 34–6, 48, 92, 97, 139, 147, 150, 169, 175, 228, 233–4, 242, 245, 253, 259
see also Empire Day
Broad Elms Lane, 139
Broad Lane, 57, 59, 68, 90, 188
Brookhill, 57, 89
Broomhill, 56, 60, 82, 240
Broomspring Lane, 71
Brown, H.L. jewellers, 64, 92, 138, 257
Brown, John and Company, 201, 205, 211, 247
Bryce Report, 149–50
Burgon and Ball, 58
Burngreave, 158, 223
Buses, 28, 55–6, 99, 117, 170, 237, 241

Cambridge Street, 76
Cammell Laird, 200, 202, 204, 209–11, 260
Canadians, 18, 25, 180, 233, 251

Canteens, 185–7, 206, 209
Carbrook, 60, 65, 238
Cardiff Street, 143
Carlisle Street East, 250
Cars, 15, 26, 55, 58–9, 75, 90, 153, 161, 172, 181, 208, 210, 215, 237–8, 259
Carterknowle Road, 139
Carterknowle School Hospital, 121, 165–6
Cartmell Road, 204
Carver Street, 254
Castle Street, 185
Casualties, 17, 19, 87, 97, 141, 160, 196, 216, 232–4, 251
see also Deaths, Disablement
Cathedral, 53, 102, 226, 228
Cemeteries, 105–106, 146
Censorship, 134, 139–41, 146, 251, 253
Channing Hall, 253
Chantrey Road, 245
Chapel Walk, 38
Chaplains, 97, 142, 145, 150, 163, 172
Chapman, J.A. and Company, 212
Charities, 33, 42, 66–7, 69, 71, 98, 126, 156, 173, 193, 198–9, 235, 240, 255, 257
see also Voluntary work
Charles Street, 76–7
Charlotte Street, 57
Chief Constable's Civilian Corps, 96, 187
see also Sheffield Volunteer Defence Corps
Children's Hospital, 68, 239
Church Street, 65, 72–3, 191
Church Street Galleries, 252
Churches, 36, 53–4, 66, 72, 76, 89, 95–100, 102–103, 137, 141, 147, 150, 156, 166, 169, 172, 177, 180, 183–7, 192, 196, 215–16, 226, 228, 237, 258, 261

Cigarettes, 93, 162, 179–80, 184, 243
Cinemas, 36, 77–8, 84, 139, 149, 241–2, 252, 261
City Council, 51–2, 55–6, 59, 60–4, 69, 71, 75, 85, 90, 96, 99, 103, 130, 138, 187, 191, 216, 222–3, 237–8, 240–2, 250, 257–8, 260
City Road, 105–106
Clarkehouse Road, 254
Class see Hierarchical society
'Clean cut', 261
Clubs, 60, 71–5, 96, 138, 184, 196, 217, 257
Coal, 46, 61–3, 99, 149, 201, 224, 258
Coal Aston, 225, 254, 261
Cockayne, T.B. and W., 92
Cole Brothers, 65, 92
Collegiate Crescent, 162–3
Colonel Connell's Fund, 193, 195, 198
'Comb-outs', 218
'Comforts', 94–5, 97, 150, 177, 180, 195, 198
see also Personal Comforts Depot, Voluntary work
Commercial Street, 61, 242
Committee on Munitions of War, 128, 205
Commonside, 69, 240
Communal kitchens, 187, 223
Comrades of the Great War, 216, 240
Conkers, 217
Conscientious objectors, 134, 148, 220–1, 261
Conscription, 134, 138, 152–6, 205, 215–21, 252
Conservative Party, 41–3, 51–2, 54, 86, 114, 134, 237
Consuls, 98, 126, 130–1, 244, 249
Control Boards, 134, 136–7, 222, 224
Controlled establishments, 9, 136, 203–206, 208, 250

Cooke, William and
   Company, 181, 255, 258
Co-operative societies, 65,
   181, 243
Corby Street, 253
Corn Exchange, 86–7, 89,
   216, 218, 253
Cornish Place, 212–13
Corporation Street, 74
Cossey Road, 253
Cost of living, 39, 137–8,
   215, 223
Cost of war, 8, 19–29, 216,
   235
Crimicar Lane, 56
Crimicar Lane Hospital,
   68–9, 240
Crookes, 24, 166, 184,
   186, 228, 240–1
Cruiser Week, 192, 216
Cutlers' Company, 162
Cutlers' Hall, 38, 150, 156,
   180, 222
Cycling, 64, 75, 113, 258

Dannemora Steel Works, 98
Danville Street, 253
Darnall, 142, 158, 240–1
Darnall Road School, 178
Darwin and Milner, 249
Davy, Arthur and Sons, 92
Daylight saving, 138
Deaths, 17, 19–21, 26–8,
   37, 87, 97, 105–106,
   122, 126, 133, 140–6,
   158–60, 215–16, 225,
   232–3, 247, 251, 253,
   257, 260, 262
Debadging, 205, 252
Defence of the Realm Act,
   95, 134–5, 147, 221, 246
Derby Scheme, 154, 252
Dilution, 206–208, 260
Disablement, 20, 24, 44,
   71, 175, 215–16, 261
Dixon, James and Sons,
   156, 212–13
Doctors, 23, 44–5, 66, 69–
   70, 138, 156, 160, 163,
   166, 169, 172, 218, 243,
   250
Dogs, 26, 28, 61, 198

Domestic servants, 46, 62,
   71, 208
Dore, 61, 150, 154, 183,
   238
Dore St John's Hospital,
   99, 165, 169, 171, 196
Dyche Lane, 261

Earsham Street, 59
East Parade, 242
Ecclesall, 60–1, 70, 98,
   128, 138, 157, 193, 244,
   255
Ecclesall Comforts and
   Entertainments
   Committee, 195
Ecclesall Road, 99, 102,
   161–3, 165, 184, 187,
   235, 254
Ecclesall Workhouse
   Hospital, 70, 98, 165,
   168, 193, 195, 240, 255
Ecclesfield, 66, 179, 255
Edgar Allen and Company,
   205
Edgar Allen Institute, 68,
   173, 239
Edmund Road, 253
Elections, 37–40, 43, 52,
   96, 235–7
Ellesmere Road, 23
Empire see British Empire
Empire Day, 35–6, 72, 235
Empire Palace of Varieties,
   76–7, 139
Empire Theatre, 76–7, 139
Endcliffe Hall Hospital,
   165, 167–9, 195, 256
Endcliffe Park, 228
Endowed beds, 255
Enlistment, 84–7, 89, 102,
   134, 154
   see also Conscription,
   Recruiting
Excess profits tax, 136, 204
Exchange Works, 75
Exchequer Bonds, 191
Exhibitions, 73, 79, 148,
   150, 190, 222, 252
'Eye-witness', 139, 251

Factories, 9, 61, 81, 136,

137, 157, 186, 192–3,
   196, 201–203, 209, 215
   see also Armament works,
   individual companies,
   National factories
Families, 15, 20, 34, 42,
   44–7, 51, 62, 70, 96,
   109, 126, 143, 147, 161,
   185, 187, 193, 219, 224,
   261
Fargate, 65, 92, 186, 227–
   8, 240
Feed the Guns Campaign,
   150, 192
Fever hospitals, 56, 68–9,
   240
Field Service Postcard,
   141–2
Films, 22, 36, 77–8, 84,
   149, 231, 241–2, 252
Fire brigade, 57, 110, 190
Firshill School Hospital,
   165
Firth, Thomas and Sons,
   187, 193, 200, 202, 211–12
Firth Park, 253
Firvale Workhouse
   Hospital, 70, 165, 168,
   193, 240, 255
Fitzwilliam, Countess, 181
Fitzwilliam, Earl, 58, 74
Fitzalan Market, 64
Fitzalan Square, 31, 77, 84,
   148, 192, 216, 239
Flag days, 193, 197–8,
   216, 259
Flu, 9, 18, 126, 215, 225,
   233, 257, 262
Food, 15, 18, 25, 47, 81,
   95, 102–103, 124, 134,
   137, 166, 169, 178, 215,
   221–4, 261
Football, 75, 96, 138, 198,
   243, 250
Freedom Road, 146
Friendly societies, 44,
   70–1, 183, 191
Friends' Ambulance Unit,
   220, 261
Fulwood, 61
Fulwood Cottage Homes,
   70, 240

Fulwood Road, 66–7, 165
Fund-raising, 25, 38, 66–7, 90, 97, 99, 102, 150, 168–9, 181, 191–3, 195–9, 216, 243, 257
  see also Colonel Connell's Fund, Flag days, Voluntary work

Gas, domestic, 46, 55–6, 62, 138, 224, 237, 258
Gas, poisonous, 23, 118, 202, 234, 246, 252, 255
Gell Street, 68, 162, 243
Germans in Sheffield, 107–32, 187, 221, 225, 244–50
Gibraltar Street, 187, 223
Girl guides, 259
Girls' Charity School, 71
Glossop Road, 73–4, 85, 162, 188, 235
Golliwogs, 195, 244
Government-controlled factories, 9, 136, 203–206, 208, 250
Greystones School, 178
Greystones School Hospital, 165
Grimesthorpe, 116, 158, 211
Guardians (Poor Law), 42, 70, 98, 168, 240
Gun Week, 192, 216

Hadfields Ltd, 200, 202, 211–12, 236, 255
Hanover Street, 104
Hawley Street, 78–9, 96, 187, 242
Haworth Street, 143
Haymarket, 60, 92–3
Health, 24–5, 34, 43–5, 66–71, 187, 209, 234–5, 238, 240
  see also Medical examinations, National Insurance, Shell-shock
Heath John and Company, 59
Heeley, 74, 102, 184, 237, 256

Helmets, 118, 128, 212–13
Hierarchical society, 33–4, 48, 52, 122, 180
High Storrs, 157, 241
High Street, 92, 138, 253
Highfield, 240
Hill Turrets, 244
Hillsborough, 55, 75, 211, 240, 253
Hillsborough Barracks, 113, 156, 162, 172, 185, 248, 254, 256
Hillsborough Park, 61, 153, 184, 253
Holly Court, 66, 128–30, 249
Holly Street, 183
Holme Lane, 211
Home rule, 40–2
Horse chestnuts, 217
Horse-meat, 27, 103, 223
Horses, 15–16, 25–7, 33, 37, 55–61, 78, 84–5, 87, 90, 92, 122, 156, 196, 199, 210, 214, 235, 237–9, 243, 256
Hospital Supply Depot, 183, 198, 217
Hospitals, 25, 45, 66–70, 95, 102, 138, 156, 160–73, 178–1, 183–4, 198, 220, 234, 253–5, 257–8
  see also Fever hospitals, individual hospitals
Hours of work, 45, 61, 90, 96, 138, 209
Housing, 46, 51, 62–3, 137, 236, 238
Howard Street, 64–5
Hunter House Road, 175
Hunter's Bar, 56, 75, 240
Hunter's Bar School, 178, 198
Huntsman's Gardens School, 178
Hutton, William and Company, 145, 256
Hyde Park, 84

Imports, 15, 18, 136, 201, 212, 217, 221–2, 238
Income tax, 29, 137, 236
Infirmary Road, 66–7

Influenza, 9, 18, 126, 215, 225, 233, 257, 262
Insurance, 44, 60, 156, 247
  see also National Insurance
Intake, 157
Internment, 107, 114, 116–18, 120–8, 187, 221, 245–6, 248–50
Invalid Soldiers' Rest Room, 185
Invalids see Casualties, Disablement
Isle of Man, 123–5
Ireland, 34, 40–2, 118, 191
Ivy Park Road, 145

Janson Street, 258
Jessop Hospital, 68, 239
Jews, 53, 84, 98, 123–4, 242, 249
Johnson and Appleyard, 178, 257
Jonas and Colver, 109, 130–1, 212, 250
Jungle, 78–9, 96, 187–8, 241–3, 253–4

Kayser, Ellison and Company, 250
Kenwood Park Road, 141
Killamarsh, 60, 144
King Edward Hospital, 31
Kitchens, 183, 187, 210, 223

Labour Party, 41, 52–3, 81, 133–4, 235–7
Laissez-faire, 42, 133, 136, 154
Langsett Road, 185
Leaving certificate, 136
Leavygreave, 68, 136
Leopold Street, 64, 78, 127, 186, 240, 257
Liberal Party, 40–3, 51–2, 54, 86, 114, 130, 133, 237, 260
Libraries, 72, 102, 183, 186, 195, 240
Lock-outs, 136, 204
Lodge Moor Hospital, 56, 69, 240

London Road, 242
Longshaw Lodge Hospital, 165, 169–71, 184, 195
Lord Mayor's Fund, 193
Lords, House of, 33, 41, 43, 236
Lydgate School Hospital, 161–2, 165–6
Lusitania, 110, 118

Malin Bridge, 253
Manor Lane, 157
Mappin and Webb, 138, 175
Mappin Art Gallery, 150, 252
Mappin Brothers, 57
Mappin Street, 57
Market Place, 64, 138
Markets, 48, 64–5
Marks and Spencer, 65
Marlborough Road, 38
Marsh Brothers, 128, 212
Meadowhall, 58
Meadowhead, 254
Medical examinations, 86, 89, 218, 243
Medical services, civilian *see* Doctors, Hospitals, National Insurance
Meersbrook, 72, 240–1
Memorials, 31, 105–106, 144, 228–30
Messines Ridge, 16
Middlesex Regiment, 247
Middlewood Hospital, 172, 240
Middlewood Road, 55, 241, 245, 256
Military Service Acts, 154, 216, 218, 252
Military tribunals, 154, 187, 218–21, 261
Ministry of Food, 222, 261
Ministry of Information, 150, 251
Ministry of Munitions, 131, 136, 201–205, 207, 209, 252, 260
Moor, the, 64–5, 114, 120, 187, 197, 223
Moor End Hospital, 240
Moss, 217

Motor cycles, 15, 90, 187
Mowbray Street, 146, 223
Munition manufacturers *see* Armament works
Munition tribunals, 9, 136, 204
Munitions of War Act, 203–204, 206, 208

Name changes, 36, 65, 109, 115–16, 171, 180, 235, 240, 244–6, 261
Napier Street, 127
National anthem, 30, 84, 103, 184
National factories, 9, 202–203
National Federation of Discharged Soldiers and Sailors, 216
National insurance, 44, 70, 133, 244
National kitchens, 223
National Relief Fund, 193, 243
National Services League, 258
Naturalization, 107, 109, 112, 114–17, 119, 122, 127–32, 242, 245–50
Neepsend power station, 139, 237
Neill, James and Company, 212
Nether Chapel, 151
Nether Edge, 62, 70, 98, 100, 240, 255
Nether Green, 168, 256 *see also* Ranmoor School Hospital
Nether Green Hospital Tobacco Fund, 257
Nether Green Soldiers' Breakfast Fund, 257
Netherthorpe, 229
No Conscription Fellowship, 148, 221
Non-Combatant Corps, 220
Norfolk Market, 64–5
Norfolk Park, 73
Norfolk Row, 103, 150

Norfolk Street, 72, 76, 105, 138, 241
Norton, 61, 80, 241
Norton Lane, 261
Nunnery colliery, 253
Nurses, 149, 162–3, 166–9, 171–2, 175, 208, 254–7 *see also* Hospitals, Voluntary Aid Detachment

Oakbrook Hospital, 165, 168, 255–6
Officer Training Corps, 85, 242
Olympia roller-skating rink, 187
'On War Service' badges, 153–5, 204–206, 252, 260

Pals Battalion, 84, 86–8, 141, 144–5, 183, 186, 232, 242, 251
Paradise Square, 71
Park Crescent, 98
Park district, 74, 238
Parks, 61, 72–3, 81, 103, 152–3, 157, 171, 187, 228–9, 253
Passchendale, battle of, 17
Peace Day, 228
Peace Garden, 53–4
Peel Terrace, 180
Pensions, 20, 43–4, 71, 96, 234–6
Personal Comforts Depot, 172, 178–80, 258
Petre Street, 253
Petrol, 94, 136–7, 215, 238
Pickford Trowne and Company, 181
Pickin, Henry (company), 214
Pigeons, 27–8
PIPS, 193–5
Pitsmoor, 20, 138
Poldi Steel Works, 127
Police, 38, 60, 81, 102, 111–13, 117, 120, 129, 135, 156, 188–9, 208, 215, 242, 248, 259

Pomona Street, 178, 186
Pond Street, 185–7
Pools, swimming, 63, 73–4, 238
Poor Law, 42, 70, 240
  see also Guardians, Workhouses
Population, 37, 51, 53, 70, 107, 127, 235–6, 245
Pork butchers, 61, 108–109, 114, 119, 247
Postcards, 64, 100, 141–2, 152, 239
Posters, 83, 86, 97, 147–8, 206–207, 222, 251
Poverty, 34, 42–3, 176, 229
Powell Street, 196
Press Bureau, 139–40, 250
Primrose Day, 197
Princess Mary's Sailors' and Soldiers' Christmas Fund, 196
Princess Road, 253
Prisoners-of-war, British, 118, 150, 180, 183, 196, 198, 251
Prisoners-of-war, German, 113, 225, 254
Proctor and Son, 94
Propaganda,146–52, 251
  see also Censorship
Protected jobs, 154, 205, 219
Psalter Lane, 71, 184, 193, 245

Quakers, 53, 124, 220–1, 261
Queen Alexandra's Imperial Military Nursing Service, 171
Queen Mary's Army Auxiliary Corps, 261
Queen Mary's Needlework Guild, 177
Queens Road, 57

Railways, 15, 40, 61, 81, 110, 134–5, 161, 201, 211, 220, 241, 246, 261
Ranfall, 244
Ranmoor, 62, 80, 98, 168, 240, 256

Ranmoor Park Road, 244
Ranmoor School Hospital, 150, 165–8, 255, 257
  see also Nether Green Hospital Tobacco Fund, Nether Green Soldiers' Breakfast Fund
Ranmoor Wesleyan School, 168
Rationing, 134, 136, 215, 221–4
Rats, 20, 23, 28, 234
Razors, 91, 210, 214, 249
Recruiting, 15, 80, 82–90, 96–7, 133–4, 146–7, 151–5, 191, 216, 218, 232, 241–3, 251, 260
Red Cross, 94, 99, 141, 149, 162, 169, 174, 177, 197, 220, 251, 256
Redgates, 103
Redmires, 86, 88, 96, 182–3, 185–6, 196, 225, 242, 254
Refugees see Belgians
Registration, 104, 111, 134, 136, 154, 190, 246
Regulation of Meals Order, 221
Relief funds, 90, 99, 176, 181–2, 193, 198, 243, 257
  see also Fundraising
Renton Street, 127
Repatriation, 107, 116, 121–2, 126–7
Restrictions, 96, 107, 111–12, 116, 133–6, 146, 221, 246, 250
  see also Control Boards, Controlled establishments, Excess profits tax
Riley's Fields, 253
Riots, 116, 118–20, 131, 229, 247, 249
Ripon, 183
Rivelin, 74, 235, 241
Rivelin Valley Road, 31, 237
River Don Works, 211

Roads, 54–6, 58, 220, 237–8, 240, 242
  see also individual names
Roll of Honour, 97, 233
Roller-skating, 78, 187, 242
Rosedale Road, 105
Royal Air Force, 18, 254
Royal Army Medical Corps, 24, 156, 160, 163, 169
Royal (from late 1918) Army Service Corps, see Army Service Corps
Royal Defence Corps, 248, 256
Royal Engineers, 27–8, 131, 153, 242, 247
Royal Field Artillery, 20, 25, 84
Royal Flying Corps, 18, 20, 152, 254
Royal Garrison Artillery, 175
Royal Horse Artillery, 25
Royal Hospital, 66–7, 160, 162–3, 165, 239, 255
Royal Infirmary, 66–7, 160, 162–3, 165–6, 239, 254–5
Royal Naval Air Service, 18, 254
Royal Naval Reserve, 156
Royal Welsh Fusiliers, 143

Sailors' and Soldiers' Rest Room, 185
Salvation Army, 71, 159, 183, 187, 198, 223
Sanderson Brothers and Newbould, 212–13
Sandygate, 60, 180, 225
'Save or Starve', 222
Savings Bonds, 191–2
Scarborough, 97, 155
Schools, 43, 46, 52, 71, 102, 150, 161, 165–6, 168, 178, 181, 193, 201, 217, 235, 244, 254, 257
Scouts, 181, 197, 258, 259
Secret Service Bureau, 111

Seebohm and Dieckstahl *see* Balfour, Arthur and Company
Servants, domestic, 46, 62, 208
Shakespeare Society, 193
Shalesmoor, 32
Shardlow, Ambrose and Company, 212
Sheaf Market, 64
Sheaf Street, 61, 86, 218, 237, 253
Sheffield City Battalion *see* Pals Battalion
Sheffield Committee on Munitions of War, 128, 205
Sheffield Distress Committee, 90, 176
Sheffield Food Control Committee, 222, 224
Sheffield Horse Repository, 59
Sheffield Military Service Tribunal, 218, 221
Sheffield Motor Volunteers, 190
Sheffield National Service Committee, 216
Sheffield Pals *see* Pals Battalion
Sheffield Prisoners of War Help Committee, 150, 183, 198
Sheffield Relief Fund, 90, 176, 257
Sheffield Soldiers' Home, 185, 198, 259
Sheffield Voluntary Association, 180
Sheffield Volunteer Defence Corps, 96, 156, 187–8, 220, 250
'Shell Scandal', 200
Shell-shock, 21–4, 166, 234–5
Sherwood Foresters, 242
Shiregreen School Hospital, 165
Shirle Hill House, 98–100
Shop stewards, 208, 252, 260

Shopping, 48, 64–5, 92, 137, 215, 239
Shortages, 17, 18, 81, 215, 221–4
Silver War Badge, 174–5
Simplex Motor Company, 58–9, 237–8, 249
Sindelfingen, 109
Smith, W.H., booksellers, 148
Smoke, 50, 61–2, 159, 238, 252–3
Smokes, 180 *see* also Cigarettes
Socks for Soldiers Day, 197
Soldiers' and Sailors' Families Association, 185
Soldiers' and Sailors' Help Society, 196
Soldiers' Home, 185, 198, 259
Solly Street, 71, 98
Somme, battle of, 17, 87, 140–1, 232, 251–2
Songs, 36, 103, 150, 152, 161, 184, 186, 231, 244, 251–2
South Street, 46
South Yorkshire Asylum, 70, 171–2, 240
Southbourne Road, 254
Special police, 188
Spencer, Matthias, and Sons, 214
Sphagnum moss, 217
Spies, 110–14, 118, 120, 129–30, 149, 249
Stag Inn, 184
St George's Terrace, 83, 242
St John's Ambulance Brigade, 156, 174, 196–7
St John's Hospital (Dore), 99, 165, 169, 171, 196
St Marie's Church, 53, 102–103, 150, 226
St Paul's Church, 53–4
St Vincent de Paul Society, 71, 102
St Vincent's Church, 98, 100, 187

St Vincent's Young Men's Society, 162
Station Road, 144
Stead, J. and Company, 212
Stephen Hill, 20
Stock Exchange, 61, 139
Stocksbridge, 99, 181, 237
Storth Lane, 168
Street lighting, 55, 96, 135, 156
Strikes, 40, 136, 155, 204, 208–209, 215, 247, 252
Strines, 82
Stringer and Company, 58, 238
Submarines, 14, 17–18, 118, 211, 221, 233
Substitution, 155, 216
Suffrage, 35, 37–9, 52, 235, 237
Suffragettes, 37–9, 81, 151–2, 216, 235
Summer Street, 229
Surrey Street, 72, 253
Swimming pools, 63, 73–4, 238
Sybry, Searles Ltd, 249

Tank Week, 192, 216
Taxes, 29, 43, 136–7, 204, 215, 236
Teachers' Training College, 162, 254
Telegrams, 63–4, 82, 138, 141, 239
Telephones, 63, 69, 102, 189, 238–9
Temperance, 72–3, 186
Temperance Hall, 76, 240
Templeborough, 211–12
Tenter Road, 224
Theatres, 30, 76, 139, 194–5, 240–1
Third Northern General Hospital base and other units, 70, 101–102, 146, 160–71, 174–5, 184, 186, 193–6, 217, 244, 254–5, 258–9
Thorntons, 64
Tinsley Park Road, 261

Totley, 150, 185, 195, 237–8
Town Hall, 50–1, 81, 85, 134, 226, 228–9, 243
Townhead Street, 72, 76
Trade unions, 39–41, 44, 52–3, 90, 191, 200, 204, 208, 237
Trams, 31, 51, 56, 58, 64, 95, 102, 137–9, 161, 164, 181, 197, 207–208, 237
Treaty of Versailles, 226
Tribunals:
  internment, 122, 127
  military, 158, 187, 218–21, 261
  munition, 136, 204
  repatriation appeals, 127
Troop numbers, 13, 90, 152, 231, 260–1
Tsar Nicholas II, 33
Tudor Square, 76
Turner, Thomas and Sons, 146

Ulster Volunteers, 41
Underage troops, 232
Unemployment, 34, 43–5, 70, 90–1, 133, 138, 219, 229
Union of Democratic Control, 148
Union Street, 76–7, 84
University, 31, 57, 85–6, 99, 102, 126–7, 130, 149, 162–3, 201, 237, 241–2, 247, 249, 254–5, 260
  see also Hospital Supply Depot
Unwin Street, 142
Upper Chapel, 98, 105
Upperthorpe, 74, 237, 240
USA see America

VAD see Voluntary Aid Detachment
Versailles, Treaty of, 226
Veterinary Service, 25–7, 60
Vickers Ltd, 131, 181–2, 198, 200, 211, 250, 252

Victoria Hall, 39, 76, 151, 226
Victoria Station, 61
Viener, E. and W., 118, 128, 246
Viner see Viener, E. and W.
Voluntary Aid Detachment (VAD), 162, 166, 168–9, 173–5, 254, 256–7
Voluntary work, 66–8, 71, 86, 97, 99, 102, 124, 156, 161–3, 166, 169, 172, 176–99, 208, 214, 217, 220, 223, 254, 256–9
  see also Charities, Fundraising, Hospital Supply Depot, Sheffield Volunteer Defence Corps, Special police
Volunteer Defence Corps see Sheffield
Voting see Suffrage
Vulcan, 50–1, 198, 236

Wadsley, 253
Wadsley Asylum, 70, 160, 171–2
Wages, 34, 39, 44, 110, 136, 138, 260
Walkley, 143–6, 240
Walsh, John retailer, 92, 138
War bonds, certificates and loans, 29, 150, 190–2, 216, 243, 259
War Propaganda Bureau, 147–8
War Savings Associations, 191–2
War Weapons Week, 192, 216
Waste paper, 183
Water supply, 46–7, 62–3, 113, 135, 238
Welfare supervisors, 209
Wesley Hall, 166
West Street, 66, 92, 145, 256
Western Bank, 68, 71, 99
Western Road School Hospital, 165
Westfield Terrace, 239

Weston Park, 103, 198
Wharncliffe War Hospital, 160–1, 171–2
Whit Sings, 72
Whiteley Wood, 165, 239
Wicker, the, 98, 102, 239, 257
Wiley and Company, 93
Wilson Peck, 94, 127, 240, 257
Wincobank, 51, 58, 63, 156, 237, 240–1
Winter Street Hospital, 69, 165, 183, 255–6
Women's Army Auxiliary Force, 260–1
Women's Defence Relief Corps, 188
Women's patrols, 188
Women's Royal Auxiliary Air Force, 260
Women's Royal Naval Service, 260
Women's Social and Political Union, 37–8, 52, 151
Women's votes, 35–9, 52, 235, 237
  see also Suffragettes
Women's work, 47, 51, 60, 137, 155, 166, 173, 183, 186, 205–209, 212, 226, 252, 256–7, 260
Woofindin Convalescent Home, 165, 239
Workhouses, 42, 44, 70, 168, 193, 195, 236, 240, 255
Writtle Street, 158

YMCA, 182–3, 185–6, 196, 198
Yorkshire Engine Company, 58, 238
Young recruits, 232

Zeppelin attacks, 20, 118, 137, 156–9, 254
Zion Chapel, 239